PROJECTED PASSION
THE HISTORY OF CINEMAS IN SALISBURY

By Richard Nash and Frogg Moody

Dedicated to the memory of Alan Richardson (1923-2018): The man who saved The Odeon, and to Cyril Jones, Roy Nash and Angela Tesch

First published in the United Kingdom in 2021 by Hobnob Press

Typesetting and origination by Frogg Moody

ISBN - 978-1-914407-13-0 (paperback)

978-1-914407-14-7 (hardback)

Special thanks to John Chandler for advice and guidance.

Cover design by Pete Leyland

email - peter.swapp1@btinternet.com

Mobile - 07970 375141

We would like to thank the following people for their kind permission to reproduce photographs. Sara Hubbard, Salisbury Museum, Alan Clarke, Salisbury Library, Salisbury Journal & Times, BBC Wiltshire, Bryan Smith, Dorothy Feltham, Ken Smith, Nigel and Bryan Rowe, Arthur Millie, Peter Brown and Geoff Lang.

CONTENTS

FOREWORD

I am delighted to have been asked to contribute a Foreword for Projected Passion, which builds on the history of Salisbury cinema as written in 'The Cinema Theatres of Salisbury' by my late father Alan Richardson in 1981.

Although as a family we grew up in west London, away from my father's native city, he ensured that my brother, sisters and I all had the opportunity to explore the wonders of Salisbury and individually we grew to love and appreciate its phenomenal architecture, wealth of history and its diverse artistic venues, not least the incomparable Odeon cinema. His passion for film, and the arts more generally lives on in each of us.

It is fascinating to read how Salisbury, a relatively small and rural city, played host to Albany Ward – one of the early pioneers of circuit cinemas – and was able to support no less than three modern state of the art cinemas in the golden era of the 1930s, not to mention the Plaza at Amesbury and other nearby garrison theatres. These subjects featured in my father's cinema history, but the extraordinary story of how he and his colleagues saved the Salisbury Odeon was yet to play out at that time. This now forms a fitting climax to Projected Passion, which my father would undoubtedly have enjoyed reading and which is a source of great pride to his family.

Sara Hubbard
Salisbury
April 2021

CHAPTER ONE:
THE FIRST PICTURE SHOWS
(The early Days)

The Lumière brothers

Leisure and popular culture stimulates widespread nostalgia, and perhaps always has, often for times before the nostalgic was even born. High-brow critics are not immune from this as they view with horror the popular art forms of today but are really caught up in their own romantic picture of the past - a past that in reality did not exist exactly as they see it.

As is also particularly the case with popular music, the 'golden age' of cinema seems to depend largely on when one was young with fewer responsibilities. For example, in 1938 cinemagoers in Salisbury had the choice of watching a range of films at three luxurious cinemas – but would those who still remember those simple happy evenings really wish to return to the harsher elements and impending horrors of that decade?

By coincidence this book was written during the onset of the biggest World crisis since those days. At the very point where the escapism provided by cinemas and other leisure and cultural outlets would have been most welcome, those outlets have been largely closed. We hope this book will provide memories that partly compensate for this – and, more so, we hope those venues in Salisbury and elsewhere are able to survive and thrive in to the future.

The story of cinema in Salisbury generally follows the pattern of many other cities in Britain. However, before we delve further into that story we thought it would be useful to first glance back at the early history of cinema generally, including the chains that had most impact in Salisbury, and the history of the one building that remains in use as a cinema in the city.

The word 'Cinema' is taken from the French, as a popular contraction of 'cinématographe'. This term had been coined by the Lumière brothers in the 1890s, with its roots in Ancient Greek kínēma (movement) and gráphein (to write or record). Therefore, in simple terms the word means 'the recording of moving images'. In this sense the history of cinema could be said to reach back around 380 years. The Optical Lantern was first produced and brought before the public by Athanasius Kircher, a German Jesuit, who in 1640 made his first 'Magic Lantern'. The Jesuit College in Rome was crowded nightly as the nobility and wealthy citizens witnessed the projection of a few crudely painted slides, mostly of demons and skeletons (sometimes referred to as 'Phantasmagoria').

Persistence of vision is the secret of seeing a moving picture upon a screen. The eye retains the image as the frame of the film is stopped and pulled down into position 28 times a second. The first person to study and indeed discover persistence of vision was Dr Peter Roget, secretary of the Royal Society, who in 1824 became interested in the phenomenon by watching the wheels of a baker's cart through the spaces between the slats of a Venetian blind.

Roget noticed that, although the wheels of the cart were revolving rapidly, by moving his gaze up and down the blind, the slats acted as a series of shutters giving a momentary impression of the wheel being stationary. His findings were published in the Society's Quarterly Journal in 1825. Dr Roget's thesis made possible the science of cinematography and over the next 30 years various scientists produced a variety of machines in an endeavour to create moving pictures.

Meanwhile, extensive research was also taking place in the United States. Thomas Edison began to take an interest in experimenting in about 1877 and by 1891 had filed a patent for his 'Kinetoscope'. This machine used the same standard size of film used today - four perforations on the margins of each frame with the actual photograph area being 1 inch by ¾ inch, providing exactly 16 frames to each foot of film. By 1896 Edison had produced his 'Projectoscope'.

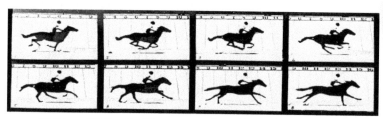

Edward Murbridge reproduced the movements of human beings and animals

In 1866 a Greenwich man named Beale invented the Choreutoscope, a clever instalment that contained practically all the elements of the present day 'Maltese Cross' projector. The Maltese Cross is a four bladed cross that is synchronised to cover the film at the time it is pulled down to the next frame. The experiments continued and in 1872 Edward Murbridge of Kingston-upon-Thames reproduced the movements of human beings and animals using a series of 48 cameras. Murbridge actually journeyed to San Francisco to settle a bet between two American millionaires, as to whether a horse could ever have four legs off the ground at once. With his 'Zoopraxiscope' Murbridge proved it could.

However, if there is one man who can be styled the inventor or father of commercial cinematography, that title should be bestowed upon William Friese-Green. In 1885 Friese-Green produced the first film upon paper using perforations down each side of the margins. After years of further experiments and having spent every penny he possessed the thought came to him to try celluloid as a base for his photographs - this he achieved in 1889.

In Britain, Robert William Paul had become interested in Edison's experiments and had developed his own projector, known as a 'Theatrograph'. On 20 February 1896 he gave the machine its first public demonstration at Finsbury Technical College. He then constructed his 'Animatograph' projector and showed moving pictures at the Alhambra Music Hall (which stood on the site of the modern Odeon Cinema in Leicester Square).

This was exactly two weeks after the French brothers Auguste and Louis Lumiere had shown their first pictures at the Empire Music Hall, also in Leicester Square. The Lumieres had held the World's first public movie screening on 28 December 1895, at the Grand Café in Paris. The film shown was La sortie des ouvriers de l'usine Lumière (Workers Leaving the Lumière Factory). Moving film and the cinema had arrived.

Born in Richmond, Virginia, USA in 1854, Birt Acres contributed much to the introduction and development of all aspects of cinema including the construction of cameras, projectors and film viewers, mobile newsreel reporting and the public projection of moving pictures. With his British partner Robert William Paul, Acres was

"... people in the theatrical business laughed at those of us who thought that there was a future for the cinema ..."

Birt Acres

Albany Ward

the first person to build and run a working 35mm moving picture camera in Britain, although the pair fell out after Acres patented their joint moving camera design in his own name.

Acres was also the first travelling newsreel reporter in the World and the first European-based film maker to have his films shown in public performances in the USA. He made very early silent films during the Victorian era, including a record of the 1895 University Boat Race. On 10 January 1896, he gave a display of moving pictures to the Lyonsdown Photographic Society, at the Lytton Road Assembly Rooms in New Barnet. This was the first public showing of moving pictures to a British audience. On 21 June 1898 Acres was among those who filmed the disastrous launch of HMS Albion at Leamouth on the Thames, when a wave caused by the launch caused a gantry to collapse, drowning 35 spectators. Birt Acres died in Whitechapel in London in 1918.

Although Acres was a great pioneer in the history of cinema, he was not a particularly good businessman. However, working for him was a man who would become the greatest pioneer of motion pictures in the Salisbury area, if not the entire country. Albany Ward was born Hannam Edward Bonner in 1879 in Stoke Newington, London, and was educated at Christ's Hospital,

but he had West Country roots and was apprenticed to a carpenter in Ilfracombe, becoming fully qualified by the age of 16.

Ward became acquainted with Birt Acres while on a family holiday in 1893, went to work with him in 1896 and was with him when he filmed the Diamond Jubilee procession of Queen Victoria near London Bridge in 1897. Although a very young man Ward recognised that the new world of film could be big business and in 1898, aged just 19, he started his own business as a projectionist, taking films to venues around the country, working in his studio during the day and showing films in the music halls in the evenings.

Whilst writing his biographical notes in the 1940s, Ward recalled 'In the early days, particularly in the 1900s, I can well recollect that the majority of important people in the theatrical business laughed at those of us who thought that there was a future for the cinema and I can well remember the late Mr George Edwardes telling me personally that it was quite hopeless and that the cinema would be dead within a year or two if it lasted as long as that.'

The Albany Ward Billboard Company in Wilton Road, Salisbury.

Mr. Albany Ward possessed extraordinary entrepreneurial skills and being in the right place at the right time. The first theatre Ward purchased was the Empire in Oxford in 1900, where he put on a mixture of variety acts and films, and in 1906 he took over a hall for conversion in Weymouth, which he opened in 1909. From this he grew his business until by 1914 he owned and ran the largest cinema circuit in the country - with his head office located in Wilton Road, Salisbury, where he also ran a successful bill-board advertising company. Ward also operated a film renting company from offices in London.

The Gaumont chain would also play a major role in the cinema in Salisbury. This World famous company was founded in France, the brain child of Leon Gaumont. On 10 August 1895 Gaumont took over an optical company in Paris and set up his own business making and selling photographic equipment – in the same year the Lumiere Brothers screened their first film and Gaumont decided to make film projectors.

In 1896 the first Gaumont projector was sold, and the following year he started to make films in order to further market his machines. Films were supplied to Britain and by 1898 a British branch of Gaumont had been established in London in Cecil Court, just off Wardour Street – this area soon became known as 'Flicker Alley' because of the number of cinema-related businesses located there. The first films from here were sold to exhibitors on the music hall circuit, and the topical newsreel styled film also developed rapidly to meet demand.

In 1906 a separate British Gaumont Company was formed and opened the first full time dedicated cinema in Britain, when a shop opposite Liverpool Street Station in Bishopsgate was converted into a cinema known as the Daily Bioscope. With upholstered chairs and a lushly decorated waiting room the Daily Bioscope was the forerunner of the luxurious cinemas of the 1920s and 1930s. Seats cost 2d and 4d, with continuous performance from noon to 9pm including a special show for office workers from 1 to 2pm.

The venture was a big success and 'the cinema' as an entity in itself was born. Leon Gaumont frowned on the London venture and separated the two companies, but by 1910 he saw the way things were going and began operating cinemas in France, laying the basis for the company that still bears his name today – Gaumont-Pathe, the major cinema chain in France. In 1914 Gaumont of London built the famous studio at Shepherds Bush that was eventually occupied by the BBC. This then was the basis for the ever growing circuit that would eventually absorb PCT and the Albany Ward circuit.

The other national cinema chain that would establish itself In Salisbury was ABC. Established in 1927 by John Maxwell, who merged three smaller Scottish cinema circuits, ABC became a wholly owned cinema subsidiary of BIP when it was merged with the production arm of British National Studios, formed by Maxwell in 1926.

During the 1930s ABC grew rapidly through acquisition of sites and an ambitious building programme under the direction of chief architect William R Glen FRIAS, who maintained a distinct house style. Existing cinemas which could not be re-modelled were usually operated separately from the main circuits. ABC also ran cinemas under the Ritz brand. In 1937 the parent company, BIP was renamed ABPC.

After John Maxwell's death in 1940, his widow Catherine sold a large number of shares to Warner Brothers, who eventually became the largest shareholders and thus able to exercise control, though ABPC was separately quoted on the London Stock Exchange. By 1945 ABPC operated over 400 cinemas (usually named 'Savoy' or 'Regal') and was second only to Rank's Odeon and Gaumont chains. By the close of the 1950s ABPC had started rebranding most cinemas as simply ABC rather than continuing with distinctive local names.

In 1967 Seven Arts, the new owners of Warner Brothers disposed of its holdings in ABPC and EMI subsequently launched a successful take-over bid for the company. ABPC was later to be renamed Thorn-EMI Screen Entertainment Ltd, although the cinema chain retained its name. In 1986, this was later divested by EMI to Australian businessman Alan Bond, who sold the chain a few days later to the Golan & Globus 'Cannon Cinemas' group for a reported £50 million profit in seven days.

The sites of what would become the four purpose-designed cinemas in Salisbury were in various uses during the Victorian era. The Picture House, New Picture House / (Fisherton Street) Odeon and Regal / ABC are discussed in the parts of the book dealing with the establishment of those cinemas, as are some of the other venues used for showing moving pictures, but the building that would become part of the Gaumont Palace / (New Canal) Odeon has a history extending back many centuries.

The foyer of the building, now Grade I listed, is a genuine medieval hall, which was once part of the home of John Halle – a very successful

JOHN HALLE.

wool merchant. John Halle was admitted as a Member of the Common Council in Salisbury in 1446, became Alderman in 1448 and was made Constable of New Street Ward in 1449. He was elected Mayor in 1451, 1458, 1464 and 1465, and represented the city in the parliaments of 1453, 1460 and 1461. In 1465 the City Corporation became involved in a quarrel with Richard de Beauchamp, the Bishop of Salisbury, over a piece of land. Halle, having taken an active part in the row, was summoned by Edward IV and the Privy Council. When he appeared before them he misbehaved himself to such an extent that he incurred Royal wrath and was ordered to the Tower of London.

The City Corporation was ordered to elect a new mayor in Halle's absence but refused to do so and he was elected for his fourth term whilst still in prison. The dispute having eventually been resolved and Halle having been released, in 1470 he provided forty men on behalf of the city to accompany Warwick the Kingmaker, for a payment of forty marks. In 1467, having accumulated considerable wealth, Halle had purchased a site in The Canal in Salisbury, to build himself a house that suited his status.

Ye Halle of John Halle

The Stained Glass Window put in to commemorate the end of the War of the Roses

John Halle died in 1479, at which time he held property at Shipton Bellinger as well as in Salisbury. His son William was attainted in 1483 for taking part in Lord Buckingham's rising (with its ghostly Salisbury connection), but this sentence was reversed in 1485. William Halle's daughter and heiress married Sir Thomas Wriothesley, Garter King-at-Arms in the reign of Henry VII. John Halle had also left a daughter, Chrystian, who married Sir Thomas Hungerford.

The Hall of John Halle was later used as an inn and from 1816 to 1819 was part of the printing offices of the Wiltshire Gazette. By the 1830s Sampson Payne was occupying the building, both as a home and a shop, having relocated there from the Market Square with his successful china and glass business. In 1834, Payne employed the noted architect Augustus Pugin to restore the building. Pugin had moved to Salisbury and was lodging in High Street while his own house, St Marie's Grange in Alderbury, was being built. The renovations to the Hall of John Halle included a mock Tudor façade, extensive restoration of the window glass, a new stone archway with a moulded, four-centred head

at the north end of the hall, a cartouche of arms painted by Pugin and the relocation of a fireplace in to the entrance hall to give it more visual prominence, even though this meant it could no longer be used.

In 1837 The Spectator magazine reported: 'When these premises were recently purchased by Mr Sampson Payne, china-man, the present owner and occupier of this ancient mansion, he, at considerable expense, removed the modern partitions, and renovated the curious hall, which is now to be seen in its original size and proportions. Its richly-storied window, its antique chimneypiece, its massive and elegant roof, framed of oak or chestnut, did suggest that this was an ancient refectory; but whether that of a religious or mercantile fraternity, or of an affluent citizen of the olden time, was utterly unknown.'

Sampson Payne became a person of consequence in Salisbury. As well as living in a prominent home and running a successful business, he was also a deacon at the Independent Chapel. Payne was however evidently keen to expand his business and in 1842 he and his brother Charles mutually agreed to dissolve their

"Facing this widening is a great curiosity, a cinema with a grossly overdone timber-framed façade of 1881...."

china and glass dealer partnership. Sampson Payne borrowed the sum of £1,000 from his father and moved to Southampton, where he opened a similar business at his 'Bazaar' in the High Street.

The Hall of John Halle was later occupied by another china business, Watson & Godden (later Watson's). An undated Watson's flyer sets out the business' full range of services from an era when high quality crockery was, in certain homes, an everyday necessity rather than for 'best' or collecting:

'Alfred Watson (late Payne) Cut and Plain Glass Dinner, Dessert, Breakfast, Tea and Toilette Services. Ornamental and General Goods. Parties Furnishing. Furnishing Orders delivered Carriage Free in any part of the Kingdom, and warranted Safe. Public and Private Parties supplied with Goods on hire to any extent. Riveting and Repairing by experienced workmen. Goods of every description matched.' Referring to the building's history the flyer also advertised models of Salisbury Cathedral and Stonehenge, and a range of Worcester china depicting local views, being displayed in the Hall of John Halle.

Watson & Godden made further changes to the building in 1881. The frontage of the building facing New Canal was replaced in wood and plaster to a design by Salisbury architect Fred Bath, carved and worked by Harry Hems of Exeter. This frontage, with a few functional later additions – most notably the Odeon signage – remains in place today. Fred Bath had worked as an assistant to the Diocesan Surveyor before setting up his own business. Among the notable local buildings he designed were Milford Manor, Blooms Department Store (at 3-5 New Canal), the Palace Theatre and Fisherton School.

The changes to the Hall of John Halle were welcomed by the local press. The Wiltshire County Mirror, which had an office opposite the site in New Canal, concluded 'Messrs Watson & Godden have had the moral courage to stand by their convictions and produce a new front worthy of ancient Salisbury every citizen will admit and give them credit for.'

A later highly respected critic was however less enamoured. As part of his comments on a perambulation around Salisbury, Nikolaus Pevsner described how New Canal widens on its north side '...as if it were a subsidiary market place. Facing this widening is a great curiosity, a cinema with a grossly overdone timber-framed façade of 1881 (by Fred Bath), and behind this façade the substantial and memorable remains of the House of John Halle.' Pevsner was kinder in his assessment of the interior of the building: 'A good deal of stained glass, shields-of-arms and scrollwork, well restored and supplemented by Willement (Dean Woodforde).'

Cinema as an industry emerged from the innovations we have seen and in the UK film-makers established small studios initially to produce short films for use by travelling show-men and in music-halls. In the first decade of the twentieth century, more than 30 film studios were established in and around London. British films rapidly established a substantial share of the market at home and abroad, including around 15% of the American market by 1910. However, this initial success rapidly faded as American

The Palace Theatre, formerly the County Hall in Endless Street

production took off, with expensive and heavily marketed feature films. The UK industry share of the home market fell from 50% to less than 10% by 1914.

Although home grown film production was waning, cinema going flourished as a pastime of the British public. Investment in cinemas surged, with the founding of many new companies and investment of £1.5 million in cinemas in 1908 alone. The Government recognised the potential of the film industry, initially as a source of revenue, when it included cinema, together with other entertainments, such as music hall and theatre, in the Entertainment Tax, introduced in 1916. The rate, which was initially set at between 25 and 50% of the price of cinema tickets, was reduced in the 1920s, but then raised during the Second World War. It was not finally abolished until 1960.

An old Salisbury resident of many years ago, Mr Harrold, recounted a time when silent movies were shown in tents at the city's annual charter fair: 'In those days there was Dooners on the Blue Boar Row, Studts by the Guildhall and Taylors by Burtons in Butcher Row. All were silent cinema shows but the fun was in watching the performances of the girls and the clowns on the outside to induce the crowds to go inside.'

Mr Harrold also claimed, in jest, that he was Salisbury's first film actor, having appeared in a film made by Mr Theodore Brown, the uncle of Bernard Brown, an architect. The film was called Christmas Waits, and was made at the rear of houses in Nelson Road. Mr Harrold was filmed playing in a band in a garden when a woman looked out from a window and threw a bucket of water over them. This film and others were shown at the Palace Theatre by a Mr Baker (who had a magic lantern) and by Mr Brown, when the Mayor entertained the schoolchildren of the city.

It was during the 1900s that a formidable rival first began to challenge the thriving live theatre scene in Salisbury. Thanks to marvellous contraptions such as the 'Bioscope' and Mr Poole's 'Pooleographs', state of the art moving pictures were shown at the County Hall.

The building that would become the County Hall, and later The Palace Theatre, was built in 1889 at the junction (south west corner) of Endless Street with Chipper Lane and was owned by Arthur Whitehead, a Salisbury solicitor who would become Mayor of the city in 1892. The building was designed by Fred Bath. The stage was 46 feet wide with a depth of 30 feet, the front being 4 feet above the floor, rising to 5 feet to the rear. The flooring was solid 3 inch batten, fixed on iron girders without joists, in order to provide a good fixing for stage properties and scenery and also of resisting the spread of fire in case of an outbreak.

"In the same year he opened the 'New Picturedrome and Theatre', next to the Avon public house in Castle Street...."

Arthur Whitehead and Assembly Rooms which today is Waterstone's bookshop

The stage curtains were of gold plush velvet with terra-cotta trimmings. The main part of the hall was 70 feet in length with a width of 30 feet and comfortably seated 650 persons, with tip-up seats at the front, behind which were benches. A large balcony stretched right across the auditorium and could accommodate a further 350. The external parts of the building were designed and freely treated in the Queen Anne style – the woodwork was of pitch-pine, the windows being painted white and the doors peacock blue. The entire building works (with the exception of the stage fit) were carried out by Messrs. Webb & Co of Salisbury.

The County Hall remained under Mr Whitehead's personal guidance until about 1910, during which time practically every local event of importance – whether artistic or social – took place within its walls. Mr Whitehead had taken his cue from the Assembly Rooms, which stood in the High Street and nowadays forms the upper floor of Waterstone's bookshop. The Assembly Rooms had been one of the city's most important centres of social life for many years and had attracted many eminent artists. The County Hall was also the home of the Salisbury Amateur Operatic Society from 1908 to 1924 and from 1928 to 1932 (the Society was based at the

Victoria Hall in Rollestone Street during the interim).

Albany Ward first exhibited his 'Imperial Electric Pictures' at the County Hall in 1908. In the winter of 1910 he leased the building, re-named it 'The Palace Theatre' and presented a combination of what he called 'Perfect Pictures and Variety'. In the same year he opened the 'New Picturedrome and Theatre', next to the Avon (Brewery) public house in Castle Street, with a showing of The Sorrow of Satan.

As the civilian cinema provision became established within Salisbury, so some of the military bases in the wider area began to be developed, with the need to provide leisure facilities in mind. A garrison theatre was opened at Tidworth in 1909 and would be managed by three generations of the same family across its 100 year history.

The Military Lands Act of 1892 gave the Government powers to lease and purchase land for military purposes. The owner of the Tedworth Estates, Sir John William Kelk, sold all his property to the Government in 1897. This included Tedworth House, subsequently used as an Army Headquarters, 13 farms, eight farm-houses, 107 cottages and the Ram Hotel, at a total cost of £95,000. Substantial permanent barracks

The Garrison Theatre, Tidworth

were built on the land and it became evident that a place of entertainment would be necessary for the men stationed there.

Herbert and Florence Pickernell were the first managers of the new theatre. In the early years silent films were shown to appreciative audiences. Over the next century the theatre was also used for plays, concerts, variety shows and even boxing matches. Henry Cooper and his brother George fought there in 1952 when the Army Boxing Trials were held in the theatre. Dame Nellie Melba sang at the venue in 1926. Stars of ballet Margot Fonteyn and Frederick Ashton appeared on stage together and a number of famous stars of stage and screen such as Will Hay, Alastair Sim, Donald Wolfit, James Mason, Brian Rix, Charlie Chester, Max Bygraves, Gracie Fields, Ray Ellington, Ronnie Scott, James Cagney and Bob Hope also performed there.

On returning from service with the Royal Air Force in 1947 Ken Pickernell took over the management of the Garrison Theatre. He remained in post until 1987 when his son Tony Pickernell carried on the family tradition. There had been a complete refurbishment of the building in the early 1980s. In 2010 the theatre was closed to be replaced by a modern 700-seater facility outside the confines of the barracks.

1912 saw the introduction of the BBFC, a non-governmental organisation funded by the film industry and responsible for the national classification and censorship of films exhibited at cinemas and associated works (such as trailers and public information films), and (in time) television programmes, adverts, videotapes and DVDs.

Previously there had been no universally agreed rating standards, and local councils imposed their own – often differing – conditions or restrictions. For cinema releases, the BBFC has no legal power (technically, films do not even have to be submitted for classification), as it falls to local authorities to decide who should be admitted to a certain film, but it is normal practice for such authorities to apply the BBFC certificates, effectively making them legally binding. Authorities do however have the right to impose their own conditions. Initially there were two levels of certificate: U (Passed for Universal Exhibition - Suitable for everyone) and; A (Approved for Adult Audiences – Not suitable for anyone under 16 years).

October 1911 had seen a remarkable number of visitors to Salisbury Fair. Kinematograph Weekly reported how over the three days Jacob Studt, Mr Taylor and Mr Dooner provided moving picture shows and 'all reaped a good harvest, notwithstanding the fact that the Palace was also crowded at each performance.' This was noteworthy as in previous years the then County Hall had been empty if anyone had booked it for shows during the fair.

In 1913 Albany Ward spent £1,500 transforming The New Picturedrome and Theatre in Castle Street and re-naming it simply 'The New Theatre'. Although films were still frequently shown there, the New Theatre gradually became the principal live theatre of the city. The shrewd businessman Ward also had a philanthropic side and the opening show at the New Theatre was a charity performance in aid of Shunter Applin, who had lost both feet in the course of his duty as a railway shunter at Fisherton station.

At the outbreak of World War I, Albany Ward realised that the tens of thousands of soldiers arriving on Salisbury Plain would need entertaining in the long tedious hours between training. He later wrote 'When war was declared..... I was of course at Salisbury which was my Headquarters and I at once decided to offer my services to the War Department, and I

"... the troops should have attractive and wholesome places of recreation at hand in their camps .."

approached General Pitcairn Campbell who was in charge of the Southern Command [based in Fisherton at Radnor House] and offered to put up and open a proper Cinema Theatre in Codford for the benefit of the Troops who were drafted there immediately, including the famous Black Watch, with the result I opened The Palace, Codford, within two days of war being declared and we actually opened the same night that the original men of the Black Watch arrived in camp.'

Ward went on to open cinemas in every camp in the Southern Command area, including Larkhill, Fovant (to the east of the main village – the cinema steps can still be seen on Green Drove), Hurdcott, Sutton Veny, Heytesbury and two at Bulford, operating a mobile cinema and theatre circuit providing films and variety acts for the troops: 'For this I built up a special organisation including our own motor transport as we ran not only Pictures but Variety Turns with a proper stage fitted with scenery, and electric light generated by our own plant at all these Theatres, which were completely equipped with Tip-up seating, central heating and every convenience that could be provided. In fact, I think I can justly say that my Theatres were the most comfortable buildings in the respective camps and the Troops were only too glad to go to them at night, knowing they would be warm and comfortable.'

This military cinema circuit was in addition to the 29 film theatres now being operated by Albany Ward in the south west. As the war progressed Ward struggled to keep staff as they enlisted or, later, were conscripted. Ward feared he too could be called up and sought reassurance from the Army that his cinema circuit for the troops was important war work. In November 1915 Lieutenant General Pitcairn Campbell agreed, writing 'I am of the opinion that in helping to entertain the men in various camps around Salisbury and in Salisbury itself, Mr Albany Ward is doing great work for the nation and I consider that he should be relieved from service with the Colours. He is giving every facility for his staff to enlist.'

The Palace, Codford

Garrison Theatre, Larkhill

Following the introduction of conscription in 1916, Ward sought further assurances on the subject in March 1917. Colonel F Wintour of Southern Command responded: 'The major general i/c administration authorises me to say that he regards it of great importance that the troops should have attractive and wholesome places of recreation at hand in their camps, and that he has no hesitation in acknowledging the value of the work you are carrying on, the utility of which is fully appreciated at Command Head-quarters.'

The First World War also brought about the provision of a cinema in Amesbury. In 1911 fire had destroyed the Ivydene guest-house. Owned by the Edwards family, the thatched cottage and adjacent malthouse on the site were completely burned to the ground and the site was left derelict. Chipperfield's circus used the site when visiting Amesbury over the next few years, and it was here that moving pictures were first shown in the town, with short films accompanied by acrobats and musicians shown on a steam-powered projector inside the big top. In 1913, silent feature movies were becoming popular and a more permanent building was required on the site, to house the projection box and seating. Then, in 1915, Canadian troops stationed on Salisbury Plain built a log cabin on the site and named it 'The Cinema'. A show was held at the venue every night at 7.00pm, plus at 2.00pm and 5.00pm on Saturdays and Sundays.

The history of the building that would now become the first purpose-designed cinema in Salisbury itself began in May 1869, on a vacant plot on the street between the city and Fisherton, when Mr S P Yates of the Wilton Carpet Factory undertook the task of laying the foundation stone for a new Primitive Methodist chapel. The Primitive Methodists had struggled to find a permanent place of worship in Salisbury and at the time were meeting in a small building at the back of nearby premises. However, £1,700 had now been raised towards the construction of a purpose designed new building.

Mr Witt of Fisherton was the designer and contractor and he made good progress as the building was ready to open with a special service on 18 November 1869. The chapel was built in the Italianate style. Inside was a fine moulded panel gallery with stained elevated seats. There was accommodation for 400 seated worshippers in total. To the rear was a schoolroom and to the side of this a classroom and a vestry 'with a place for boiling water for tea meetings'. Two adjoining houses, one of which was for the use of the minister, were built to match the chapel.

Services continued at the Primitive Methodist chapel for more than 45 years. However, the building suffered extensive damage, mainly caused by flooding, and it proved expensive to keep it in good repair. Worshippers complained that the side entrance was practically impassable

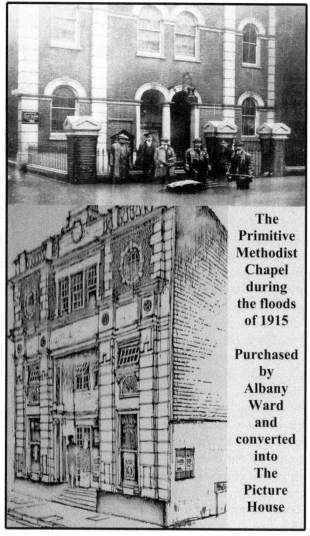

The Primitive Methodist Chapel during the floods of 1915

Purchased by Albany Ward and converted into The Picture House

owing to there being no footpath, nor the likelihood of finding funds to provide one. The upshot was that the Methodists relocated to a new site in Dews Road.

The last service was held at the Fisherton Street chapel on 25 October 1915. The chapel trustees then agreed to dispose of the premises to Albany Ward, on the understanding that he was going to convert the building into a garage. Considering the extent and success of Ward's principal business, this seems to have been very naïve, and in fact he spent £7,000 converting the building into a 514 seat cinema - to be known as 'The Picture House'. The trustees were angry that their place of worship was going to become a place of entertainment. However, with no written undertakings in place as to any particular future usage, there was nothing they could do to prevent Ward's plans.

Under the direction of architect Michael Harding (who also designed the Duke Of York public house in York Road), the conversion included several alterations and underpinning to the front of the building, and it is possible that the original foundation stone of the chapel building was lost or destroyed at this time. The Salisbury Times and South Wilts Gazette described the new cinema as 'Salisbury's new hall of delight'. £7,000 had been spent on the project and '...a pleasing feature of the work is that it is practically [all] the outcome of local talent'. Alongside the work of local designers and builders, leading Salisbury department store Style & Gerrish had provided upholstery and Albany Ward's own staff had completed the decorating.

such offerings as The Perils of Pauline and The Adventures of Pearl White. The projection room was at the back of the stalls and the projectionist was assisted during school holidays by a boy named Francis Pullen.

In June 1918 The Picture House was showing The Crisis – 'a magnificent drama founded on Winston Churchill's well known book' – this crisis relating to the American Civil War and the author being a best-selling Missourian novelist, and no relation to the more famous Winston. The potential Picture House audience was enticed by promotional material explaining the film lasted for two and a half hours and was 'one of the finest productions of modern times.'

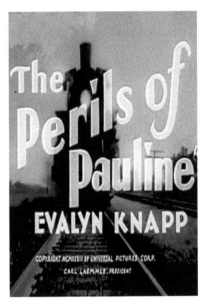

The Picture House opened on 11 December 1916 with a new official war film The King and His Armies on The Somme together with 'an amusing and unique cartoon' entitled The Tanks. Tea would be served free at all matinee performances and the performance receipts from that first day were given to the Mayor's Fund for the Salisbury Infirmary.

This opening presentation was followed later the same week with Mrs Plum's Pudding starring Marie Tempest. The films shown were silent but accompanied by a piano to lend dramatic effect to

Other productions followed throughout the year including The Life of Lord Kitchener, The War at First Hand (under the auspices of the Ministry of Information) which was claimed to be 'the finest war film ever produced' and My Four Years in Germany, the first film to be produced by the celebrated Warner brothers, based on the memoirs of James W Gerard, a former US Ambassador in Berlin.

Something of a novelty was a series of war pictures shown to open-air audiences in Salisbury (including at the Market Place) and the surrounding area during 1918. The events were arranged by the Ministry of Information and used fully equipped apparatus mounted on an ordinary army truck, and accompanied by a speaker, an operator and a driver. The Salisbury Journal reported that 'the pictures filmed show what our men are doing in the army, the navy and the air service, what munition workers have done, and how women are helping to win the war.'

Albany Ward (far right) at The Picture House

At the end of the war, the authorities decided to take over garrison entertainment directly. Albany Ward was offered a Commission so that he could continue working in the theatres he had established but 'did not feel disposed to accept this appointment, feeling that I would prefer to remain independent.' Then, in December 1918, he was involved in a near fatal accident, following which he was incapacitated for almost 12 months. During this time he decided to sell his cinema circuit.

In 1919 the first national cinema chain, PCT, increased its capital with a heavily oversubscribed issue of new shares - Lord Beaverbrook alone taking a £400,000 stake in the company. In 1920 PCT issued more new shares and used this capital to buy up existing cinemas including, at the seemingly small amount of £226,296, the cinemas owned by Albany Ward. PCT retained the services of Ward to run the cinemas, because of his great knowledge of the southern region.

Excluding the 'Albany Ward' circuit, PCT was recording some 20 million admissions a year in its 72 cinemas and showed a substantial profit of £224,000 in the year ending January 1921. However, a slump followed in 1922 and 1923 and PCT's fortunes declined to the extent that it became effectively bankrupt. During this crisis Albany Ward broke away from PCT but regained control of 26 cinemas. However, he was dogged by ill health and in 1924 he allowed PCT to take back 19 of the cinemas, keeping the remainder for himself. By 1927 Albany Ward had had enough of the business and sold all his retained cinemas back to PCT. However his name was still on the Board of PCT until it was bought out by the Gaumont Company in 1929. 'Albany Ward Theatres Ltd' was finally wound up in 1951.

Albany Ward remained in Salisbury focusing on developing houses in the Hulse Road area, and his successful printing business, Salisbury Press, at Fisherton (established in 1907 when Ward became frustrated by the vagaries of using local printers for his various cinemas), until moving to Bristol in 1931 and then Stroud, Torquay and Weymouth . He remains something of a legend and in 1954 claimed to be the oldest living representative of the cinema industry in the country. He died in Torquay in 1966.

The rapid growth of Durrington village during the early 1920s saw the development of houses, banks and shops, two new schools and a village hall. Some of these structures were initially of a temporary nature, built from huts and tin moved from the nearby Larkhill camp. At this time a cinema was built on the south side of Larkhill Road, on a plot opposite what is now Rangers Garage and filling station. There are now private dwellings on the site.

" To make a good impression on a new girlfriend we paid 1s 3d to sit in the balcony."

In 1978, Mrs A R Whittall wrote to Alan Richardson with her recollection of the Durrington cinema, which was built in galvanised iron: 'I have a very hazy recollection of it, but know I was taken there to see silent films such as The Virgin Queen, with a piano tinkling away in the corner. I should imagine it was built towards or at the end of the Great War, before all the troops were demobilised and while there was still a demand for such entertainment in this area. When they left, or perhaps because of the garrison cinemas, depending on the relative dates, this cinema went out of business, but I believe the old building remained there for some years.'

By 1925, British film production declined to a point where fewer than 40 feature films a year were being made - compared with over 150 in 1920. The vast majority of films being shown in the UK were American. In May of that year Lord Newton raised the issue in the House of Lords, citing the 'industrial, commercial, educational and Imperial interests' involved, and calling for a Committee of inquiry. In 1927, the Government recognised the importance of film production to the British economy and its role in stimulating exports of other goods and services, and acted to protect the home market from American domination by means of the Cinematograph Films Act.

The Act recognised the interdependency of film production, distribution and exhibition, and sought to encourage home production by setting quotas for British-made films, to be met by both distributors and exhibitors. The 1927 Act was a success - production of films in the UK more than doubled by the end of the decade, and several new production companies were established, including BIP at Elstree, Warner's at Teddington and Fox's at Wembley. The Act was however also blamed for creating a market for poor quality, low cost films (these films were sometimes known as 'quota quickies').

The American authorities had already recognised the importance of cinema as an export industry and overseas missions were reporting on foreign film market opportunities as early as the 1910s. In 1926, the US Congress set up the Motion Picture Section within the Bureau of Foreign and Domestic Commerce of the Department of Commerce, which collected market information through 44 foreign offices and 300 consular offices.

The Perfect Alibi
Salisbury's first 'talkie'

In Salisbury, films continued to be shown at The Picture House throughout the 1920s. On 23 December 1929, the local press advertised The Perfect Alibi starring Chester Morris and Mae Bush. Punters were promised 'The 100% Dialogue Film Sensation with Singing and Dancing! See! Hear! And Marvel!' – 'talkies' had arrived in Salisbury. In a letter to the Salisbury Times, published in 1974, Mr J H Rideout of Alderbury recalled the happy times had at the cinema during this period: 'We used to pay nine pence in the back row downstairs. To make a good impression on a new girlfriend we paid 1s 3d to sit in the balcony.'

On his retirement in 1967, projectionist Jack Overton gave the following account to the Salisbury Journal: 'I was born in Exeter Terrace [then off Exeter Street], Salisbury, in 1904 and started work as an assistant projectionist for the Palace Theatre in November 1918. I was there for only eight months when I moved to the Picture House in Fisherton Street. I stayed there for eight years as chief projectionist and during this time I became the first projectionist in Salisbury to introduce 'Talkie' films.'

Salisbury audiences soon developed a strong taste for the talkies. The Perfect Alibi was a huge success, but its immediate successor, The Broadway Melody, proved even more popular, with heavy pre-booking and many people being turned away at every performance. This pattern continued into 1930 as the Picture House was crowded three times a day to see and hear Al Jolson singing Sonny Boy in The Singing Fool.

Earlier in 1929 the owner of a property elsewhere in the city had received an unusual visit. Alan Richardson documented the history of cinema in Salisbury better than anyone, and is someone to whom the city and its cinemagoers owe a great debt - as we will see later. Writing in 1981 Alan recalled: 'My mother owned a needlework shop in Catherine Street, grandly listed in Kelly's Directory as an 'Art Needlework Repository', and one day when I was very small I dimly recall a visit to our house by a man with a large Alsatian dog. He talked with my mother about buying our shop!'

'It transpired he wanted our home and garden to make an entrance to the front stalls of a brand new super cinema he planned to build around the corner in The Canal. The main entrance was to be through a china shop that was housed in the Hall of John Halle. My mother must have been gently persuaded on the merits of a cinema being good for Salisbury for shortly afterwards we left our Catherine Street home.'

The prospectus sent to would-be shareholders in the new cinema venture left no doubt that the age and beauty of the Hall of John Halle was a major and probably unique selling point for the proposal, describing the property as 'a very valuable freehold building situated in the centre of the city', which was 'a part of the land and buildings acquired for the purpose of erecting this new super cinema... the Hall would be used as a grand entrance to the new cinema and restaurant...to be erected behind the Hall. The Hall was erected around 1470 by John Halle and with the exception of some slight restoration work in 1836 the building stands as it was originally built. Among its features, apart from its general antiquity, are its richly-storied windows, its antique chimney-piece, its beautifully carved oak screen, its elegant framed roof of oak, and its fine minstrel gallery.'

The Catherine Street entrance to the front stalls - once a needlework shop

'In 1925 the building was scheduled under the Protection of Ancient Buildings Act. From this fact may be gathered it's historical and antiquarian interest, and the Hall will be open to the public as in the past. The directors have every confidence in recommending the undertaking and the shareholders will possess a cinema and restaurant unrivalled in the unique beauty of its entrance hall and the luxurious comfort of its accommodation which, combined with the first class entertainment to be provided, will make it the recognised rendezvous of the City of Salisbury.'

CHAPTER TWO:
THOSE GLORY, GLORY YEARS
(The 1930s)

The arrival of the 'talkies' in the late 1920s had a positive effect in the UK. British films were protected in the home market and, unlike the French and German film industries, able to compete with American sound films without the need for dubbing. The result was that the industry experienced uplift. However, in the late 1930s, the boom in British film production came to a sudden end as over-rapid expansion led to bankruptcies. The number of feature film productions peaked in 1936 at just below 200, and fell by two thirds over the next four years.

In 1932 the BBFC reviewed its 20 year old system of certifications for films in the light of the rise of the horror genre. The two existing levels of certification were revised and a third added: U (Passed for Universal Exhibition – Patrons of all ages are admitted); A (Passed for Public Exhibition – Patrons under 12 cannot be admitted unless accompanied by a parent or guardian) and; H (Horrific – Only patrons aged 16 or over are admitted).

National cinema attendance records are available from 1935 onwards and show admissions to have been over 900 million per year for the second half of the decade, rising to just short of one billion in 1939. The quota provisions for British films in the Cinematograph Films Act 1927 had been agreed for ten years. In 1936, the Government set up a Committee chaired by Lord Moyne to investigate what assistance the industry now required. Moyne warned of the dangers of foreign (essentially American) control of the industry, particularly the exhibition sector, and recommended both that financial institutions be encouraged to fund film production and that quotas be extended for a further ten years. The Committee also condemned the 'quota quickies' practice and recommended that quota rules should include a quality test.

The Cinematographic Films Act 1938 confirmed the retention of quotas, at 15% for distributors and 12.5% for exhibitors. This was intended to encourage bigger budget films, which could compete internationally. It also encouraged American film companies to make films in the UK, thus getting around the quota restrictions. Warner Brothers and Twentieth Century Fox had already established production facilities in the UK and MGM now established a British subsidiary.

Many of the original pioneers of moving films went out of business in the face of fierce competition from larger organisations. In Salisbury, although both the Palace and the New Theatres had continued in their dual functions in the 1920s - putting on both live and film shows - modern purpose-built cinemas would eventually spell the end for the more individual enterprises.

With the concept of sound at 'the flicks' causing great excitement, in June 1930 Picture House manager Arthur Craven had the novel idea of broadcasting music from the film Hollywood Review to passers-by in Fisherton Street. The music was relayed by a speaker fitted above the box office and connected to the main amplifier of the theatre's 'Cinephone' talkie equipment. Potential patrons were also enticed by a poster reading 'You have been listening to the musical items from the Hollywood Review. Now come in and see it as well.'

The Palace Theatre closed, with a stage revue entitled Eve's Daughters, in May 1931. In October that year Leonard Sheldrake, who had been a projectionist at the theatre, moved on to the newly opened Gaumont in Barnstaple. On leaving school at Easter 1921, aged 14, Mr Sheldrake had started work as a trainee projectionist at the Picture House in Salisbury. In 1922 he moved to the New Theatre where he stayed until 1926. He later recalled that events other than film and theatre took place at the venue, including a talk by John Alcock and Arthur Brown, the first aviators to complete a non-stop transatlantic flight. The Misses Pinniger always booked the theatre for one day every year for their Deux Dansants show.

Mr Sheldrake was paid 12/6 per week but with little hope of promotion moved to a cinema in Frome for £2 per week, before returning to the New Theatre in 1928, as Chief Projectionist and manager of the lighting plant. Around a year later he moved to the Palace which by now mainly presented stage shows. Every Saturday morning though there were children's film matinees where Mr Sheldrake would show what were advertised as 'super epics' such as The Gold Rush with Charlie Chaplin, Way Down East with the Gish sisters, Orphans Of The Storm and The Four Horsemen of The Apocalpyse.

Whilst working in Barnstaple Mr Sheldrake met Winifred Cann, who was working as an usherette at the cinema. The couple married at Salisbury Registry Office in 1932, by which time Mr Sheldrake had returned to Salisbury to work at the Gaumont, where he would stay until he retired in 1971. The couple lived in Rectory Road and later in Mr Sheldrake's boyhood home in Cecil Terrace. On his retirement Mr Sheldrake had no regrets about his 50 years and one month as a projectionist, saying 'I loved it except for the last few years when it became too much like big business.'

" ....there was not another theatre quite like it in the whole world...."

With the necessary land (or at least options on it) having been accumulated, a scheme for a new cinema with frontages to The Canal and Catherine Street, submitted by Messrs O'Donoghue and Halfhide, was approved by Salisbury City Council in May 1929. This scheme was never implemented but a year later an alternative proposal was submitted by the Chief Architect for Gaumont, William Edward Trent, on behalf of Albany Ward Theatres Ltd.

Albany Ward Theatres Ltd.

THEATRES, CINEMAS, VAUDEVILLE THEATRES.

Please reply to
Architect.

Accountant's Office:
NEW GALLERY HOUSE,
6 VIGO STREET,
LONDON. W.I

16th May, 1930.

C. Notley, Esq.,
Assistant Surveyor,
Council Offices,
Salisbury.

Dear Sir,
re:- John Halle Cinema.

As arranged at our recent interview I beg to enclose herewith plans for submission to your Council for the building of the above Cinema. You will remember that approval was given by the Council on May 6th, 1929 to a scheme submitted by Messrs. O'Donoghue & Halfhide. Since this date my Company have acquired this property and in order to improve the scheme they have purchased an additional 12 feet in width of the site and some property in Catherine St.,

It will be noticed that the present scheme submitted very greatly improves the exits, whilst the number of persons in the Theatre is only very slightly increased from the previous scheme, this being very largely due to the increased space allowed for the seats.

My Company will be applying for a Cinematograph, Music and Dancing and Stage Play license for the building, and I shall be glad if you will kindly inform me if it is necessary for me to forward you any additional copies of the plans to go before the various Authorities interested. You will notice that on the ground plan it is stated that various matters such as drainage, steel construction, concrete floors, fire appliances etc., will all be to the satisfaction of the Surveyor or the official concerned.

As my Company is desirous of putting this work in hand as early as possible, I shall be glad to have the sanction of your Council as soon as convenient.

Yours faithfully,
FOR: A L B A N Y   W A R D   T H E A T R E S   L T D.,

W.E.Trent

In a covering letter Mr Trent wrote '...the present scheme submitted very greatly improves the exits, whilst the number of persons in the theatre is only very slightly increased from the previous scheme, this being very largely due to the increased space allowed for the seats... My Company will be applying for a Cinematograph, Music and Dancing and Stage Play licence for the building...As my Company is desirous of putting this work in hand as early as possible, I shall be glad to have the sanction of your Council as soon as convenient.' William Edward Trent played a major part in designing the buildings that helped to make up the Gaumont-British Empire. He had an eye for detail and was keen to ensure his buildings were fit for purpose, and he strived for improvements with each new design.

Within 18 months the new Salisbury cinema was complete and on 7 September 1931 the 'Gaumont-British Wonder Theatre' opened with showings - to a full house paying between 8d and two shillings - of The Chance of a Night Time, starring Ralph Lynn and Winifred Shorter, A Yank at King Arthur's Court, Mickey Mouse's Birthday Party and the Movietone News.

The Salisbury Times estimated that nearly 5,000 people visited the theatre during the day, and it was formally declared open by the Countess of Pembroke in the afternoon. The hall was also crowded in the evening, with its seating capacity being taxed to the limit. 'Expressions of appreciation were heard on all sides, and, indeed, nothing but praise could be given concerning an undertaking so perfectly carried out.'

'The Hall of John Halle has been carefully restored, and now forms a charming vestibule for the theatre, which although an entirely new building has been admirably designed to represent a hall of the Tudor age to harmonise with the vestibule. In its prevailing rich brown colour with panelled ceiling and walls decorated with beautifully painted pictures in tapestry style, the theatre immediately appeals to the visitor. Moreover it has concealed lights which give a soft yet sufficient lighting effect, the floor and stairs are nicely carpeted and the seats are most comfortably upholstered so that all together the place is full of interest and in itself is an addition to the entertainment houses of the city that will be increasingly appreciated.'

Ye Halle of John Halle
1470

Gaumont Palace
:: Salisbury ::

:: :: Grand Opening :: ::
Monday, September 7th,
at 2-30 p.m. Doors 1-30

Opening Ceremony by the
Countess of Pembroke
and Montgomery

GAUMONT PALACE

GB 1931

The first manager of the Gaumont Palace was Mr Victor Hydn, previously well known to local theatregoers as manager of the Palace Theatre for many years. Mr Hydn was remembered locally as being very smart in appearance, with dark hair and a small moustache, and whose wife was a talented violinist. Fred Martin was the doorman at the Gaumont for the first two years of its existence.

For the opening ceremony Mr J D Saunders (Supervisor of the Western Circuit of the Gaumont-British Picture Corporation Limited) presided, supported by the Countess of Pembroke, the Honourable David Herbert, Miss Guendolen Wilkinson, Major Despenser-Robertson MP, Mr H G Ware (Archdeacon Carpenter), Mr Mark Ostrer (Managing Director) Mr W Jarrett (Assistant Managing Director), Mr and Mrs Albany Ward, Mr A J Francis (Publicity Supervisor) Mr W E Trent (Architect), Mr F Barnes (Artist) Mr E C C Nichols and others.

Mr Saunders said that as a representative of Gaumont it gave him great pleasure to welcome all present. He thanked them for coming to assist at the opening ceremony. He regretted that the Mayor and Corporation were unable to be with them because the opening happened to clash with the monthly meeting of the City Council, but Members had promised to attend in the evening. Mr Saunders was certain that everyone present would be surprised and somewhat amazed at what they saw in the Gaumont Palace. He thought Mr Trent was to be very heartily congratulated on his skill and conception, which gave them such a wonderful theatre.

'Without fear of contradiction' Mr Saunders thought he could say the Gaumont Palace in Salisbury was unique in its general principles and there was not another theatre quite like it in the whole World. Mr Trent had very cleverly kept within the atmosphere of the 15th century, so the new building would not interfere with the amenities of what he knew everyone in Salisbury revered, the old Hall of John Halle. It was an easy matter for a clever architect to design a modern theatre but if they asked one to design a theatre, which must not deviate from the style of a 15th century building, then they were really giving him something to do.

Mr Saunders continued, interrupted only by outbreaks of applause, noting that formerly there had been some little reproach resting on Salisbury for not having a first class up-to-date cinema, with the result that a number of people had been going outside the city to take their entertainment. He was certain there would no longer be any justification for that reproach for none of the big cities had anything that need now attract them from their own city. It was hardly necessary to say that his company had gone to enormous expense but they had done it gladly and with every confidence they could rely on the support of the people of Salisbury and district to justify the expense. Gaumont was one of the largest companies in the World and controlled about 350 theatres across the country, so he could assure Salisbury that its future entertainment would be well looked after.

Next Mr Saunders, 'with great pleasure', introduced Lady Pembroke, 'who had graciously consented to perform the opening ceremony.'

Lady Pembroke, who was first presented with a beautiful bouquet by Miss Nancy Mosselmans, said she was highly gratified and immensely pleased to be asked to declare the Gaumont Palace open. She had for some years taken a great interest in films, not only in the pictures but in the industry itself. She was quite certain that the theatre would be a landmark in the South of England for those who enjoyed the cinema as much as she did.

Mr Saunders had referred to the 'wonderful' work of Mr Trent and Lady Pembroke could not help feeling that if old John Halle were there to see his once loved little home turned 400 years later into a magnificent Palace, he would rejoice with them to see it used for such a purpose. She was sure they would agree that Mr Trent deserved some such recognition as was accorded Inigo Jones and Sir Christopher Wren.

Those present were aware of the 'immense value of film to the general public throughout the World.' Lady Pembroke continued, 'No amount of reading alone could give the same vivid pictures that films gave, and from an educational point of view they were invaluable. When turned in the right direction - as they always were by the Gaumont-British Picture Corporation - films did an immense amount of good.' Lady Pembroke was glad that the finest cinema in the World was a British one. There had been too great a monopoly of American films and she was glad to think that in a short time British films would be uppermost in the eyes of the world. She had great pleasure in declaring the Gaumont Palace open.

Retaining its magnificent medieval hall entrance and well deserving of its description as a 'palace', the old building had been converted into a state of the art cinema, designed with a Tudor theme, with seating for 1,687 people. The heavy looking 'wooden rafters and stone panels' that remain today on the ceiling of the modern Screen 1 auditorium are in fact made of plaster. This Screen room also still contains the remaining original canvas murals by Frank Barnes, representing tapestries, of which there were originally 40.

Highly decorated stage curtains showed (according to local legend) the Spanish Armada. There have been suggestions that at least two sets of these curtains were originally installed with different pictures. For many years local tradition had it that the first curtains were originally made for the London premiere of Laurence Olivier's Henry V, in recent years some doubt has been cast on this as the premiere did not take place until 1944.

No trace remains of the curtains today, but an item published in Kinematograph Weekly in 1945 appears to resolve the Henry V connection. Mrs H Dodge, the Assistant Manager at the Gaumont (in the absence of manager Mr Leddra, who was on sick leave) told the magazine that 'the original stage curtains which were specially made for the London premiere of Eagle-Lion's Henry V have been installed.' The implication was that this

The only known picture of The New Theatre in Castle Street

had only just occurred – presumably requiring the removal of the first set of Gaumont curtains - and this fits well with the premiere date.

The cinema was built with full stage facilities and a large fly tower. Most of the old equipment, including the Tannoy, still survive and under the stage the dressing rooms and connecting corridors remain in place, as does the old 35mm projector - in the main projection room although no longer in use.

The New Theatre struggled on a little longer than the Palace, having been fitted up with 'talkie' apparatus during February of 1931 and re-opening later that year. It continued to be licensed up until 1933 for the screening of films but found it hard to compete with the Gaumont Palace 'super cinema' and finally closed on 20 April 1932 with a feature film entitled Mother And Son, starring Clare Kimball Young. By this time the New Theatre had a reputation as something of a 'fleapit' and closing it down was perhaps the kindest thing to do.

This did however leave Salisbury with no dedicated live theatre space for the time being and despite its apparent deterioration the New Theatre was fondly remembered by its patrons. It had specialised in showing Westerns, particularly episodic adventures starring Pearl White, accompanied by Miss Violet Southey on the piano. Live artists would perform in the intervals between films. The long narrow building seated about 600 people, with a stage located at the western 'river' end. There was no balcony as such, though the rear seats were raised above the gangway level.

In more recent times Joan Coombs recalled how a bull once escaped on market day and ran loose along Castle Street and in to the New Theatre. Talking to the Salisbury Times in 1981, Tom Hutchins – by then retired and living with his wife Millicent in Park Street – recalled how he and his friends sometimes got into the film shows at the New Theatre 'on the cheap'. As a boy, Mr Hutchins and his gang would earn a few pennies here and there by selling bottles and rabbit skins at Miss Tylee's haberdashers in Gigant Street. Then, at the side door of the theatre, along a passageway, they would be let in by an employee for a bit of 'beer money'.

The vacant building was taken over by Wilton's in 1935 before another builder's merchant, William Dibben & Sons, owned the site for many years. The building had been gutted but the stage remained in use as a storage space until the demolition of the building in 1957. An office building named Cheviot House now stands on the site.

.... He built up business to the extent that the building of the new cinema was justified ....

Meanwhile, the popularity of the First World War era cinema in Amesbury had continued to the point where a more permanent brick building was commissioned, resulting in the construction of the Plaza. During the building work the old 'log cabin' cinema building was temporarily re-located on the site of the original Wilts & Dorset Bus Station in Salisbury Street, approximately where Peacocks and Dominos now stand.

Constructed by James & Crockerell Ltd of Durrington, the Plaza opened on 11 November 1935, and could seat 500 people in stalls and a circle. The cinema was equipped with a 16 feet deep stage and a proscenium of 24 feet in width. There was also a small café in the building.

The Amesbury Plaza and old cabin cinema

Manager Lieutenant-Colonel Hugh Robert S Duncan MBE had opened his first cinema in Hampshire, having converted it himself from a theatre. It proved to be successful and it was from this cinema that he was the first to broadcast as such, from Radio Normandy in 1928. He then took over at the Plaza's predecessor the 'Little Hut', where he built up business to the extent that the building of the new cinema was justified.

Before moving into the cinema industry Lieutenant-Colonel Duncan had connections in the theatrical world. As the First World War ended he was given an introduction to the Royalty Theatre, London, where he acted with the likes of Leslie Howard before moving on to other theatres, working with Sir Frank Benson, Arthur Bouchier, Sybil and Russell Thorndike, Gladys Cooper, Godfrey Tearle and De Vere Stackpoole. Moving into theatrical management, he still found time to write successful plays, to be an umpire for more than 20 years at Wimbledon and to play Lancashire League cricket. With the coming of the 'talkies' in the 1920s Mr Duncan moved into the cinema business - 'It was an easy jump' he commented many years later.

Most of the temporary army camps in the Salisbury area were dismantled after the end of the war, but in 1938 the press reported that work had recently commenced on the erection of new cinemas at the permanent Bulford and Larkhill camps. The cinemas would accommodate about 450 persons each and were scheduled to be completed in the spring of 1939.

Back in the city, in March 1936, during the showing of the film RAF, Picture House manager George A Howes (also known as 'Ted') had held a special morning matinee, to which he invited cadets of the RAF stationed in the local area. Several hundred attended having marched to the theatre, where they were received by Mr Howes.

During the same month Mr Howes had arranged for a personal appearance of Hyde Park Corner star Gordon Harker at the cinema before the showing of the film. Kinematograph Weekly reported that Harker's visit 'aroused considerable interest in the city. In the theatre a packed audience greeted the star, while crowds thronged the street outside.'

Mr Howes continued his innovative approach to film promotion in April that year, with a campaign to publicise Peg Of Old Drury. Mr Howes had heard that Salisbury's leading department store, Style & Gerrish, had coincidentally planned a series of fashion parades during the week prior to the film's screening. With the help of Jack Francis, of United Artists, Mr Howes obtained the actual costumes worn by Anna Neagle in the film, and these were paraded each day as a finale to the main fashion shows. This generated extensive coverage in the local press and Kinematograph Weekly reported 'The local police had a struggle with the large crowds who created obstructions in order to see the costumes on display at Style & Gerrish.'

In 1935, there had been talk of refurbishing the Palace Theatre building as a modern cinema, and also of building a brand new cinema, opposite the Palace. Nothing came of the refurbishment proposal, and in 1937 the building was converted into a motor garage – named 'The Palace Garage'. During World War Two the building was also used as a police garage, with an entrance off Chipper Lane.

However, the alternative proposal eventually materialised in the form of the Regal Cinema, operated by ABPC. The site had previously been occupied by L Blackford Hickman, a dental surgeon, to its Endless Street frontage, with a garden area along the Chipper Lane frontage.

Opened by Sir James Macklin on 22 February 1937, and designed by William R Glen FRIAS, the Regal was a warm red brick building with pleasing curves, very much in the then contemporary style of cinema design. A full house of 1,608 patrons attended on the opening night – 964 in the stalls and 644 in the circle, to see the latest Shirley Temple film, Captain January, supported by a second feature entitled A Star Fell From Heaven, with Joseph Schmidt in the lead role.

.... Mr Burge announced his principal aim was to make the Regal the social and entertainment centre of Salisbury ...

It was reported that 'In planning a theatre for the town of Salisbury's particular amenities' Mr Glen had 'fully realised that the building must not clash with the dignity of the nearby cathedral, and at the same time must provide the population with a kinema [this spelling still being in common usage at the time] that possesses the finer points of modern design. In the Regal he has produced a praiseworthy layout with a frontage occupying a corner site, in red brick, the corner piece forming a neat rounded setting for six elongated windows, intersected by strips of neon. A long canopy completely encircles the façade. Immediately above the canopy and entrance doors are two sets of windows above which is an interchangeable programme sign, and high up the façade in red neon are the letters of the theatre's name.'

'Inside the theatre is decorated in tones of red and two great lighting troughs run across the theatre and the main ventilating grills on either side are floodlit. The grilles give a hint of gothic heraldry as a reminder of the cathedral city in which the theatre is built.' One oddity was an organ pit constructed for an instrument that would never arrive due – it was suggested – to objections that it might in some way 'compete' with the Father Willis organ in the cathedral.

The surveyor for the project was Arthur G Yuile FFS. The main contractors were L F Richardson of Streatham and, with the few exceptions as noted, most of the sub-contractors and suppliers were based in the London area: Ornamental ironwork and canopies etc - Garton & Thorne Ltd; Carpets - James Templeton & Co; Carpeting, curtains and rubber mats - Hall & Dixon Ltd; Internal telephones - British Home and Office Telephone Co; Electric fittings - F H Pride; Seating and operating box equipment - Pathe Equipment Co Ltd; Electrical installation—W Draper & Co Ltd; Heating, ventilation (the 'Turnaire' system) and gas - Norman Turner Engineering Co Ltd; Joinery, doors etc - The Broomhall Joinery Co Ltd; Terrazzio, faience and tiling - Standard Pavements Co; Asbestos roofing - The Universal Asbestos Manufacturing Co; Fibrous plaster decorations - Ker Lindsay Ltd; Talkie installation – RCA; Vacuum cleaning - The Lamson Pneumatic Tube Co; Granolithic steps - Block-crete Co (Northam, Southampton); Cat ladders - S A Norris & Co Ltd; Plumbing - E Howes (Iver, Buckinghamshire); Bio shutters - W J Furse & Co Ltd (Nottingham); Steelwork - Boulton & Paul Ltd (Norwich); Neon - Boro Electric Signs; Balcony steppings - Girlings Ferro-Concrete Co;

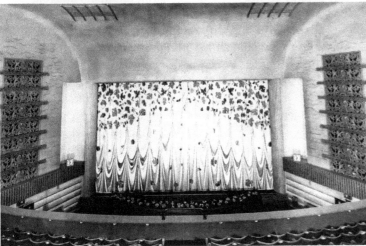

Sanitary ware - John Bolding & Sons Ltd; Metal casements - Standard Metal Window Co Ltd; Locks and door handles - Walter Cassey Ltd; Lantern lights - Haywards Ltd.

As well as its pleasing modern design, ABPC was keen to set out the state of the art, high specifications of the Regal's projection and sound equipment: 'Perfect projection is essential for a theatre wishing to give only the very finest screen results, and to please its patrons by showing a clear and brightly-defined picture. The Ross Kinematographic Projectors and Lamps which have been installed have undoubtedly earned for themselves the reputation of being the finest in the World, both from a projection standpoint and with regard to their mechanical perfection. The installation at the Regal completely eliminates eye discomfort.'

'The average picture-goer is not usually interested in the technical equipment in his favourite cinema. He seeks relaxation and entertainment and a too intimate knowledge of the mechanical means to this desirable end, might detract from the illusion. Nevertheless, he is definitely interested in the results given by the sound equipment. The RCA Photophone 'High Fidelity' System which is installed in this theatre reproduces a range of sound frequencies which ensure that every vocal and tonal quality is heard exactly as in the original. It is, therefore, with great pride and pleasure that Messrs Associated British Cinemas Ltd present talking pictures that will equal the finest in the World.

Comfort and safety were paramount: 'The seats are of the very latest type, designed to give the maximum of comfort, and the carpets and appointments of the cinema generally are on the most modern lines, in keeping with the importance of the theatre. In order to maintain an even temperature, millions of cubic feet of air per hour, pass into the auditorium. The closest co-operation between the Architect and the Engineer has dispensed with the usual unsightly grilles and produced a system in this theatre, which, it is claimed is one of the most successful in Great Britain.'

'The cinema is constructed throughout of steel and concrete and is absolutely fire-proof. The construction of the operating chamber on the roof of the building carries the risk, which is occasioned by the use of films, entirely away from the auditorium and from any place where patrons have access. The situation of this chamber and the provision of fire shutters render it impossible for fire from the projection booth to get into the auditorium. The exits are so situated that a full house can be cleared comfortably in two minutes.'

Mr H.M. Burge

The first manager of the Regal was Hugh Melville Burge, who held the position for 31 years. Born in Wales, at the tender age of ten young Hugh became the proprietor, manager, projectionist, bill-poster and attendant of Burge's Cinema – created in a shed in the back garden of his home! Having worked at the Windsor and Hippodrome Cinemas, Penarth, and the Vandyck, Bristol, he arrived at the Regal via the King's, Bristol. In the programme for its opening, Mr Burge announced his principal aim was to make the Regal the social and entertainment centre of Salisbury

On opening, admission prices for the Regal ranged from 6d (Front Stalls), through 1 shilling (Back Stalls) and 1/6 (Back Circle) to 2 shillings (Front Circle). In these days of expectant instant availability at all hours, a service offered by the cinema seems rather quaint: 'Doctors or professional people expecting messages should leave their names at the Pay Office and also with the attendant, before taking their seat.'

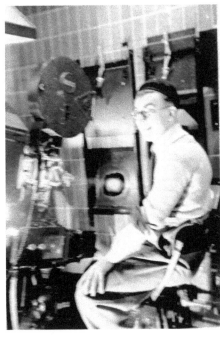

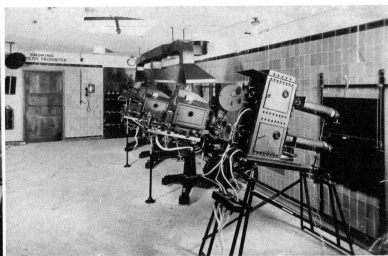

**Jim Smith who became projectionist at the Regal.
The hat was worn to stop hair getting onto the film**

Recently returned to the Salisbury area, Joe Smith heard there was a vacancy for a commissionaire at the newly opened cinema. With his smart appearance and his Great War medal ribbons, Joe got the job and was given an appropriately impressive uniform to wear. Joe later heard that the Regal was looking for a trainee projectionist. His son Jim went along for an interview and was accepted for the post.

Jim Smith soon learned the basics of his new trade. Taking delivery of the large reels of film and checking them for breaks, he would then spool the film through the projector, making sure that it was not too tight. All of this had to be carried out in the morning, ready for the 2.30pm performance. Each projector carried a single film reel, which lasted about 30-40 minutes. As one projector neared the end of a reel, a second projector came in with the next reel. The skill was to merge the changeover so the audience would not notice. Any delays or jams would soon result in catcalls, boos and feet drumming on seat backs followed by a visit from an irate Mr Burge. If the film was a particularly long one, further projector switchovers would be needed.

Many films arrived in poor condition with numerous breaks. This meant running the entire reel through a hand-wound system to find and splice the breaks together before loading. As a break in a hard morning's work in the projection box, Jim and his workmates would often go up on to the roof of the Regal with their morning coffee. On one such occasion, they saw smoke rising from the eastern part of the city. Jim recalled saying to one of the others 'it looks like someone's chimney is on fire.' The sound of the siren and then the fire engine speeding out of its nearby Salt Lane head-quarters soon followed. When Jim got home that night, he learned that it was his own home that had been badly damaged in the fire.

March 1937 saw another high profile publicity campaign arising from the imagination of George Howes at the Picture House, in connection with the showing of trapeze act drama The Three Maxims. Mr Howes engaged an artist friend to paint figures of the three gymnast characters onto three-ply wood. The figures were then cut out and assembled on a trapeze suspended on a rope across Fisherton Street. Mr Howes obtained the permission of the police beforehand and the stunt created considerable interest.

Page 27

The old Picture House above and the new Picture House below

The 1930s was proving to be the heyday of cinema in Salisbury, with the Gaumont and the Regal now strongly competing with the old Picture House. In fact though, the facilities at the Fisherton Street venue were poor by comparison to the modern buildings and, despite George Howes' best efforts, the Picture House doors were closed for the last time on 18 September 1937 with a showing of Sea Devils, starring Victor McLagen and Ida Lupino. This meant that all three of the original Albany Ward cinemas in Salisbury had now closed.

However, in February 1936, the local press had announced news of another new cinema, to be built by Gaumont-British, just 30 yards or so from the Picture House. The site had previously been the old Griffin sawmills and timber yard (later Wright's building materials premises), together with part of the back garden of the Angel Hotel, and proved to be ideal - on a busy road, only a short walk from the town centre and easily accessible to the population of the city. The purchase of the land was completed in September 1936 and the clearance of the area began. It was promised that the new cinema would '...include all the up - to - date amenities for which the Gaumont-British Corporation are noted.'

As with the Canal Gaumont, the new building in Fisherton Street was designed by William Sidney Trent, this time alongside his son William Sidney Trent and R C H Golding.

The development was carried out to a high specification by McLaughlin and Harvey Ltd, general contractors then based in Highbury Grove, London, whose foreman Mr G Gratwick oversaw the project. The foundations were constructed by Franki Compressed Pile Co Ltd of Victoria Street SW1. The technical engineering and electrical works were carried out by Messrs A Anderson of Middlesbrough, under the direction of Mr S Hart MIEE, Gaumont's Chief Engineer, assisted by R T Dealey and W F Peerless.

.... it was of a scale that dwarfed neighbouring shops and the previously prominent Angel Hotel ....

The most notable external feature of the new building was a very attractive Art Deco frontage framed by twin brick pillars topped with ornate towers. Three flag poles adorned the roof, giving the building a stately appearance. Kinematograph Weekly considered that 'With a low façade in red and multi-coloured brickwork, the new building bears definite touches of Dutch styles, and is a dignified addition to the well-known architectural beauties of the Wiltshire city.'

This is perhaps debatable as the style of the building was very different from older buildings in the city. Indeed, it was of a scale that dwarfed neighbouring shops and the previously prominent Angel Hotel. However, its brick frontage was of its time and made an imposing addition – although like most cinemas and functional buildings of the era, little detailed design was considered for the more functional rear and sides of the building. The new cinema seems to have been generally welcomed, although there was objection to initial plans to use Chapel Place to access car parking, with residents pointing out the street only had a pavement of nine inches and a road of six feet in width.

The cinema's main entrance, then from Fisherton Street, led into a long vestibule, which housed the box office. The floor was lavishly carpeted in a terrazzo design and the walls were painted in various shades of fawn, blue and silver.

Settees and palm trees added to a comfortable and palatial atmosphere, creating a decadent and somewhat exotic ambience.

The vestibule in turn led to a lavishly decorated 50 feet by 30 feet foyer with a chocolate kiosk. The walls were elegantly veneered in wood and the whole effect was finished in friezes of daffodil yellow and apple green with the odd touch of silver. Above, a panelled glass and stepped ceiling housed lighting fixtures designed by F H Pride Ltd of Clapham and manufactured by Blunt & Wray of Kilburn.

Three doors led from the foyer into the spacious auditorium, which was built in a style known as 'the stadium design' with banked seating to the rear. This design was principally chosen with economy in mind, as the provision of a balcony would have added considerably to the cost of construction and may have possibly resulted in a reduced capacity overall. W W Turner & Co of Birmingham provided the 1,311 seats and furnishing.

The walls of the auditorium were panelled in rich, warm tones of peach, relieved with lemon yellow, green and silver, each panel terminating in a rose tinted dado rail. The ceiling was painted in similar colours to complement the effect and was crowned with an ornamental light fitting. Silk curtains lined the walls at intervals and the ceiling was painted in the same colour as the walls.

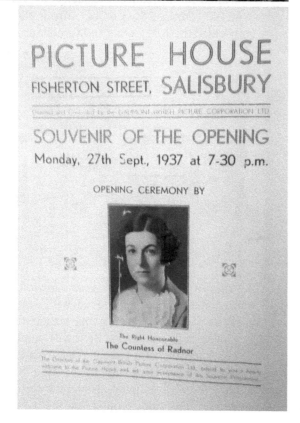

PICTURE HOUSE
FISHERTON STREET, SALISBURY

Owned and Conducted by the GAUMONT-BRITISH PICTURE CORPORATION LTD

SOUVENIR OF THE OPENING
Monday, 27th Sept., 1937 at 7-30 p.m.

OPENING CEREMONY BY

The Right Honourable
The Countess of Radnor

The stage and screen curtains, also made of silk, in peach and cream with green and gold trimming, complemented the décor.

The whole auditorium was designed to give customers a feeling of warmth and comfort. With few home comforts or luxuries in this era of austerity, the cinema was a way of escaping as punters spent a few hours in surroundings they could never hope to match in their own home. The new cinema boasted a state of the art screen – made by H V Polley Ltd of Shaftesbury Avenue in London, Gaumont Magnus projectors and the latest 'Duosonic' sound system, and a telephone link between the auditorium and the pay boxes to assist in filling particular seated areas when there were queues. The building could, it was claimed, be cleared in less than 2½ minutes in the event of an emergency and there was even free parking at the adjoining Griffin's Court.

On 27 September 1937, just over a year after building work began – and less than 10 days after the closure of the old Picture House, the 'New Picture House' opened. The opening night (for which a souvenir programme was published with the title 'Progress') had a carnival atmosphere with people queueing five abreast as far as Chapel Place on one side and Griffin's Court on the other. The main opening film was King Solomon's Mines with Paul Robeson. This was to be preceded by a Mickey Mouse cartoon - Magician Mickey, a supporting feature entitled Can This Be Dixie and the British Movietone News.

By 7.30pm the 'House Full' boards were put out by the doormen. Those remaining outside gathered around the front entrance to watch the guests arrive. The trumpeters of the 12th Royal Lancers played as the Right Honourable the Countess of Radnor, six Gaumont-British starlets and the star of the evening, actress Nova Pilbeam, were escorted into the vestibule. Also present on the night were Mr Ecles, the Area Advertising Manager for Gaumont, Mr and Mrs C Scammell, the deputy Mayor and Mayoress of Salisbury, other local dignitaries and the architects William E and William S Trent.

Addressing a packed auditorium, J D Saunders, Gaumont's Circuit Supervisor, introduced the new theatre to the people of Salisbury, saying it gave him great pleasure to attend the opening ceremony and thanking the audience on behalf of

".... Salisbury is lucky to have such lovely buildings as this and the Gaumont, I wish this theatre the very best of luck ...."

the directors of the Gaumont-British Picture Corporation. Mr Saunders had just one regret, which was that the Mayor, Charles Thomas, was unable to attend owing to a previous engagement – the Mayor had asked him to express his 'regret'. It is an interesting coincidence that the then Mayor had been unable to attend the opening ceremony of the Gaumont six years earlier. Mr Saunders noted his company had had the pleasure of providing entertainment for the people of Salisbury for 'more years than he could remember' and he also pointed out that the gentleman who opened the very first cinema in Salisbury was in the audience. This was of course Albany Ward, former proprietor of the original Picture House, who received a warm round of applause.

Mr Saunders went on to say that the closure of the old Picture House had caused a tinge of regret in the hearts of the regular patrons, but his company knew that the modern picture-going public demanded something much better than the old cinema could offer. Gaumont-British, realising that demand, had erected a new theatre which he was quite sure would meet with their approbation. Mr Saunders also introduced former (old) Picture House manager Mr George A Howes as the manager of The New Picture House.

This may have been of some comfort for any cinemagoer that might have missed the old venue. Mr Howes had built a reputation as a strong manager who ran a tight ship. Also known as 'Ted', George Howes started work in 1917 aged 14 in what he thought was a lawyer's office in London. However, it was in fact a property company that owned four theatres forming the Davis Circuit. The company was bought out by PCT in 1927. Mr Howes was sent to train as a manager in King's Cross, following which he took up relief work in Dorchester before spending three years in the Channel Islands. There was then more relief work in Swindon and Frome, before he arrived at the Picture House in Salisbury, in 1935.

Howes was a man of tremendous character and great charm, who addressed the usherettes as 'missy' (taken as a perfectly acceptable informal greeting in those days). Despite this the staff were careful to gauge his temperament by the colour of the suit he was wearing – if he was wearing a brown pin-striped suit, he would be both amenable and approachable but if he was wearing a black pin-striped suit...

Mr George A. Howes

Next on opening night, there were speeches from Major Robson MP and Nova Pilbeam, who was presented with a bouquet of flowers by a young girl named Betty Street. Ms Pilbeam told the audience 'I am very glad to be here tonight for this gala performance, and may I thank you for the wonderful reception you have given me. This is the first time I have been to Salisbury and during my short stay here I have been greatly impressed by the wonderful buildings. I am sure you will agree with me that this is a wonderful theatre, and I think Salisbury is lucky to have such lovely buildings as this and the Gaumont, I wish this theatre the very best of luck.'

The building was then officially opened by the Countess of Radnor, who expressed her pleasure at being asked to open such a fine theatre. In her opening speech, she declared she felt 'sure that The New Picture House would not only serve Salisbury but also the outlying villages, and that the perfect photography, good sound and ideal conditions of the cinema would establish it as a popular house for entertainment.'

Lady Radnor and Nova Pilbeam watched the start of the main film but were then transported to the Gaumont Palace in New Canal at around nine o'clock. Here they both addressed the audience from the stage before returning to their seats in the upper circle at The New Picture House. At the end of the programme, Nova Pilbeam was driven off in a car, waving to the crowds as she left the city.

In November 1938 and June 1939 Hugh Melville Burge, manager of the Regal, ran two publicity campaigns in conjunction with the Wiltshire School of Flying, based at High Post. Firstly, during the week prior to the screening of Test Pilot, thousands of 'flyers' were distributed asking: 'Have you ever flown an aeroplane? If not all you have to do to win one of four trial flying lessons at the Wiltshire School of Flying is to see the film Test Pilot and then send to the manager of the Regal a short account of what you consider to be the film's greatest thrill, and why.' The local press gave the contest valuable publicity and many hundreds of entries were judged by A H Clement of the Flying School, who personally conducted the free lessons.

Seven months later a 'Free Flight Contest' was run in support of the screening of The Dawn Patrol at the Regal. 5,000 handbills were distributed to patrons over a wide area, explaining that the School of Flying was offering five free flights over Salisbury to draw attention to the opportunity of joining the Civil Air Guard and learning to fly at the inclusive cost of £5. Patrons were invited to write a short criticism of The Dawn Patrol, with the five best efforts being rewarded with the prize free flights above the city. A tie-up was also arranged with the makers of Beverley Hills shirts, Randalls of Endless Street, which resulted in attractive displays at the outfitters' premises and in the theatre's foyer.

Kinematograph Weekly also reported that more than 50 column inches of editorial space

The 1939 George Formby film 'No Limit'

were given in the local press to the Regal screening of The Warning – an air raids precautionary film 'for which Mr Burge went all out with a most commendable campaign.' All the official departments connected with Air Raid Precautions and National Defence in the city supported the screening alongside a comprehensive display of equipment in the cinema foyer. The film had been given a civic premiere locally, to a party consisting of the Mayor of Salisbury, Lady Eyre Coote, Major J Houghton Brown, and representatives of every National Service department.

During the following month, July 1939, Ted Howes at the New Picture House took advantage of a popular local sporting event to secure publicity for George Formby's motorcycling comedy No Limit. Sunday grass track meetings were popular in the Salisbury area, attracting crowds of several thousands, and Mr Howes organised a special race at one of these meetings for a 'George Formby No Limit' cup. He put the proposition before the Salisbury Motor Club who agreed to co-operate with what they considered to be an excellent idea.

Mr Howes arranged for the film to be booked to run at his cinema during the week following the race meeting and he secured a cup for the prize through the Gaumont publicity department. The Motor Club announced the event on all their bills and programmes with streamers and bills also being displayed all around the track and on the public address system.

.... Even after World War Two started in September 1939 cinemas were nearly always full ....

The New Picture House which later became The Odeon

Mr Howes borrowed a grass track motorcycle and kept this on display alongside the cup in the cinema foyer, backed by a collection of stills of scenes from the film and one of the flags used on the track. During the film's run a recruiting campaign for cyclists for the Corps of Military Police was being held in the city and Mr Howes lent his support to this, using the slogan 'There is 'No Limit' to the possibilities if you join.'

Early in 1939 the City Council Watch Committee had considered an application from the Gaumont for permission to exhibit a film entitled The Son of Frankenstein, classified H by the BBFC as a 'horror film'. The Committee resolved that permission to exhibit the film be not granted. Councillor Bigwood said he did not know whether the Committee was horrified with the title but he wondered how many members had seen it.

About four years previously, the Councillor remembered, The Invisible Man was banned in a similar way. As he left the Council meeting on that occasion Alderman Hudson had said to him: 'Come over to Bulford with me. They are showing that film and we'll see what it's like.' They went and had 'never had such a hearty laugh in their life.' Councillor Bigwood challenged anyone to say The Invisible Man was frightening, or that there was anything in it that a child or

anyone else could object to. Any child could have seen it (pun perhaps not intended). Before the Committee got frightened at the titles of films, he hoped some members would go and see them, because it looked rather stupid and in the case of The Invisible Man made the Council the laughing stock of the district!

The New Picture House became an overnight success, providing stiff competition for the Regal and the Gaumont Palace. Its popularity owed as much to the luxury and comfort of the surroundings as it did to the superb and varied selection of films supplied by the Gaumont chain at the time. In fact all the Salisbury cinemas performed very well in this golden era of films. Even after World War Two started in September 1939 cinemas were nearly always full – an escape for a few hours from the bleakness of war, just as Albany Ward had provided some 25 years before.

This was despite an initial nationwide ban aimed at preventing large gatherings of people, which as it transpired only lasted one week. The Government soon realised that cinema would be a vital weapon in the propaganda war, keeping the public abreast of developments overseas as well as maintaining morale, with newsreels presenting 'The truth to the free people of the World' (as claimed by Gaumont-British). In fact, there was never any significant loss of life as a result of any direct bombing hits on any British cinema during the war, although there was some structural damage to the many that were hit during raids, which generally tended to take place during the dark hours following closure of the venues for the night.

Locally, the job of bringing 'the truth to the free people of Salisbury' was not as straight-forward as it may have seemed. Gaumont-British would only send one newsreel to Salisbury, to be shared between The New Picture House and the Gaumont Palace. It was customary for the reels to be shown first at the Gaumont, before being raced across town by the apprentice projectionist (or occasionally one of the usherettes) to The New Picture House. The deliverer would often arrive exhausted and out of breath, sometimes with just minutes to spare!

In his 1981 history of the cinema in Salisbury, Alan Richardson described a trip to the cinema in 1939 that was so descriptive and evocative we have simply repeated it below:

'For my generation the cinema of the thirties and forties will always hold a special and happy memory. In those days we children had no television to fill in the long hours of the evenings, visits to the theatre were rare and extensive treats, mostly confined to the Christmas pantomime and the annual display of dancing that sisters took part in, and brothers dutifully attended. So it was to the silver screen of the super cinema that we looked for the make-believe world that all young people seek at some time in their young lives.'

'I remember in 1939 a winter afternoon at the end of that bitter first year of war, muffled and over-coated against the snow a long queue shuffled along the New Canal in Salisbury towards the enticing entrance to the Gaumont Palace, surely the most incongruous yet magnificent entrance to any cinema in the Kingdom. The Gaumont Palace was entered by going through the door of a house that once belonged to a wealthy wool merchant who lived in the fifteenth century by the name of John Halle.'

'You paid your precious one shilling and threepence at the ticket box just inside, and stepped beneath his minstrel gallery into the superb hall that served as a foyer, and walked into an age of long ago. This ancient hall would have done justice to any film-set designed for the historical drama about to be unfolded upon the screen inside. Passing on across the tiled floor, admiring the stained glass windows and the armour upon the walls you walked through time beneath a magnificent carved oak screen into the inner foyer, and back to the present.'

'Here the heady perfume particular to real super cinemas assailed the senses with a combination of rich aromas, fragrant cigar smoke (or was it Woodbines?) hung suspended above the deep pile carpeting creating an aura of slightly decadent but highly pleasing excitement. Up and round the soft-treaded stairs to the circle (a birthday was the excuse for being posh that day) pictures of the stars upon the walls, and then into the main auditorium, splendid in its décor of mediaeval England, designed specifically to harmonise with the real thing in the entrance hall.'

'Then followed three hours of delight, in company with fifteen hundred others, all enjoying their weekly visit to the cinema, a glimpse of another world, savouring it all the more because you knew that while you were sitting there warm and snug, outside many unlucky ones were waiting patiently for you to give up your seat

"…. what a pleasure the ritual had for those of us just beginning to feel the freedom of growing up …."

The staff proudly parading outside the Gaumont Palace shortly after opening in 1931

when the show was ended. Then reluctantly you dragged yourself away from your comfortable armchair, broke the thread of imagination that linked you with the silver screen, and turned to go, but the pleasures of the day were not entirely over, for on your way down the stairs you turned right and into the café-restaurant, and on a war-time evening with blacked-out streets and cold homes the hour in the café made a very special ending to the weekly cinema visit.'

'Deep inside the café there was a long panelled gallery with secluded alcoves at each end, with benches and tables inside them, rather like inglenook fireplaces. At these tables our group of young people invariably gathered, and we would meet in the mornings for coffee and talk. Fathers were at work or in the forces, mothers were busy at home, and ever understanding, would let us youngsters on school holidays, or awaiting call-up into the services off the chores for an hour or two, and we would make this café and these tables our rendezvous.'

'What romances, real or imagined, started here. What disappointments were suffered, but what a pleasure the ritual had for those of us just beginning to feel the freedom of growing-up, and forming new relationships. On this wartime evening soft music sang on the air, animated chatter filled the restaurant, food over and above your ration was served piping hot, and the company was good, life really did mean some-thing after all. There must have been lots of Americans around before they joined the war because copies of the Saturday Evening Post circulated freely between the tables, their glossy advertisements and stories seemed to tell of another world as remote and unobtainable as that on the silver screen we had just left.'

'The Gaumont Palace was aptly named in those days, for cinema-going had a richness, a plushness missing from the everyday lives of many of us who lived in the thirties and certainly missing from those austere wartime years.'

The Gaumont Palace staff on stage at the time when the 'Henry V' curtain was sent to Salisbury for permanent use. The design represented the British setting forth across the Channel for the battle of Agincourt. Below shows some of the younger members of staff (date unknown)

CINEMATOGRAPH ACT, 1909.

Licence where Enclosure Permanent.

The *Mayor Aldermen & Citizens of the City of New Sarum* —— being the Licensing Authority under the above-mentioned Act hereby grant unto *Albany Ward Theatres Limited* —— of *New Gallery House, 123, Regent Street London W.1* this Licence authorising *them* to use the building and premises known as *The Gaumont Palace* situated at *The Canal* —————————————————————— in the said —— *City* ———————— for the purpose of an exhibition of pictures or other optical effects by means of a Cinematograph, or other similar apparatus, for the purposes of which inflammable films are used, subject to the regulations for the time being of the Secretary of State made under the said Act and to the conditions and regulations endorsed hereon.

This Licence shall be in force from the *Seventh* —— day of *September* 1931, until the —— *31st* —— day of *December* — 1931.

This Licence will be suspended by the Licensing Authority in the event of the Licensee failing to carry out the Regulations of the Secretary of State or of the building becoming otherwise unsafe or of any material alteration being made in the building or enclosure without the sanction of the Licensing Authority.

Arthur Smart
Town Clerk to the Licensing Authority.

The 1931 licence granted to Albany Ward to show films at the Gaumont Palace

CHAPTER THREE:
CARRY ON DREAMING
(The 1940s and 1950s)

Cinemas remained popular throughout the Second World War – even during the traditionally quiet Cinemas periods - providing an escape, morale lift and attendant boost to the war effort for civilians and the services alike. Despite the privations of the decade, national cinema attendances exceeded one billion in every year of the 1940s, rising to an all - time high of 1.635 billion in 1946. Although various techniques of colouring of films had been developed over the previous 40 years, this was still a novelty by this time. It is interesting to note that of the 52 weekly feature films shown at the Salisbury Gaumont in 1940, only four were in colour.

The decade saw the rise of the first British company to attempt to compete with the Holly-wood studios in size and scope. Starting in 1936, J Arthur Rank had built an integrated film organisation, buying up distributors, cinema chains and production companies. Between 1941 and 1947, The Rank Organisation financed half the films made in the UK, controlled over 600 cinemas and was the largest film distributor. Rank also ensured American distribution for their productions and a supply of American films for their cinemas, by securing a 25% stake in Universal film studios through the General Cinema Finance Corporation.

Salisbury was not completely immune to bombing, but its three cinemas thrived. Attendance was greatly boosted by the influx of evacuees to the area within weeks of the outbreak of war, with thousands arriving from Portsmouth, a prime target because of its Royal Navy base. Then, as the war progressed, British and Allied forces flooded the area, joining the already swollen population. This made Salisbury a very

busy and, in some respects, cosmopolitan city during this era. Odstock Hospital (now Salisbury District Hospital) was especially built (by the Americans) to provide care for wounded soldiers, and during recuperation they could often be found at the cinemas in town, particularly the afternoon shows at the New Picture House, where they were allowed in at a reduced rate.

Running a war time cinema was an important business and it was with this in mind that the Government of the day sanctioned a number of key posts as reserved occupations - an occupation considered to be so important to the country that those serving in such roles would be exempt from military service. Among the most important aspects of the war were propaganda and morale, hence the list of reserved occupations included Chief Projectionists.

At the New Picture House this role was filled by Len 'Chiefy' Adams. The second projectionist was Dave Weston, who not long after joining was promoted to Chief Projectionist at a Trowbridge cinema. The third projectionist was Ken Robson, but his post was not senior enough to warrant being classed as a reserved occupation. It would have been a hugely onerous task for Len Adams to keep the two Magnum projectors at the cinema running on his own, so he enlisted two helpers - Myrtle Penny and Nora Jerrard, the latter an usherette at the cinema, both of whom played an invaluable role in keeping the New Picture House in business throughout the war years.

Despite his considerable day-to-day workload and the task of training his two new recruits, Len Adams played a full part in the war effort, joining the Home Guard and serving in the local fire watch. One of the key fire watch observation posts during the war was the roof of the New Picture House, which afforded a good view across parts of the city.

The Gaumont Palace's first offering of 1940 was a comedy – Where's That Fire being the latest vehicle for the noted trio of Will Hay, Moore Marriott and Graham Moffatt. Despite being 20 years old, Moffatt had continued with his portrayal of 'Albert', an insolent, overweight, overgrown - schoolboy sidekick to Hay and Marriott, loosely reminiscent of Billy Bunter.

Moffatt made a personal visit to Salisbury during the film's run. After lunching at the Gaumont Palace Café he was met by some members of the Salisbury Fire Brigade, wearing false beards and comic noses, aboard the ancient manual fire pump which had been shown at the time of the brigade's recent Silver Jubilee celebrations. Graham Moffatt was also in uniform – that of the 'Bishop's Wallop Brigade' (the fictional fire brigade featured in the film) - and he boarded the pump, which was

Graham Moffatt (right) in 'Where's That Fire'

towed to the fire station in Salt Lane. Here he saw the brigade carry out two drills, made an inspection of the station, and was introduced to the members of the brigade.

In the evening Moffatt was introduced to the audience at the Gaumont Palace by the manager, R M Leddra, who said that Moore Marriott was to have been present but was prevented by illness from coming. He had sent a telegram, however, wishing them all a happy new year. Graham Moffatt was given a hearty reception and stayed on the stage for about ten minutes, telling stories and singing a topical song. Later he appeared on the stage of the New Picture House, where he was introduced by the manager, Mr Howes, before himself introducing the main feature there - Inspector Holmleigh on Holiday, starring Gordon Harker. Later in the evening Moffatt attended a party at the Red Lion Hotel.

Page 39

" .... it was always loud applause as the cowboys dashed to the rescue ...."

Up until now the showing of films in Salisbury had not been permitted on a Sunday. However, live performances were allowed and on 11 February 1940 Jack Hylton and his Full Band took to the Gaumont stage alongside Dolly Elsie, Bruce Trent, June Malko and Johnny Lockwood. Seats were available for two or five shillings, in aid of the Naval Amenities Fund, and the event was sold out. On the same date the Regal put on the band of The Rifles Brigade with ticket prices ranging from sixpence to two shillings.

Both shows involved a little unscripted off-stage drama. At the Gaumont the curtain rose ten minutes later than advertised. Rail travel could be somewhat unpredictable during the war years and, on this occasion, whilst the artistes were on their way to Salisbury their instruments were heading for Didcot. The GWR made amends by rushing the instruments to the venue by road, but the band manager was still frantically making telephone calls from the front foyer while they were being loaded in through the Catherine Street entrance.

Meanwhile, outside the Regal, customers who had been queuing in the cold for the sixpennys but had (at the suggestion of staff) opted to pay for more expensive seats in order to get inside more quickly, were annoyed to find there were in fact plenty of cheap seats available. Some accused the Regal of sharp practice and no response was made when the local press invited comment from the manager.

The press was also airing the views of angry filmgoers objecting to the 'ban' on Sunday movies. By now Swindon was the only other town in Wiltshire taking this approach. Under some pressure from the local police, concerned perhaps about the thousands of off duty servicemen kicking their heels around the city on a Sunday with nothing to do but drink, the authorities eventually relented and 25 February 1940 saw Sunday films at all three Salisbury cinemas.

The City Councillors nevertheless retained a degree of control. As was the case for Easter week, films to be shown on a Sunday had to be vetted as to their 'suitability' for the Sabbath. This led to what became a convention of offering a completely different programme of films to those on the established six-day run. Sunday showings very often comprised the return of a popular feature from a year or so before, supported by one of the many (and variable in quality) 'B' pictures held in the London vaults of the film companies. This offered a wider weekly choice to the customer...but also of course encouraged a twice-weekly spend at the cinema.

In August 1940, the Salisbury Times reported on an apparent change of behaviour amongst cinemagoers: 'In the early days of the cinema when melodrama held sway, the patrons who had had experience of the music hall were quick to cheer the brave deeds of the hero and to hiss the dirty doings of the villain. It was always loud applause as the Cowboys dashed to the rescue and as the struggling girl was saved in the nick of time from a horrible death.'

'As these types of film gave place to more sophisticated entertainment cinema audiences gave less and less vent to their feelings until even the most exciting episode was treated as just another piece of entertainment, and it was considered silly to applaud. The fact that opportunities of watching stage shows grew rarer and rarer encouraged people into immobility with regard to expressing pleasure, or displeasure, until the time came when actors and actresses on the legitimate stage and in other forms of live entertainment no longer could judge whether their efforts were appreciated by the amount of applause they received.'

'Now the war is changing things and no longer do people feel that is the wrong thing to applaud in the cinema. The newsreels brought to this country the defeat of the Graf Spee, the gallant deeds of the Navy, Army and Air Force, and more recently there have been shown fine pictures of the wonderful work of the British pilots as they break up the Nazi formations.'

'There are rounds of applause and cheers in the local cinemas and not only does the applause come when the news pictures are shown but during the feature films. It is not uncommon now for there to be a good round of clapping at the end of a picture which has met with approval. This is all to the good and it is also good to hear cat - calls, whistles and derogatory remarks about films which are bad. Self-expression rarely did any harm insofar as the cinema is concerned. The reactions of the audience may yet play an important part in influencing those who make the films.'

Given the huge military presence around the city, Salisbury was fortunate in escaping the intensive level of bombing that other cities suffered, not least Southampton and Portsmouth. The common theory is that this was in part thanks to Salisbury Cathedral, as the tallest spire in the country was believed to act as a great navigation point for incoming Luftwaffe aircrew.

However, the New Picture House fell under threat during the city's first air raid. On 11 August 1942 two German Focke - Wulf FW 190s approached Salisbury via Fordingbridge and Broad Chalke, before sweeping over the city and dumping their bombs. The first pilot opened fire on the city gas holder at Fisherton, puncturing the skin, which was subsequently temporarily patched up with thick mud pending permanent repair. Gas workers worked alongside the Auxiliary Fire Service – based in the old police station at the corner of Gas Lane and Devizes Road – who extinguished small fires and cooled the gas holders. The pilot of this aircraft next dropped a 250kg bomb on allotments (in the area now occupied by Waitrose). Mr J H J Witt, a local builder, had a lucky escape as he worked in his office in Middleton Road when this bomb fell. He took cover under his desk as the force of the explosions entirely demolished the building around him. Most of the injuries and damage sustained from this bomb were as a consequence of flying glass.

The second pilot dropped his bomb in Cherry Orchard Road. Due to the low altitude and the slope of the road, this bomb skidded through a wooden fence and came to rest in allotments before exploding. In all seven people were injured, none seriously, and damage was caused to houses and shops. A hole was also made in the roof of the Old Manor Hospital and a scattering of shell cases sprayed across the grounds.

At the time of the bombings, the New Picture House was showing a double feature of One Of Our Aircraft Is Missing and Weekend In Havana. The former film depicts the escape of a British air crew from the occupied Netherlands following the crash landing of their aeroplane. During the escape sequence the airmen hide out in a harbour and, under cover of an air raid, make their break for freedom. At the precise time the audience watched the bombs dropping on the screen, Salisbury came under attack and a 'real life' soundtrack accompanied the presentation. The film was interrupted and the house lights raised before a member of staff ran to the front of the auditorium shouting: 'It's alright, it's alright - they have all gone!' The lights were once again dimmed and everyone then stayed on to watch the rest of the film.

In September 1942 the Regal showed two military training films on a Monday morning. The screening was for the benefit of Civil Defence and National Fire Service personnel from Salisbury and Wilton. The first film dealt with the handling of unexploded bombs, and the second with the threat of airborne invasion. In the interval the local ARP Controller expressed his gratitude for the way organisations were working together and said he thought 'the morale of the citizens was never higher than it is today.' Later that year Salisbury cinemas opened on Christmas Day for the first time.

In January 1943 the New Picture House put on a special showing of My Friend Flicka to more than 800 children aged five to nine, who were accompanied by locally - based American servicemen playing the role of 'Daddy For The Day'. American army vehicles had been used to transport those children who lived outside the city to the cinema - with a Military Police escort as a safety precaution. All the expenses were met by the Americans, who had been making contributions to the event over the previous month – partly through use of a 'swear box' and some having forfeited a month's candy ration to provide sweets and chocolate.

Despite wartime restrictions, Salisbury's cinemas continued pulling the stops out occasionally. In August 1943 Kinematograph Weekly reported how 'Civic, Ecclesiastical and Military personages of high rank were present at a gala of The Gentle Sex' at the Gaumont, held on the opening night of the film's run in aid of the ATS benevolent fund.

Before the screening a parade of around 300 ATS women was held, with the salute being taken by Lieutenant - General Sir Charles Lloyd, KCB DSO MC, commander of Southern Command, who was accompanied by Controller Vera Farrow, Director of the ATS Southern Command, Senior Commander Sylvia Crawley, Deputy Assistant Director, officers of the Southern Command and of the American Army, the Mayor of Salisbury, the Earl of Pembroke and others.

Following the parade the whole company, headed by the ATS band, proceeded to the cinema, the entrance to which was 'dressed with flags and gay with flowers.' The ATS band went onstage and played the house in. Before the screening of the film cinema manager Mr Leddra introduced Joyce Howard, who played a leading part in the film.

Joyce Howard

In a brief speech, Miss Howard told how she had enjoyed her days in the ATS training centre and in other units during the making of the picture. Then a 'diminutive page boy' walked on to the stage and presented a bouquet of carnations to the star, and was rewarded with a kiss. It was estimated that the fund would benefit by about £250 raised on the night. The film was director/ narrator Leslie Howard's (no relation) tribute to the women who were helping to win the war. This was in fact Howard's last film in a successful 30-year career, as he was among the passengers killed when a civilian plane was shot down by the Luftwaffe over the Bay of Biscay.

As the war progressed, the cinemas continued to offer other forms of entertainment. In September 1943 the noted pianist Frank Merrick gave a Sunday afternoon piano recital at the Regal under the auspices of Musical Culture Ltd. The Salisbury Times reported that, although the audience was lower than anticipated, those that did attend witnessed 'a joy from beginning to end... this writer has not missed one of Mr Merrick's Salisbury recitals, and he has rarely heard his artistic playing to higher advantage.'

After its closure in 1937 the old Picture House building in Fisherton Street was put up for sale but stood empty for many years. The war saw the building brought back into use. The Government were searching for premises that could be requisitioned for military purposes and the Picture House became a drill hall for No 1 Company 43rd (Wessex) Division Signals Regiment, and also an army recruitment centre.

During the first winter of the war the unit moved to Mere, but unfortunately the last man out neglected to turn off the radiators, which resulted in flooding after the building was vacated. In April 1940 Wilfred Nobbs, who had been the corporal left in charge, faced an enquiry as to why £350 worth of damage had been caused to a Government building during wartime – he had been on leave at the time in question but was apparently 'ragged mercilessly by my section' about how long he would have to serve to pay the debt off. The building then stood empty again apart from a brief period in May 1943 when, during Wings For Victory week, film shows were presented by a mobile unit of the National Savings Committee.

The future for the building became somewhat brighter with the arrival of Basil Dean, who had created the Entertainment and National Service Association (ENSA) with Leslie Henson. Mr Dean was looking for premises in Salisbury that could be transformed into a garrison theatre, similar to others already established on military bases in the area. Service personnel with time to fill were seemingly prepared to watch pretty much anything including plays, ballet and concerts - perhaps for the first time in many cases - and discovered that they sometimes enjoyed what they were seeing, notwithstanding the alternative name of 'Every Night Something Awful' given to the ENSA acronym.

The Royal Engineers were engaged to refurbish the old Picture House and in four weeks thoroughly cleaned and redecorated the interior, including providing new pastel - shaded curtains for the stage. The stage space was increased by removing two walls. A new lighting system was installed and the old projection box beneath the balcony became the theatre's 'Box'. Behind the stage four dressing rooms were constructed to accommodate 20 people. The rooms behind the balcony, from which refreshments were served in the days when the building was a cinema, became offices. Seating accommodation was provided for about 500 theatregoers.

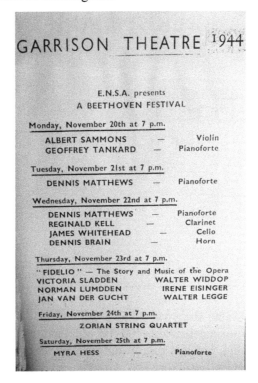

The Salisbury Garrison Theatre (Southern Command) opened on 31 October 1943 with the gala show You Asked For It, which starred John Clements, Fay Compton, Constance Cummings and Naunton Wayne. Most of the subsequent shows were organised directly by ENSA or organisations such as Stars In Battledress and The Central Pool of Artists. The garrison theatres proved to be a training ground for numerous personalities of the mid to late 20th Century - Peter Ustinov, Edith Evans, Flora Robson, James Mason, Glynis Johns, Eric Portman, Bryan Forbes, Laurence Olivier and Vivien Leigh were among those who appeared in Salisbury.

.... Each day the usherettes would go on parade in the auditorium ready for inspection by the manager ....

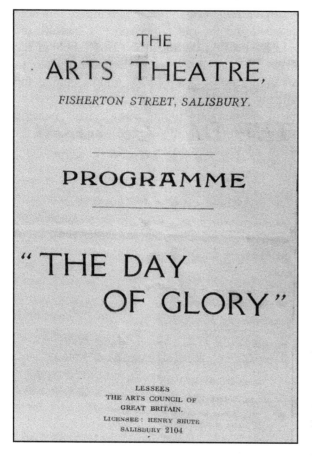

THE
ARTS THEATRE,
FISHERTON STREET, SALISBURY.

PROGRAMME

"THE DAY
OF GLORY"

LESSEES
THE ARTS COUNCIL OF
GREAT BRITAIN.
LICENSEE : HENRY SHUTE
SALISBURY 2104

When the war ended in 1945, ENSA relinquished the lease of the old Picture House building, but this time it did not stay empty and silent for too long. The Arts Council agreed to take over the running of the building and created an arts theatre with a resident repertory company. The newly named Arts Theatre opened on 31 October 1945 with H E Bates new play The Day Of Glory.

Despite the income arising from the large numbers of filmgoers during the war, the cinemas in Salisbury had received little attention to their physical condition. At the end of hostilities redecoration and repair became the top priority. However, funding was scarce and matters such as pre-war industrial actions raised their head again to hinder progress. On top of this the cinema would now face competition from a new form of home entertainment – the television.

In late 1946 George Howes, the New Picture House manager, was promoted to regional circuit manager, giving him overall responsibility for the Gaumont - British cinemas in Salisbury, Swindon, Trowbridge, Chippenham and Frome. Howes was replaced in Salisbury by Mr H B Walker, who had recently been demobbed from the Royal Navy, having served since May 1940. Prior to joining the Navy he had managed the Gaumont-British cinema in Cirencester.

Also on the staff at the New Picture House was a large-framed doorman named Reg Blake, who was assisted by Roger Emm, David Stone and in later years Roy Serviour. Mr Blake also had a young runner named Dennis. The team was regularly seen standing in the forecourt outside the main entrance of the building, once everything was up and running for the day. Their job was to organise the queues (of which there were many) and deal with any queries. As with the top hotels, the doormen, resplendent in their smart uniforms and peaked caps added to the feeling of opulence and grandeur, creating a sense of occasion for the punters. This all helped to make a trip to the cinema something very special.

Each day the usherettes would go on parade in the auditorium ready for inspection by the manager, who would ensure that everyone was properly turned out. Torches were regularly inspected and usherettes had to ensure the front of the torch was always twisted to produce a sharp spotlight. Reg Blake was charged with looking after the batteries, the usherettes having to put in a plea when their torches began to fail.

The chief usherette was Muriel Burns (later Eldridge), who was tasked with reading out the rotas each day so that the usherettes knew where they should stand. Once the positions were allocated, usherettes were prohibited from moving or swopping posts. There were also strict guidelines for showing patrons to their seats, and it was considered a major faux pas to shine a torch directly into the face of a customer. For an usherette, being placed for a shift in the stalls meant they had to sit on seats that pulled down from the wall. A shift in the balcony guaranteed far more comfortable seating and for this reason was considered preferable. Breaks in a shift were always welcome and the usherettes would often take turns to go out for fish and chips to Yorkshire Fisheries. Perhaps the worst job was the cleaning up of the cinema between films – especially the ash trays.

Although the majority of staff members were the responsibility of the management, the projectionists were in many respects autonomous. They reported directly to the area engineer, a Mr Peerless, assisted by the area sound engineer, Mr Best. Len Adams remained in charge of the projectors and Myrtle Penny and Nora Jerrard stepped down as Ken Robson safely returned to the New Picture House after military service. Ken had in fact spent some of his time overseas showing films to the forces. Now, rather than return to his pre - war role as third projectionist, he was promoted to second projectionist and the third post was abolished. This also meant a substantial pay rise – up from around £3 to £6 15s.

Len Adams and Ken Robson were joined by an apprentice who was given the responsibility of winding the films, checking the joins and ensuring that the reels were properly spliced in order to avoid any unnecessary breakdowns during a showing. Monday was the day when the new reels would arrive for the week. They were always delivered by train to Salisbury station where the apprentice would load up his wooden trolley before towing it back to the cinema.

Jim Smith had found checking of the newly delivered film reels at the Regal to be somewhat laborious, and the task was no less onerous for staff at the New Picture House. Films would often have been wound inside out having been shown at another cinema the previous week. Once the reels were checked and corrected as appropriate, they were placed into numbered, sliding bins so that everyone knew in which order the reels had to be shown. During the showing of a film neither projectionist could abandon their post since the projectors needed constant monitoring and adjustment to ensure the 'carbon arcs' did not burn out.

Two carbon rods were connected to an electric power source. When the rods were pulled apart slightly, this produced a bright light (the 'carbon arc'), caused by the carbon particles burning between the points. The projectionist had to keep a close eye because the carbon rods were gradually consumed by the burning, so they had to be regularly adjusted to maintain the correct distance between them, and the correct position relative to the optical centre of the lantern, during the showing of a film. In later years, this manual process was replaced by an automatic regulator but for now it was very labour intensive. Furthermore, the projectors from this era gave off a tremendous amount of heat, turning the projection room into a sweatbox.

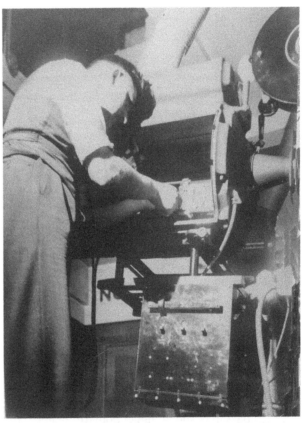

A 1940s projectionist at The New Picture House

As well as maintaining a close eye on the carbon rods, the projectionists also had to watch for breakages in the film. Whenever these occurrences arose, New Picture House audiences were apparently good natured - there was rarely any chanting or booing. The projectionists worked an average of a 60 hour week and the shifts could be gruelling. Whilst they often worked a five day week, a 'day' could be from 9.30am to 11.00pm. It was not until the late 1950s that the average working day was divided into a split shift.

The New Picture House advertising The Man in Half Moon Street and Winged Victory in 1945

On the evening of 23 June 1946, following a day of intense heat, a storm closing in from the north - east of Salisbury merged with another approaching from the north, causing the city's worst downpour in years. From about 7.00pm over two inches of rain fell in as little as 45 minutes, causing flooding between 18 inches and two feet deep. Castle Road and Castle Street were rendered impassable and a huge pool of water formed under the Fisherton Street railway bridge, stranding a coach on its way to Southsea and numerous private motor vehicles.

At the New Picture House, patrons were watching the latest double feature, Manhattan Music Box and Come On Leathernecks, but the noise of the driving rain and ensuing storm rendered the soundtrack inaudible. To make matters worse water began to flow through the side doors of the cinema auditorium, forming a lake beneath the screen and flooding out the seats at the front. This was probably as a result of the stream adjacent to Water Lane overflowing and some reports indicated that water may have come

in through the foyer as well. Despite the problem, the cinema remained open for business. Children stomped around in the puddles and on the squelchy carpet until the water receded and staff could clear up the mess.

During the war and its aftermath, cinemas had enjoyed the benefit of Sunday opening under Defence Regulation 42B, which was scheduled to remain in full force and effect, unless otherwise revoked, until 31 December 1947. It was down to Salisbury City Council to decide whether Sunday opening should be banned once again, or whether what had become the norm should be maintained.

At the time the Church still held a great moral influence and debate raged in the Council chamber and the local press for many weeks. The view of the local clergy was that 'the rest day is a fundamental law binding on all men which can only be disregarded at peril.' The Church wanted the Council to hold a referendum on the subject, but it soon became clear that they were in the minority, with not one single letter to the local press coming out in support of their views.

One Journal correspondent, T M Broomgrove, had a suggestion: 'May I suggest that the clergyman should hold later Sunday services, otherwise people are left to their own devices very early. Failing this let some enterprising clergyman attend the cinemas to conduct community hymn singing or hold a short service. One thing the Sunday cinemas have done is to keep their patrons interested and off the streets. It must be remembered that a number of people have few home comforts to hurry home to after the early finish of church services. Until the churches can offer something to take the cinemas' place, then it is my submission that they have no case for cinemas to be closed on Sunday.'

**Staff lined up on February 8th 1945
with manager Mr Leddra**

The Reverend Maulvererer, vicar of St Francis' Church, took a pragmatic and modern view in his parish magazine. He felt there was nothing wrong with Sunday football, golf, cinema or any other wholesome recreation for that matter, provided the individual had first been to church. He did however stress that any trip to the cinema should be to see 'decent' films!

These viewpoints reflected the view of many local residents. Sunday cinema had become a way of life for the local population people of Salisbury and the troops posted in the area. With not only economic but also social issues to consider, the choice to keep the cinemas open on Sundays was in many respects a foregone conclusion.

Although the local issue of Sunday opening was resolved, a crisis was raising its head in the film industry nationally. During the war years American cinema had continued to thrive, with a high percentage of its income coming from British audiences craving glamour and escapism. By contrast, many British films had lacked the quality of the pre - war period. Rather than being used as main features many British films were now paired with superior Hollywood releases.

In 1947, Sir Stafford Cripps, the President of the Board of Trade, had spoken out against the 'over-Americanisation of British culture' and on 6 August an ad valorem tax (i.e. a tax 'according to value') of 75% of expected earnings was placed on all future film imports. This became known as 'Dalton Duty' after the then Chancellor of the Exchequer, Hugh Dalton. The Government had been warned that the British film industry could collapse without American support, but this fell on deaf ears and Hollywood launched a boycott on the British market. This was exacerbated by a general slump in the British economy.

In Salisbury the Gaumont hosted a meeting on the subject. It was suggested to manager Mr Leddra that the British film industry would go under without the Americans, to which he responded 'Stuff and nonsense!' Mr Leddra spoke about there being a 'season' of crises – the dollar crisis, the coal crisis, the food crisis and now the film crisis. He put the case that the absence of American films could in fact provide British cinema with a golden opportunity to capitalise on the gap in the market.

Mr F Sanders, The Mayor of Salisbury told the meeting 'If anyone steps on the British lion's tail, it turns, and tonight we are accepting the challenge which has been thrown out to us by the Americans.' He was convinced there was enough talent, energy and enterprise in the British film industry to ride out the crisis. The simple economic truth though, was that Britain needed the American blockbusters and the impasse between the Government and Hollywood was resolved in 1948, when a settlement was reached.

.... Dick Barton grabbed the receiver, heard the voice of his dreaded enemy and rushed away into another adventure ....

Despite making losses due to the crisis, J Arthur Rank planned to merge the Gaumont-British chain with the rival Odeon chain, which had fallen under Rank control in 1941 following the death of its founder, Oscar Deutsch (the name 'Odeon' being an acronym of 'Oscar Deutsch Entertains Our Nation'). The Government had repeatedly resisted this move to effectively create a massive near-monopoly in mainstream British cinema. However, during 1948 and 1949, Rank formed a separate company named Circuits Management Association (CMA), which controlled the running of both Gaumont-British and Odeon.

As well as the turmoil in the British cinema industry, there were also changes at the New Picture House in Salisbury. Firstly, with the cinema now more than 10 years old, the 'New' was dropped from its official name. At around the same time staff welcomed the return of the highly popular George Howes as manager, although this was to prove short lived as Gaumont - British soon appointed him manager of the more prestigious Gaumont Palace, where he succeeded Mr Leddra as manager.

George Howes' former assistant, Mr Close, took over as acting manager of the Picture House, until December 1949 saw the arrival of Charles Tappy. Mr Tappy had spent 22 years in service to Gaumont-British, starting as a film boy in the days of the silent films. He had previously managed the Gaumont at Frome, where he had been in charge for five years. Mr Close in turn took on his own first full managerial role as manager at Frome.

Radio hero 'Dick Barton' had visited the Picture House in 1948, as the actor Don Stannard pulled up outside the cinema in what was described by the Salisbury Times as a 'super-streamlined two - seater sports car'. Stannard spoke from the stage to mark the provincial release of Dick Barton – Special Agent, which was intended to be the first in a new series of Hammer films. Unfortunately Stannard was killed in a car crash in 1949 and the series was discontinued after only three films.

His time in Salisbury was a busy one, beginning with a visit to the Wellworthy piston rings factory at West Harnham, where he spoke to workers in their canteen during the lunch hour. Stannard then drove off to Harnwood Hospital, where he visited all the wards and chatted to patients before continuing his tour to the General Infirmary children's wards, where he received a great welcome and signed autographs.

Returning to the Picture House in the evening, Stannard was greeted by hundreds of children who cheered as he sprang from his car and ran through the foyer to be greeted by Sir Reginald Kennedy - Cox. He then entertained another 1000 children and more adults inside the theatre before a telephone sited on the stage suddenly rang. 'Dick Barton' grabbed the receiver, heard the voice of his dreaded enemy and rushed away into another fictional adventure, with the children's further cheering ringing in his ears.

In a letter to Alan Richardson in 1980, John Robertson of the North West Cinema Preservation Society remembered visiting garrison cinemas while based in the Salisbury area in the immediate post-war years: 'The two cinemas at Bulford and the one at Larkhill were owned by the Kendall circuit. I think it was based somewhere in Sussex.'

'The garrisons at the two camps were to all intents and purposes identical from the outside. I would think they were built around 1938 and were from all respects plush little theatres. They were as well equipped as any 'civvy' shows at the time and had the full complement of tabs and lights that one would expect at a city cinema. The projection at the Bulford one was in all ways immaculate. Tabs always cued spot on and records timed to perfection. Focus and light beautiful. As a projectionist in Civvy Street I used to look for faults, but I could not find any. The sound was B.T-H and, if I remember rightly the mechs Kalee 12 with Kalee Vulcan arcs. The one at Larkhill was equipped with RCS sound, but I do not know what the rest of it was.'

'The Larkhill theatre had a fire I think about 1945, but I do not know the extent of the damage. Purely internal I would think. Both of these theatres were taken over by the AKC and renamed 'Globe'. I should think both would still have been running. Also in Bulford and also owned by Kendalls was the Beacon, known locally as 'The Bug 'utch.' This made a complete contrast with the other two. It was drab, dingy and dirty. The house lights had no dimmer, just a switch, there were no tabs or stage lighting and the projection was from behind the screen, the light was dim and the sound awful. But we used to patronise it because it was the Salisbury Plain home of Warner Brothers' gangster movies and MGM musicals. I think it closed just before I was demobbed in 1948.

In early 1948 former Regal projectionist Jim Smith returned to the area from his wartime service, during which he had spent some time as a prisoner of war in the Far East. He took on the post of projectionist at the Globe garrison cinema at Westdown Camp near Tilshead, where he and his wife Mary lived in converted dressing rooms with their kitten Tootie.

Jim used coloured lights to set the ambience in the cinema before the films began. If a thriller was showing, then reds and yellows would be used and if a horror film, blues and greens. He also chose recorded classical music to complement the coloured lights - dramatic pieces for a western or gangster film and perhaps a romantic Chopin extract for a love story. Mary sold tickets in the box office and then sat in the back row to enjoy the film once the audience was seated – often accompanied by Tootie.

Projectionist Jim Smith

The Smiths enjoyed their time on the Plain but with the imminent arrival of their first child in the spring of 1949, they moved in with Jim's parents in Fairfield Road, Salisbury. Jim now found work with the AKC based nearby in Stratford Road. He travelled all over the south-west of England, repairing and servicing projectors in army camp cinemas. If travelling very far west Jim would be scheduled to take a meal at the camp's sergeant's mess and then sleep in a barrack bed overnight, with the next day allowed for returning to Salisbury. However, Jim would invariably complete his work with enough time to drive home into the early hours, thus securing himself a free day.

The 1940s had been a chaotic and tumultuous decade for the World and for cinema. To see the decade out the staff of the three Salisbury cinemas joined together for a party at the Assembly Rooms, with entertainment provided by up and coming local singer Rosemary Squires.

.... the men said they were soldiers and had taken the helmet for 'a bit of fun' ....

The 1950s saw cinema begin to lose its appeal. During the 1930s and 1940s heyday it was an essential form of entertainment and, within living memory, still something of a novelty – especially in the case of 'the talkies', but tastes were now rapidly changing. Live entertainment was making a big comeback and this, coupled with the growing popularity of both radio and television, was eating in to cinema audience figures.

Maudie Smith outside the New Picture House, Fisherton Street in 1947. The film showing was the historical drama, Captain Boycott

The Coronation of Elizabeth II on 2 June 1953 particularly helped popularise the sale of television sets. By 1958 eight million households had television licences and many film studios had been closed or sold to broadcasters. Annual national cinema attendances did though continue to top one billion for most of the 1950s, but then dropped off dramatically over the last three years of the decade to just over 581 million in 1959.

The BBFC Certificates dating from 1932 were revised in 1951 to: U (Passed for Universal Exhibition – Patrons of all ages are admitted; A (Passed for Public Exhibition to Adult Audiences – Patrons under 12 must be accompanied by a parent or guardian) and; X (Passed for Public Exhibition When No Children under 16 are present – Only patrons aged 16 or over are admitted). The latter replaced the H ('Horrific') certificate to accommodate other violent genres and 'adult' content).

In the early 1950s an alternative to the main Salisbury cinemas was offered by Sarum Mobile Film Shows, operated by Arthur Wingrove out of the Old Castle Inn and his second hand shop in Devizes Road. The start of the decade saw technical improvements at the Picture House. Gaumont - British decided it was time to replace the old Magnus projectors with new GB Kalee projection equipment, which was modern, far more efficient and a lot more pleasant for the projectionists to operate. This meant a certain amount of retraining, with staff having to learn new film lacing techniques and loops to ensure there was constant synchronisation between the picture being shown on the screen and the sound-track coming through the speakers. The benefits of the new projectors were immediately apparent. They were much quieter than their predecessors and gave off much less heat. The Magnus projectors were virtually untouchable when they were running at their hottest. One disadvantage however was that the carbon arcs on the new Kalee projectors could produce unpleasant fumes.

A more significant change was a complete rebranding of the Picture House as CMA decided to transfer ownership of the cinema wholly to the Odeon chain. This only happened to one other cinema at the time - the Angel at Islington. This change meant the newly branded cinemas could now take Odeon film releases, placing them on a different film circuit to the Gaumont - British cinema and providing more options for the customer. From 27 February 1950, the old neon signs were removed from the cinema's Fisherton Street frontage and the famous Odeon lettering was erected in its place.

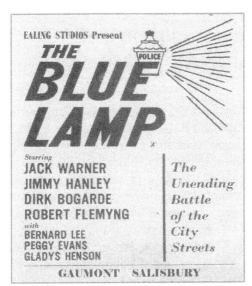

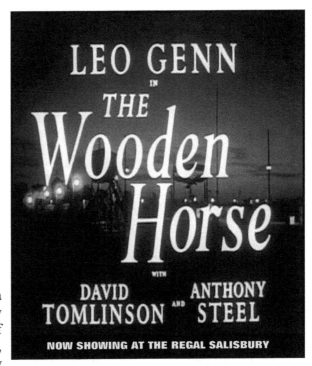

Released in 1950, The Blue Lamp attracted a lot of publicity as its representation of the sleazy side of London centred on the shocking murder of PC George Dixon (played by Jack Warner who, despite the character's 'death', went on to play the part on TV for a period of 20 years). The film proved popular at the Salisbury Gaumont, where representatives of the police force also viewed the film, at the invitation of the cinema management. Chief Inspector Scorey commented 'It depicts the true-life of the present day police officer and the nature of the work he is called upon to perform. It shows a wide variety of subjects and the film should hold the interest of both police officer and public, and allow the latter an insight into the rather obscure machinations of the police force behind the scenes.'

To help publicise the film, a tailor's dummy dressed as a police sergeant was stood outside the Gaumont. At one stage William Parsons, who was selling newspapers on the street, witnessed two men walking around the dummy. Noticing afterwards that the police helmet had gone missing Mr Parsons followed the men along Milford Street. When challenged, and in the presence of PC Gosney, the men denied taking the helmet even though one of them had a bulge under his overcoat. They were taken to the police station where the overcoat was ripped open to display the helmet - the men said they were soldiers and had taken the helmet for 'a bit of fun.' In Court, the Mayor (presiding) said the defendants had committed a crime – the very thing the film sought to prevent. Each man was given a fine of 15 shillings.

Later that year, wartime classic The Wooden Horse was shown at the Regal, bringing back memories for a Salisbury man. The film told the story of how three men escaped from Stalag III, a German prisoner of war camp, by digging a tunnel under cover of a wooden horse. The film was based on a remarkable book written by Eric Williams, who was one of the three men that escaped - alongside Oliver Philpot and Michael Codner.

Prior to the film first being shown in Salisbury, Regal manager Hugh Melville Burge invited Mr Williams on to the stage, where he described his experiences during the dramatic escape. Appearing with him was Mr E W Walker, of Wordsworth Road, Salisbury, who had been a prisoner with Mr Williams. A replica of the wooden vaulting horse was brought on to the stage. Mr Walker then described life in Stalag III before Mr Williams related how during the escape the men had improvised tunnel lamps from can bases, filled with cooking oil and with pyjama cord wicks, while bed boards and stolen planks were used to shore up the tunnel's sides and roof.

On 10 March 1951, the Odeon was the first in Salisbury to publicly exhibit an X-rated film – the sultry adaptation of Tennessee Williams' A Streetcar Named Desire, with Vivien Leigh and Marlon Brando.

.... The Gaumont-British junior cinema club was first introduced in Salisbury in 1943 ....

The ABC Minors at the Regal with Saucebox the dog (above) and Coco the Clown (below)

Despite the general downward trend in attendance, there was one initiative that remained popular with youngsters over several decades - Saturday morning cinema. In the 1940s, ABC had set up the first major Saturday cinema club for children - The ABC Minors. The Gaumont - British junior cinema club was first introduced in Salisbury in 1943, at what was still then known as the New Picture House. The club cost six pence a time and attracted 700 to 800 children per week.

The programme would normally comprise a cartoon, a short film, a serialised programme such as Flash Gordon, then an interval, another cartoon and a full length feature such as a Lassie movie.

Local entertainers would often appear, including John Batt and Ralph Francis, the Punch and Judy man. Each week there was a quiz, with children being notified of the subject the previous week (for example history or geography) and prizes were awarded to the winners. It was also normal for there to be sing-a-longs, with Mrs Nugent on piano or, if she was unavailable, the children would sing along to a gramophone player. Typical songs included Land of Hope and Glory, You Are My Sunshine and Bless You.

The popularity of the club continued in to the Odeon era, with some changes in format, with children often loading up beforehand at the sweet shop run by the Misses Ling in Fisherton Street. Saturday morning cinema could provide a challenge for the usherettes, who often had to dodge missiles being thrown from one side of the auditorium to the other.

Just along Fisherton Street financial problems had continued to dog the Arts Theatre, based in the old Picture House building. In 1951 the Arts Council decided it could no longer bear the burden of the company and withdrew from its management. However, the people of Salisbury rallied round to form a non-distributing company under the chairmanship of Sir Reginald Kennedy Cox and the theatre was saved. Gradually though, the touring element was abandoned in favour of weekly repertory. The name 'Arts Theatre' remained until July 1953 when, following criticism that the word 'Arts' could be putting a lot of people off, it was decided to change the name to 'Salisbury Playhouse'.

In 1952 teenaged Petula Clark appeared live on the stage at the Gaumont. At the time she told the Salisbury Journal a delightful story about a previous appearance in Salisbury, as a child star of the 1940s: 'I expect Daddy would remember it better, but I do recall a night during the war when we arrived late in Salisbury and found our hotel locked. Of course, we couldn't get in, and then one of your policemen came along and helped us out by taking us to the police station, where Daddy and I spent the night in a cell. It was during the blackout I think.'

In June 1952 film star Richard Todd, who had been stationed on Salisbury Plain whilst serving in the Parachute Regiment during World War II, visited the city to open an exhibition celebrating the centenary of the 1852 Salisbury Exhibition. The ceremony took place in sunshine on a platform in front of the Guildhall steps and the Salisbury Times reported that a crowd of more than 2,000 witnessed the event.

After the ceremony 'Bright eyed teenage girls and clamouring women' broke through police cordons and 'reached the Guildhall steps just as Mr Todd, sun - tanned and smiling, was leaving with the Mayor and others for a brief preview of the section of the exhibition... housed in the Market Square. Police officers rescued him from his insistent admirers and he was able to continue a triumphant walk through a narrow corridor formed in the dense throngs'.

There were also personal appearances by film stars at the Gaumont including (in 1953) a visit from Jack Hawkins, who was promoting his film The Cruel Sea. Hundreds of people queued for hours to see the 42 year old star and when he stepped onto the stage there were 'gasps and oohs' from the girls in the audience.

With all three city cinemas competing for a diminishing audience, novel promotional ideas were always being tested. In 1955 the Odeon presentation of Laurence Olivier's Richard III was advertised by a banner and the tying of a large crown to the central flag pole. Large external displays were often placed across the canopy of the Odeon, and for one film a huge parachute was draped over the frontage to catch the eye of punters. Competitions were regularly run at the cinema and families were invited as guests if they had something in common with a particular film. For instance, Mr and Mrs Scott of Endless Street and their five sons were invited to see a film called All My Sons.

Personalities connected with the films also occasionally made a special appearance at the Fisherton Street venue, including Jerry Desmonde, who also visited Odstock Hospital whilst promoting The Cardboard Cavalier, accompanied by an usherette dressed as the film's female lead Margaret Lockwood. Another visitor to Odstock was 'Uncle Remus', alias James Baskett, who

The bandleader Ted Heath who together with his orchestra, appeared at the Gaumont in February 1956. Fifth from the right is Dorothy Feltham who provided the photograph.

starred in the Disney classic Song of the South, and Derrick de Marney visited the cinema to promote She Shall Have Murder and answered questions from the stage.

In 1952 Regal manager Hugh Melville Burge had the novel idea of climbing Salisbury Cathedral and broadcasting live to the cinema's audience by relay. Unfortunately this could not be arranged but instead the team of steeplejacks who were working on the spire were invited to the cinema for an evening, answering questions from the audience during the interval. This proved very popular and even earned headlines in the London Evening Standard.

In May 1953 a touch of Hollywood glamour briefly came to Harnham. A chauffeur driven Rolls Royce pulled up outside the Old Mill Hotel and out stepped film stars Lana Turner and her husband Lex Barker, better known as 'Tarzan'. Miss Turner was wearing a light fawn woollen frock, a 'shimmering' fur stole and heavy jewellery. The couple stayed at the hotel for around 90 minutes, entertained by Mr & Mrs R M Sutherland. Lex Barker was familiar with the area, having been stationed at Longford Castle during the war. The couple were apparently touring in the area and had motored to Salisbury from Beaulieu.

".... Patrons could stay in the cinema for as long as they wanted to and see the films over again ...."

In July 1953, on leaving school at the age of 15, Bryan Rowe began working as a trainee projectionist at the Gaumont. Bryan recalls that the main film being screened that week was Thunder Bay, with James Stewart. The job was not all about showing films though: 'The working day was from 9.30am to 10.45pm with an hour break for lunch and a half hour tea break. An average day would begin by cleaning down the projectors with special attention to the arc lamp compartment. The carbons that were used to create the flame for the light to illuminate the film sent off fumes left a deposit of dust that had to be cleaned off, including the large mirror that reflected the light.'

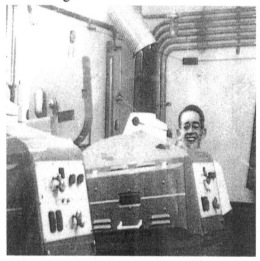

Bryan Rowe behind the projectors at the Odeon

'The main projection booth (known in the trade as 'the box') had to be kept scrupulously clean, the main floor hoovered and polished every morning - any dust particles could damage the surface of the 35mm film being put into the projectors throughout the main shows. Once a week, a major task was the preparation of the new programme of films. The films would arrive in very heavy metal boxes, delivered by a special carrier. Each box contained one feature film, normally consisting of five 2000 - foot spools of film on a central bobbin, each in its own tin with the name and part of the film on a label.'

'A member of the projection staff had to transfer the film off the bobbins on to the main spools for the week's show. This was often a painstaking task as every foot of film had to be checked by hand for any tears or faulty repair joins that could have been made at the cinema which had previously shown the film. The Sunday evening programmes were often a nightmare, as these were always older films distributed maybe some 20 years or so and were in a particularly poor condition.'

'Once a week the stage area had to be hoovered and debris thrown at the screen by members of the audience had to be cleared. A daily morning routine was the checking of all of the cinema's lighting to see if bulbs needed changing. You had to have a head for heights for this, as some of the ceiling alcove lights in the main auditorium that needed replacing had to be reached by a ladder set up at the edge of the main balcony. The person precariously changing the bulb had to look down on the area of the stalls some 60 feet below!'

'The film programmes would start each day at around 2.00pm and finish around 10.20pm. Projection staff had to then shut down generating and extractor fan equipment, bring down the iron safety curtain, which for fire purposes sealed off the screen and stage area from the auditorium, assist other staff in checking all toilets were vacated throughout the building and shut down the main lighting system.'

'In that period of the history of the cinema in Salisbury, all film programmes were shown continuously throughout the day. Patrons could stay in the cinema for as long as they wanted to and see the films over again. In the winter this was particularly attractive as patrons and families could bring in their snack food and sit in a warm environment for as long as they wanted to. More work for the cleaners next morning to clear up the rubbish!'

'One of the major changes I experienced at my time at the Gaumont was the installation of the Cinemascope screen system. The old postage stamp screen format was replaced by a screen that took up the complete width of the cinema's large stage. The installation process took place overnight [in 1954] and was in place for the first Cinemascope film to be shown in Salisbury - Tony Curtis in The Black Shield of Falworth - an all action, swashbuckling, technicolour drama.'

'The only change for the projectionist, was that the projectors had to be fitted with two inter - changeable lenses, to enable the different film image to be viewed as normal on the large screen. The main new lens could be adjusted to fit any of the alternative formats that film studios were introducing at the time - Paramount... Vistavision...RKO Superscope !'

'An integral part of all the film programmes was the Gaumont British News. In Salisbury, one copy had to be shared between the Gaumont and the Odeon cinemas. It was the job of the junior members of staff to take the newsreel to the cinema that was going to screen it next. Many is the time I braved all weathers riding my bike with the special film container balanced on my handlebars - normally twice a day!'

'I have often been asked whether we ever put on a wrong reel of film during a show. My answer is we did once! Universal Pictures used to put out a double-bill feature programme, normally with one being a drama and the other a comedy. On this particular week one feature was a drama starring Jeff Chandler and the other a comedy starring Abbot and Costello. On this particular night we were about to change over from one projector to another. The scene on the outgoing projector showed Jeff Chandler slowly climbing some stairs in the dark. We switched over to the incoming projector which showed Abbott and Costello driving across the desert in a jeep!'

Across town at the Regal, Friday 13 April 1956 was a lucky day for manager Hugh Melville Burge as he celebrated 25 years with ABC, most of them having been spent at the Salisbury cinema. Welshman Burge had grown to love Salisbury and told the Salisbury Journal 'Although I have been offered various other managerial appointments and even an executive position – that would have meant travelling around – I have preferred to stay comfortably with my wife in Salisbury.'

At the time Burge was busy preparing for the following day's celebration of ten years of the ABC Minors cinema club. The reporter noted that in Burge's office there were many framed awards, the latest of which had only recently been presented to him by ABC Managing Director D J Goodlatte in London. This was a certificate for the Outstanding Manager in the Bournemouth district in 1955. 'It's the first time I've won it' said Burge, 'and as there are 20 other ABC cinemas in the district I feel very proud.'

Guests of honour attend the screening of 'The Dam Busters' at The Regal

During World War Two, there had been a local link to the real story of 617 Squadron – 'The Dam Busters' - as the 'bouncing bomb' prototypes were tried out at Ashley Walk in the New Forest. Relics including a small viewing shelter remain today – who knows what eyes may have looked through that slot and across the experimental bombing range?

When The Dam Busters film (starring Richard Todd as Wing-Commander Guy Gibson) opened at the Salisbury Regal, in 1955, it was something of an event. The Air Cadets Band marched through the streets and formed a guard of honour at the cinema where a host of top military persons attended the screening. Two people who were also invited but unable to attend, were Mrs F Durnford, of Southampton, who had been Wing-Commander Gibson's childhood nanny, and Mr John Sykes of Woodside Road, Salisbury, who had flown as an air gunner in the night raid on the Möhne and Elder dams and lived to tell the tale.

.... The Robot naturally stole the show when the film was released much to the disdain of leading actor Walter Pidgeon ....

In 1956, Robbie the Robot, the mechanical star of MGMs Forbidden Planet, made a personal appearance at the Regal. The cinema pulled out all the stops to advertise the event and the Salisbury Times captured the scene as excited children crowded Endless Street trying to get a glimpse of this 'ingenious example of intellectual ironmongery who eventually turned up on the back of a Land Rover.' Eight foot - tall Robbie had featured largely in a nationwide MGM promotional campaign with window displays, children's competitions, Robbie the Robot balloons and displays of flying saucers. The robot naturally stole the show when the film was released 'much to the disdain of leading actor Walter Pidgeon!'

That same year, the Regal also received a Royal visitor, albeit in off - duty guise, when the Duke of Kent - at that time serving with the Scots Greys at Aldershot – and two friends went to the cinema to see wartime thriller The Man Who Never Was. The Duke was recognised by the doorman when he arrived at the cinema in time to see the last complete performance. Beforehand the Duke and his companions had spent half an hour in the Salisbury Arms in Endless Street, where they were served by the licensee, Mr E G Gough.

In the spring of 1956 Bryan Rowe gained promotion and moved from the Gaumont to become second projectionist at the Odeon: 'This was quite an easy employment transfer as both the Odeon and the Gaumont cinemas came within the management of the Rank Organisation. At the time of my move the union had negotiated a new shift system for projectionists. Rather than working long days five days a week, staff would now do a split day shift - 9.00am to 4.00pm and 4.00pm to 11.00pm. This was a big improvement as it meant when your shift ended at 4.00pm on a Friday you were off until 4.00pm on the following Monday - thus giving us every other weekend off !'

'Although in 1956, television was starting to move into most households, the cinema was still in its prime. That year the Kenneth More, Douglas Bader epic Reach for the Sky broke all records. Long queues would form along Fisherton Street at lunch time to see the matinee performance and the cinema was full for the six day run of the film. By this time the Odeon had the new Cinemascope format. Strangely both cinemas still only operated mono sound - clearly Rank had not seen this as important!'

'One great memory I have is when Len Adams, the chief projectionist, set up a stereo speaker system to coincide with the great Cinemascope musical Oklahoma. The sight and sound of Gordon Macrae singing Oh What A Beautiful Morning brought home the ultimate in screen presentation within the experience of cinema.'

'A key part of the cinema programme was the sale of ice cream at the interval. It was the job of the projectionist to train an arc spotlight on the sales girls standing at the front of the stalls or balcony. To the annoyance of the girls we would often keep the bright spotlight on them for a good length of time so that they were dazzled by the light and had to take time to adjust and re - focus to serve the patrons, who by this time had formed a long queue.'

'On Good Fridays it had been a tradition that a local priest or vicar would come on the stage during the evening performance and give a short address. I was never sure how this went down with the audience intent on watching the latest blockbuster. On one such occasion when there was a full house a vicar in a black cassock bounced on to the stage and pointed to the audience shouting 'This is the day we murdered God'… not a murmur could be heard from the audience - such drama!'

'One health hazard that was never seen as a risk factor was the amount of cigarette smoke generated by a full house. A large proportion of the audience would light up throughout the programme and the thick clouds of smoke pervading the cinema would be picked up by the beam from the projector. There was an extractor fan system but this could not cope with numbers of people smoking.'

The Plaza at Amesbury hosted its 21st Anniversary on 11 November 1956. The cinema produced a special souvenir programme for the event, with manager Lieutenant - Colonel Duncan writing: 'What is the motivation in the assembly and presentation of Films at the Plaza? Simply, it has been and always will be this: We assume our Patrons come to the Plaza, sit down, look at the Stage, and expect one thing from us, if they voiced it they would say – 'NOW ENTERTAIN US'. To do just that is our basic aim. Coupled to that, our constant endeavour is to keep you in the forefront of Pictorial presentation, give the best in

Left to right: Magda Miller, Peter Arne and Dorothy Allison, who presented the giant silver key to Mr. H.R.S Duncan, the cinema manager.

Sound, allied to comfort, environment, cleanliness and courtesy to the best of our ability. May we continue at your Service in the future in accordance with that aim.'

The programme also included some fascinating statistics about the cinema. It was claimed that to date 5,678,400 seats had been sold for 6,552 feature films, news reels and short films. 917,280 of these patrons had climbed the 36 stairs to see the films from the circle. Approximately 14,000 feet of film had been exhibited per performance (approximately 28,000 feet per night, 196,000 feet per week, 10,192,000 per year and 214,032,000 in 21 years). 62,496 programmes had been posted to patrons who had applied to be put on the mailing list.

15 tons of paper had been used in Plaza advertising. 658 tons of coke had been burnt for heating and the equivalent of supplying London with lighting for 31½ hours continuously had been consumed. In all, customers had apparently consumed 742,560 Lyons ice creams (representing 18,000 gallons), 3,822 gallons of Kia Ora soft drinks, 124,802 packets of Sun Pat nuts (in the previous six years - representing 4¼ tons) and 854,760 packets of cigarettes (representing 15,000,840 individual cigarettes!) No wonder the cleaners had disposed of more than 182 tons of paper!

.... From its opening in 1935, MGM pictures were shown at the Plaza before Salisbury ....

6.00 p.m.	NATIONAL ANTHEM
6.05 p.m.	THE NEWS—1935 - 1956
	1935—The original Newsreel shewn at the Plaza, Amesbury, at 6 p.m. on Monday, 11th November, 1935.
	1956—The latest Newsreel issued but a few hours ago.
	We pay tribute to great makers of various techniques
6.25 p.m.	The favourite travelogue of FITZPATRICK
	Copenhagen, City of Towers (u)
6.35 p.m.	The favourite cartoon of WALT DISNEY, The Lonely Chipmunk
6.45 p.m.	One of the earliest successes of the great master (u)
	CHARLES CHAPLIN in THE TRAMP (u)
7.05 p.m.	The favourite short feature of PETE SMITH, Global Quiz (u)
7.15 p.m.	Tom and Jerry in Touche Pussycat CinemaScope (u)
7.25 p.m.	Trailers
7.35 p.m.	IN THE VILLAGE TO-NIGHT—
	We stop the roar of Amesbury's Traffic to bring you some stars who are in the Village tonight. Presented by a Duncan but not Peter
	Miss DOROTHY ALISON Mr. PETER ARNE Miss MAGDA MILLER
	(for biographies see page 5)
7.55 p.m.	Interval
8.00 p.m.	PHONE CALL from The Empire, Leicester Square
8.10 p.m.	Concurrent with The Empire
	Metro-Goldwyn-Mayers Latest Film
	SOMEBODY UP THERE LIKES ME
	with Pier Angeli and Paul Newman
10.10 p.m.	Finale by the Amesbury Town Silver Band

93 people had been employed at the Plaza, one original member of staff remained, with the next longest server having completed 10 years. During the Second World War members of the Plaza staff, both male and female, had served in the Royal Navy, the Army and the Royal Air Force - Lieutenant-Colonel Duncan had served as a Special Constable for Amesbury. Snowball, a black cat, started employment at the cinema on 12 November 1935. He remained in service for three years before leaving, having destroyed 'all his enemies' and was not replaced.

The famous 'Leo' had roared at the beginning of 3,328 MGM pictures at the cinema and the gong of J Arthur Rank had been struck 1,982 times. From its opening in 1935, MGM pictures were shown at the Plaza before Salisbury – by now, in 1956, this also applied to most 20th Century Fox films.

The film of the 1937 Coronation of King George VI was exhibited at the Plaza at 6 o'clock on the evening of the actual event. Captain Sir

Malcolm Campbell made one of his first Territorial Recruiting Speeches accompanied by his mobile patrol at the cinema in 1938. The RAF Dance Orchestra, under the direction of Jimmy Miller, gave a midnight matinee at the Plaza for charity in 1941. During the war the cinema's office was used as an Army Welfare Office for troops in the Salisbury Plain district - the foyer housed the Night - watchers and many National Savings Campaigns and similar were opened from the Plaza stage. In all, £2,680 had been raised in the cinema for charities, and three wedding anniversaries - two Silver and one Golden - had been celebrated there.

The celebrations were varied and imaginative. After the playing of the National Anthem at 6.00pm came the very first 1935 newsreel shown at the Plaza followed by the very latest newsreel issued but a few hours before. Then there was a tribute to great makers of various film techniques: The favourite travelogue of Fitzpatrick, Copenhagen, City of Towers; The favourite cartoon of Walt Disney, The Lonely Chipmunk; One of the earliest successes of the 'great master' Charles Chaplin in The Tramp; The favourite short feature of Pete Smith, Global Quiz and; Tom and Jerry in Touche Pussycat. After some up to date trailers three film stars – Dorothy Allison, Peter Arne and Magda Miller – were presented to a 'large and enthusiastic audience' by Lieutenant - Colonel Duncan. Miss Alison then handed Lieutenant-Colonel Duncan a giant key on behalf of the Rank Organisation.

Following a short interval a congratulatory phone call was taken from the Empire, Leicester Square before the main feature, MGM's latest film Somebody Up There Likes Me, was shown concurrently with the London venue. More than four hours entertainment was rounded off with a finale performance by the Amesbury Town Silver Band.

Among the many congratulatory messages and advertisements contained in the programme, some were of local interest: James & Crockerell Ltd, building and civil engineering contractors of Durrington, had built the cinema in 1935 and maintained the building in the meantime; The Greyhound Inn, Amesbury (bang opposite the cinema and handy for a pre or post film jar); Macey & Jeffrey Ltd, tobacconists of Salisbury (who presumably supplied most of those 15 million gaspers); H J Cooper, coal merchants of Amesbury (ditto the 650 tons of coke); The George Hotel, Amesbury; The Hants & Wilts Film Transport Co Ltd ('who have delivered our films for 21 years despite bombing, snow and come what may, 'Bang on Time''); John Hall & Co (Warminster) Ltd ('Paints used when the cinema was built and for all decorating since'); Shepherd and Hedger of Salisbury (furnishings) and; F Jay & Son, Salisbury ('printers to the Plaza for the past 21 years').

The Plaza had organised a 21st birthday competition, inviting patrons to write in with amusing stories surrounding the cinema. The best two entries would be rewarded with a visit to the ABC studios at Elstree, to see films being made and be entertained to lunch. The 1st Prize Winner was C S Deall of The Abbey, Amesbury, who recalled 'An incident in connection with the Plaza is still good for a laugh. On this particular occasion an X film was being shown and during the week a distinguished local gentleman discussed with indignation that such films were not suitable for British entertainment, and I wholeheartedly agreed with every word. Later in the week I furtively entered the cinema and smugly sank into my seat, protected by the darkness. At the end of the picture the lights went up, I glanced at the man in the next seat – it was my distinguished friend. Yes! Our faces were red.'

The 2nd Prize went to the story submitted by Frank S Wallace of Antrobus Road: 'Brevity being considered the soul of wit, I think the following little story should fit the bill. One evening a couple of years ago I was seated in the 2/3 front row when a lady seated beside me had occasion to leave her seat for a few minutes. When she returned to the dark auditorium the usherette was showing someone to a front 2/7, full of confidence she turned left, stopped in front

GENERAL MANAGER'S OFFICE

ASSOCIATED BRITISH-PATHE LTD.

PRODUCTION LABORATORIES DISTRIBUTION

FILM HOUSE · WARDOUR STREET · LONDON W.I.

10th November, 1956.

I wish to extend heartiest congratulations to you for your Birthday Week.

You must feel justifiably proud of the knowledge that the Plaza has given 21 years pleasure, relaxation and entertainment to the people of Amesbury.

During all this time, we at Associated British-Pathe have worked in very close and happy association with you and we have been particularly gratified by the way our films have been so generously received by your patrons. May this happy association of distribution and exhibition long continue.

With kindest regards,

Yours very sincerely,
ASSOCIATED BRITISH-PATHE LTD.

[Signed] W. A. FIELDER,
Director and General Manager.

of me, faced the screen and sat on my knees! I promptly said 'If you're quite comfy I don't mind at all.' She gasped out 'Oh I'm sorry' and took the proper seat, chuckling quietly. When the lights came on we looked at each other, and recognition was mutual. For some time afterwards a certain very austere lady who is employed beside me, blushed to the roots of her hair every time I greeted her in the morning! You know, the discovery that she could chuckle over her embarrassment reminded me of the old Army saying 'on parade, on parade' etc.'

At Christmas 1959, the Salisbury Times reported on how Jimmy, the Regal cat, who preferred to stay in the cinema rather than be taken home for the holidays, had his Christmas dinner brought to him by the under - foreman David Stone. Jimmy enjoyed roast beef and vegetables followed by a nice saucer of milk, which he no doubt deserved having served the Regal well for 15 years.

Buddy Holly and the Crickets performed at the Gaumont on 22 March 1958

CHAPTER FOUR:
AND THEN THERE WAS ONE
(The 1960s and 1970s)

At the start of the 1960s Salisbury retained three apparently thriving cinemas – indeed this had been the case for approaching a quarter of a century. However, during the decade national cinema attendances continued the trend of the late 1950s, dropping every year to hit a new low of 215 million in 1969. The Golden Age of cinema was passing and there were to be drastic changes in Salisbury.

December 1960 saw the Odeon involved in a worthwhile community project. The scheme involved children attending the cinema on Saturday mornings bringing along donations of coal and potatoes for local pensioners at Christmas. Among the donations was a £1 note with a handwritten message: 'Will you please put this with the gifts? It must be terrible to be cold' signed by 'A Wiltshire Moonraker'. Odeon manager David Watts told the Salisbury Times about this generous gesture and said the cash would be used to buy two hundredweight of coal.

The Young Savages, starring Burt Lancaster and released in 1961, tackled the controversial subject of a racially motivated murder. In Salisbury the City Council Watch Committee recommended to the Full Council that the film should be prohibited in the city. However, members resolved not to follow this recommendation, but to arrange a viewing for the Council – and to adopt a policy that this should also be the case in considering future adult rated films.

The continuing decline in audiences placed CMA in a position whereby it was becoming impracticable for them to keep their two Salisbury cinemas running in direct competition. At the Odeon attendances of as few as 50 people had become a regular occurrence and departing staff such as the doorman, boiler man and car park

Wilton Road 1961 and an advertising stunt for the film The Facts of Life which was being shown at the Odeon in Fisherton Street.

attendant were not replaced, leaving the projection team, which by now comprised Bryan Rowe, John Adlam, Dennis Lavender and Pat O'Meara, to carry out additional duties.

When Bryan Rowe had moved to the Odeon in 1956, he had of course not anticipated that the cinema would be in such decline just a few years later but, he says, 'In 1960 and onwards the audience numbers fell dramatically. The introduction of a change of film programme mid - week did not attract more people. It was very sad and disheartening for staff throughout the final year that most evenings there would be only 50 or 60 people scattered around the cinema's 1500 seats.'

In 1961 CMA made the decision to axe one of the cinemas. Despite the luxurious surroundings of the Odeon, it was not particularly surprising that the decision was to retain the Gaumont, with its history and architecture, and a better location in the city centre. On 30 December 1961, the last Odeon feature was shown for the final time. Just as the cinema had opened with a Disney production (a Mickey Mouse short supporting King Solomon's Mines) so it closed with another – One Hundred and One Dalmatians.

Of the 12 remaining staff, most were either laid off or found employment elsewhere within the city. Former projectionist Len 'Chiefy' Adams was to return to become the first manager of the new City Hall, while chief usherette Muriel Eldridge and part time usherette Yvonne Oliver were transferred to the Gaumont along with the last manager of the Fisherton Street cinema era, Bill Case.

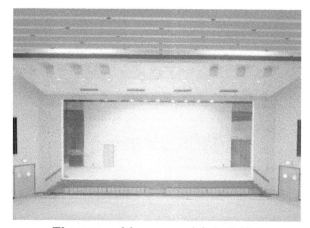

The new multi-purpose civic hall 1962

The Odeon officially closed on 31 December 1961 and was purchased by the City of New Sarum for conversion to a multi - purpose civic hall, to be dedicated as a memorial to the local men and women who lost their lives during World War II. The sale was subject to a legal restriction that films would not be shown to a paying audience at the venue.

Extensive works were required to convert the cinema into a functional civic hall. The auditorium was re - modelled to provide a semi-sprung dance floor, tiered seating, a restaurant and smaller function room and a new main staircase, pay box, bar and lounge area were installed in the foyer and entrance hall. The existing staircases were cut out to provide cloak-

room and toilet facilities and a new scenery dock constructed at the stage end of the hall. The cost of purchasing and converting the building was £81,800, but this was met by the city's Victory Fund and additional funds built up over a number of years through the sale of Council owned property, with none of the costs being borne directly by the rate payers.

The hall was opened with an official luncheon on 30 January 1963. A plaque was unveiled in the foyer, which read 'As a lasting tribute to the citizens of Salisbury who served in the Second World War 1939 - 45 the provision of this hall was made possible by the united efforts of our community'. The opening, dedication and luncheon was led by Alderman Francis Moore (the Chairman of the Victory Fund Committee), hosted by the Mayor and Corporation, and invited guests included officials and magistrates, representatives of the city's business community and members of ex - service associations.

The official luncheon on 30 January 1963

Through the 1960s and early 1970s the City Hall hosted concerts by many of the most famous names in British music. Less regular concerts and comedy shows continued through subsequent decades, during which time many other events and dances, including wrestling and Salisbury Amateur Operatic Society productions were hosted. Further physical changes were made to the building over the years. The hall was closed during the first national Covid-19 lockdown in 2020 and used as a regional vaccination centre in 2021. At the time of writing it has recently been announced the hall will not be re - opened as an entertainment venue until at least 2022.

" .... Can any cinemagoer really say he prefers to see his film in a building called 'Odeon', instead of the 'Palace'...."

In 1964 a local resident was, for a second and third time, recognised by the international film industry at the highest level. Cecil Beaton, whose home was at Reddish House in Broad Chalke, won Academy Awards for both his costume design and his art direction in My Fair Lady, following the Award for his costume design in Gigi in 1958.

During the spring of 1966 Rank undertook the most significant investment in the Gaumont building since the cinema had opened 35 years earlier. Two months of work were undertaken to provide £20,000 worth of improvements. Redecoration was carried out throughout and 200 downstairs seats were removed to provide more legroom and comfort, reducing the overall capacity to 1,501. A new screen was also installed and oil heating provided. The work was carried out at night, so the cinema could remain open to filmgoers, the only evidence being scaffolding erected within the theatre, and manager George Howes arranged an open day where interested parties could take a two - hour tour around the revamped premises.

These physical improvements were followed in December 1966 by a name change, which self-styled 'Exiled citizen and ardent campaigner' Alan Richardson, living in Ruislip, saw as an ominous step. In a letter published by the Salisbury Times, Alan recalled 'In 1931 it was called the Gaumont Palace. A night out at the pictures meant something in those days. 'Palace' conjured up luxury and entertainment. In later years, in the interests of accountancy, for the sake of a punch hole in a computer card they significantly dropped the 'Palace' [this had happened in 1955] and called it simply the Gaumont! Now they call it Odeon! without so much as a 'by your leave' from the most important person of all, the patron.'

'Can any cinemagoer really say he prefers to see his film in a building called 'Odeon', instead of the 'Palace' of treasured memory? Does Mr Rank realise the confusion of the veteran cinemagoer who returning to his home town, makes his way to the Picture House and finds the

Playhouse, walks on to the Odeon and finds the City Hall, hurries to the Gaumont Palace and finds the Odeon? Next 'Ye Old Hall of John Halle' will be ripped apart and chrome and jazzy décor will take its place! Watch out citizens! Perhaps Sarum, that became the Salisbury we love, will for the sake of the computers of centralised government be simply known as PCW1 (Provincial City Wilts One). It's later than you think!'

Odeon manager George Howes with assistant Eileen

Spring 1967 saw one of the sporadic flurries of letters to the Salisbury Times regarding particularly controversial films. On this occasion correspondents were concerned with Peter Watkins' film The War Game, depicting the prelude to, and the immediate weeks of the after-math of, a nuclear attack against Britain.

The City Council's Civil Defence Committee had proposed that the film be shown in Salisbury – mainly for the benefit of Councillors. However, Councillors had seemingly objected on the grounds of the technical 'quality' of the film, which had a documentary style, rather than its' content. The paper reported that Councillor Snook stated people who had seen the film had said it was badly produced, very far - fetched, not official, fiction not fact and 'very horrible', whilst

Councillor Mrs Benson asked if the film had been made by the CND. Alderman Lambert assured her it had not but added it was 'not made by a recognised firm either' (the film was in fact produced by the reasonably recognisable BBC). In his opinion the film was 'frightening and any young adult would be scared – it was just rubbish.'

Derek Warner of Winterslow found the report on the Council meeting 'more disturbing than the film itself.' He sounded a warning that 'unless one is fortified in some way against complete despair one should not see the film' but even so that 'censorship of this kind should be so peremptory and ill - informed is sad indeed.'

The controversial film The War Game

Alan Richardson wrote a furious letter in response to the decision, calling the comments made by Councillors 'irresponsible'. In his view it was a matter of individual opinion as to whether the film was 'far - fetched'. He also saw the comments regarding the CND as 'prejudiced' and 'ill - informed' – the latter particularly so given the degree of media coverage and debate around the film's initial release some 12 months earlier.

Michael Haugh of New Zealand Avenue had already seen The War Game, at a packed Southampton Classic Cinema screening. He agreed that the film was indeed made on a shoe-string budget, with all but a handful of its cast of 7,000 having any serious acting experience. However, he compared this approach to the work of D W Griffith in Birth Of A Nation (1915) and Intolerance (1916) 'probably the two greatest films of all time.' Mr Haugh noted that, in contrast to the city elders, Amesbury RDC had written to the BBC demanding the film be put on general release. In conclusion Mr Haugh felt 'it might increase the chances – if any – of survival in a Nuclear War for the citizens of Salisbury. We have a right to see this film.'

Letters were also received from J T Howden of Sidney Street who 'read with absolute amazement…the Councillors and Alderman who were quoted seemed to have no factual information at all, and what information they did have was second hand…' and Hugh Abel of Queen Alexandra Road: 'It would appear that some members of the City Council live in a cloud cuckoo land of their own…the facile dismissal of the film as 'just rubbish' seems a particularly ostrich - like move in view of the serious consideration it has received by many responsible bodies, including Members of Parliament.' Writing jointly, Jeanette Tee and Pam Golding of Salisbury stated 'The public should be allowed to judge for itself as this is an issue which concerns everybody, and it should not be left to such a small minority of apparently disinterested and unaware people.'

During the week between the Times' report of the Council decision and the publication of the various letters The War Game won the 1967 Academy Award for Best Documentary Feature. The film is now looked on as a classic of the drama - documentary genre.

"…. I think the reason is that the standard of films has gone up and television has lost some of its glamour …."

September 1967 saw the 30th anniversary of the opening of the Salisbury Regal (which in 1963 had been renamed the ABC in accordance with the company's policy that any distinctive local names should be changed to the chain brand). Four people were particularly excited, having worked at the cinema since the day it opened: The manager Hugh Melville Burge, the assistant manageress Miss Ruth Chapman, projectionist Frederick May and head usherette Florence Foord (with the exception of a short period during World War II after she married).

The stalwarts recalled how comedian Bob Hope and singer Richard Tauber were among those who had appeared live at the venue, Mr Burge's particular favourite show having featured a Royal Marines band. One of the big successes had been the introduction of the Saturday morning ABC Minors matinees in 1946 – Mr Burge noting that parents were thankful to have somewhere safe to leave their children when they went shopping. He had experienced one particular disappointment though when, along with his wife, he had been due to dine with John Wayne in London. The date was cancelled when the actor was suddenly recalled to Hollywood, but he later sent Mr Burge an inscribed marble pen and ink stand.

Mr Burge told the Salisbury Times he felt that cinema was recovering from a period of challenge, particularly from the growth of television: 'When ITV started in this area admissions went down for a period but we find today that for an entertaining film we get big audiences. I think the reason is that the standard of films has gone up and television has lost some of its glamour. The quality and standard of production progresses and improves every year. People who are enjoying their first visit for some years are really surprised by the standard.' Although – with admission charges having risen to five or six shillings – the days of the sixpenny seats had long gone, Mr Burge felt the cinema still offered value for money, given the general rise in the cost of living.

The 30th anniversary of the opening of the Regal

The reporter noted how the manager always spoke in terms of what 'We' had achieved, rather than 'I'. Mr Burge stressed that the success of the cinema had been due to teamwork, starting at the top with the London office of ABC: 'We really have a team spirit here. As well as Miss Chapman, Mr May and Mrs Foord, several others of the 33 staff have given long service, and that has helped me a great deal.'

September 1967 also saw the retirement of another long-serving Salisbury cinema employee, as Jack Overton left his post as chief projectionist at the Odeon after 50 years in the business. As we have previously seen, Mr Overton started out at the Palace Theatre before moving to the then New Picture House in Fisherton Street for eight years, during which time he became the first projectionist in Salisbury to show a 'talkie'. After travelling around as a relief projectionist he returned to the city for the opening of the Gaumont in 1931 but after eight months was transferred to Taunton for the opening of another new venue. After five years he moved to the Gaumont in Barnstaple before returning to the Salisbury Gaumont in 1941 for the rest of his impressive career.

A new manager, George Chantrey, was appointed at the Salisbury Odeon in late 1967. Mr Chantrey had been involved in cinema for most of his working life. Starting with Gaumont, he moved to the Rank Organisation in 1947 and had formerly managed the Glasgow Odeon, Cardiff Gaumont and Dundee Odeon.

The late 1960s and 1970s would see great changes to the physical character of Salisbury, with many now affectionately remembered buildings lost in the drive to improve living and working conditions and implement large projects. In 1968, the magnificent old County Hall/Palace Theatre building – where the first indoor moving picture shows in Salisbury were held 60 years earlier was among the casualties.

On 28 May 1968, The Hollies headlined the last major live show on the old Gaumont/Odeon stage (so far as our research has found). The venue had seen some of the American greats, including The Platters, Gene Vincent, Little Richard, The Everly Brothers, Bo Diddley and, perhaps most famously of all, Buddy Holly and The Crickets in March 1958.

Salisbury
Electric Palace

Bryan Rowe recalls: 'One of the main non - film attractions presented at the Gaumont on a Sunday afternoon was the jazz and pop concerts - Johnny Dankworth, Eric Delaney and Acker Bilk all strutted their stuff on the main stage to a packed audience. One concert I will always remember was the special guest appearance of singer Sandie Shaw. I remember standing in the wings of the stage virtually rubbing shoulders with this very attractive woman intrigued by how sexy she looked in bare feet!'

After the name change to Odeon live shows at the venue had diminished, with the 'club' at the Alex Disco and the 'dancehall' atmosphere of the City Hall perhaps more suited to the emerging musical styles. Nevertheless, as well as the American stars, for over a decade the Gaumont/Odeon had hosted a 'who's who' of British popular music of the day, with Cliff Richard and The Shadows, Lonnie Donegan, Chris Barber, Ruby Murray, Ted Heath, Billy Fury, Adam Faith, Joe Brown, The Rolling Stones, Cilla Black, Dusty Springfield and the Bee Gees representing just some of the other bigger names to have performed there. However, despite assertions that have been repeated so often they sometimes appear to be treated as facts, there is no evidence that The Beatles ever graced the Gaumont stage – 15 June 1963 at the City Hall was their only Salisbury date.

The building had been occupied by Palace Garages for 30 years and the Salisbury Times reported the demolition '...will have brought a touch of sadness to some, but none more than 78 year old Tom Bromham of Hulse Road, who trod the boards there as Tom Clifford, the famous ventriloquist, in 1908. It was well over half a century ago when Tom appeared before Salisbury audiences as a star in his own right having shared the bill with Marie Lloyd, George Robey, Harry Lauder and an up and coming star called Charlie Chaplin.' In 1968 Tom's local was the Rising Sun in Castle Street where he would often sing the old music hall songs from the past. The building on the site of the old theatre has most recently been occupied by The Karma Centre.

As well as personal appearances at the cinemas and occasional location work, stars of the silver and small screens often visited the Salisbury area for other reasons. In October 1968 Avenger and future Bond Girl (and Dame) Diana Rigg opened the Boscombe Down Fair 'looking glamorous in sleek brown slacks, autumn coloured blouse and snake - skin jacket' according to the Salisbury Times.

.... Helga was described as a 'film of sexual explanation in the true sense ...."

The potential for controversy raised its head again in November 1968 when the sex education film Helga came to the ABC for a week long run. Made under the auspices of the German Ministry of Health, and featuring 'the inquisitive stages, the courtship, the sexual problems, the physiology of sex, childbirth and the miracle of life itself', this was the first full length film on the subject to be widely shown in the UK. The BBFC saw the film as being 'educational' and consequently awarded an X certificate, meaning under - 16s could view it if accompanied by an adult.

Helga was described as a 'film of sexual explanation in the true sense' aimed at adolescents, young couples, parents and educationalists, and new ABC manager R P Street wrote to local schools and woman's organisations, advising them of the screening of the film and offering a special rate to school children under the supervision of a teacher. It was perhaps a sign of the changing times that the showing of this film in Salisbury apparently passed without much comment. However, the Salisbury Times thought the publicity posters gave the wrong impression, suggesting that Helga was a 'sexy' film, rather than a serious production that 'gives cause for careful thought and should be seen by young people especially.'

Also in 1968, ABC applied to the City Council to change the use of its Salisbury cinema to include 'indoor games'. It was denied at the time that there was any intention to no longer show films. However, just seven months later it was announced that films would indeed cease to be shown at the venue from 25 January 1969. Despite public petitions the closure went ahead - the final week saw packed houses for the showing of Bullitt, starring Steve McQueen, where outbursts of jeering greeted screen notices about the future operation of a bingo club at the premises.

The London office of ABC issued a statement on the matter: 'Circumstances alter cases. Patronage of the ABC Salisbury did not justify the continuation of the theatre as a cinema and it was considered that a Bingo Club would appeal to a larger number of local citizens. We understand that a public petition is being prepared and in view of this the matter will be considered in any future plans for the theatre, although the present plan to operate bingo cannot be changed at this stage.'

The building re - opened for bingo on 14 February and remains in the same use today (most recently operated by Buzz Bingo). 200 seats had been ripped out from the stalls to make way for the bingo tables. The vast silver screen - at one time the largest in Salisbury – had been removed, as had the orchestra pit from where, if the old story was to be believed, a neon - lit organ would have risen if it had not been forbidden by the city fathers. A snack bar had been installed and the floor was built up to meet the stage, and in its centre sat the bingo caller's rostrum. The old balcony became out of bounds but the original seats remain there to this day, still with their horse - hair filling and alongside the art - deco wall mountings.

In its piece on the ABC closure, the Salisbury Times also reported that the BFI, with the backing of the Arts Council, was interested in opening a cinema in Salisbury as part of a nationwide 'art' cinema project. The City Hall was identified as a possibility for occasional showings. However, once the BFI discovered the clause preventing films being shown to a paying audience at the venue remained in place and was unlikely to be lifted, the proposal wasn't followed up.

The closure of the Regal meant that, after more than 20 years, the local ABC Minors would have to find a new venue for their Saturday morning entertainment, as Neil Tonge recalls: 'From a young age I attended 'Saturday Morning Pictures', firstly at the ABC Regal in Endless Street and later the Odeon in New Canal. It was one of the week's highlights and my mother would walk me down before leaving me at the cinema with my friends. It was probably quite chaotic with kids running about but I remain blissfully unaware of that.'

'At the Regal the show began, or finished, with the ABC Minors' song, the words were played on the screen and the bouncing ball used to show where we were, or were supposed to be, in the song. As ABC Minors we could buy ABC Minor badges which had a luminous ring around the circumference and would glow in the dark. The morning's entertainment followed a fairly standard programme with a serial or show, something like Hopalong Cassidy or The Three Musketeers, there would also be a cartoon, and a feature film, usually an adventure and swashbuckling; I remember being overwhelmed by the colour, remember we only had a black and white TV at home, I knew nobody who had a colour set! Thinking back to the films some seemed quite gory to be shown to kids - The Man In The Iron Mask I remember was pretty sinister.'

'When the ABC closed in January 1969 we moved en masse to the Odeon. In our strange young boys' way the Odeon was seen as being a little bit 'posher' and rumours abounded in the week prior to the move about a forthcoming fight or battle between the ABC Minors and the Odeon gangs. Nothing happened but I do remember we ran about a lot, even venturing into the Circle (now Screen One) before being evicted; there was an extra cost for sitting there which I could never afford.'

Salisbury ABC Minors at the Regal

'Years later, stationed in Cyprus, I took my sons to the RAF Akrotiri cinema for the equivalent experience. They loved it, I just remember the noise of a hundred young kids running about and screaming, I think the duty staff just turned up the volume to drown them out.'

'Over the years I have looked back on those early cinematic experiences with a true fondness and my mother and I still chuckle at this story: I was taken to see Batman (the [1966] movie) at the ABC and I sat in the dark, next to my mother, with a brown paper bag of peanuts; had we been to Woolworth's or were they sold in the cinema? I don't remember. I sat eating these nuts, mesmerised by the action on the big screen, and occasionally being nudged by my mother to pass her a peanut. I also had a loose tooth, my first, and I was also wiggling this when it came out. I passed it to Mum, never taking my eyes off of the screen. At the end I asked for it back eager to put it under my pillow and claim the sixpence the tooth fairy would bring that night. I will never forget the look of horror on Mum's face - she thought it was another peanut! I was distraught but calmed down as the fairy visited after all!'

Sad though the closure of the old Regal undoubtedly was, the initial response to bingo at the venue proved the business reasoning for the change was sound. R P Street, who had stayed at the venue as manager, told the Salisbury Times 'The response has been fantastic...when we opened there wasn't a seat to be had in the house.'

.... It was resolved that the showing of late night films at the Odeon should be limited to four per year ....

In a letter to the paper Alan Richardson felt that although there was nothing wrong with bingo as such 'What the people of Salisbury should find disconcerting is...that the cinemagoer is getting less and less choice or say in what he wants to see.' He was supportive of the petitioners but disappointed that to date only 200 had signed up out of a potential catchment of 100,000, and warned 'Amenity after amenity is fast disappearing in Salisbury... Most citizens are in ignorance of the changes authorised in their names until it is too late.'

Perhaps not surprisingly, the provision of a dedicated bingo club in the city sounded the death knell for regular sessions of the game at the Odeon. Sunday afternoon bingo had been provided by Top Rank in the lower floor of the cinema since as early as November 1961 and had been well supported. In 1966 evening bingo was introduced in the restaurant. The Top Rank daily national top prize for a full house had been won by Salisbury club members on several occasions - most notably by Mrs C Drake of Stanley Little Road who won a bumper £1,388 on the penultimate Top Rank session in the city. Another unfortunate collateral impact was that the John Halle restaurant has to date never been generally open to public use again.

At the time of the closure the Top Rank club membership stood at a healthy 13,000. However, a spokesman said 'In view of the facilities that the ABC are able to offer with a full time bingo hall, we agreed with ABC that we would close down.' The closure of the club meant that ten part - time jobs were lost, including that of the caller, Gordon Beavis of George Street.

Salisbury's Chief of Police, Chief Superintendent J G Fisher, came under fire after the February 1969 meeting of the Watch Committee, where it was resolved that the showing of late night films at the Odeon should be limited to four per year. Chief Superintendent Fisher was described as 'stuffy' and accused of seeking to dictate Council policy on the subject matter of films, as most late night showings had involved the horror genre.

In response, he explained to the Salisbury Times that his recommendations had been made as a result of 'many complaints from members of the public concerning excessive noise late at night. If endeavouring to prevent trouble in this city, and having regard for hard working people who have to get up in the mornings and who are entitled to a night's rest uninterrupted by unnecessary disturbances, then I am stuffy. If I am asked on behalf of the City Council for my views on such things as late cinema shows...then, as always, I give my views to them without fear or favour.'

Referring to the reduced choice for Salisbury cinemagoers, Chief Superintendent Fisher continued: 'I fully appreciate the necessity for the only cinema now operating in the city to maintain business without undue restrictions. Above all things I appreciate more than some perhaps the need of providing adequate entertainment for the young people of this city. If the best we can do in this direction, however, is to provide X certificate horror films commencing at 11.00pm and running into the small hours of the morning, then I think this is a poor effort on our part and suggest that certain people have got their priorities a little mixed.'

Any lingering hopes that films might return to the old Regal were dashed in May 1969, when ABC announced it was ending its interests in Salisbury, with Star Associated Holdings taking over the bingo club. Bemoaning the lack of choice for cinemagoers in the city, the Salisbury

Times felt this was 'Fine for bingo enthusiasts – but a dismal prospect indeed for film fans. In fact, this probably leaves Salisbury the worst - served for cinema entertainment of any town of comparable size in the whole of the country.'

'It now sees a tiny part of the film industry's output. The only remaining cinema – the Odeon – purses a policy of showing X certificate films for teenagers and re - runs (often re-re-runs) of established favourites.' This lack of choice was exacerbated by the refusal of Rank to consider agreeing to the lifting of the restriction on films at the City Hall – the City Council apparently being reluctant to press Rank on the issue as, more generally, the organisation had agreed to favourable terms in originally agreeing to sell the site for civic use.

In the early 1970s the introduction of new American tax rules on exports, combined with opportunities for Hollywood companies to invest in television, led to a severe reduction in American financing of British films. Between 1965 and 1971, annual inflows of American capital for filmmaking averaged £19 million. Between 1972 and 1979 they averaged £6 million. With the exception of a few years, the decade saw national cinema attendances continuing the 20+ year trend of dropping year-on-year to eventually hit a new all - time low of 101 million in 1980.

In July 1970 the BBFC A film certification level was split into two. An A certificate now allowed those of all ages to be admitted, but warned parents that they may not wish children under eight to watch the film, while the new AA certificate allowed only those aged 14 or over to be admitted. In addition the X certificate was modified to a minimum age of 18. The full certification list now read: U (Passed for Universal Exhibition – Suitable for all ages); A (Passed as Adult Supervision Recommended for Young Children – Not suitable for children under 8 years of age); AA (Passed as Adult Accompaniment Required Children Under 14 – Not suitable for children under 14 years of age); X (Passed as Extremely Graphic – Suitable only for anyone aged 18 or over).

In a letter published in the Salisbury Times in February 1970 Alan Richardson asked whether, in the intervening 12 months since the ABC had closed, 'anything [had] really been done to attempt to find alternative outlets for the showing of films to Salisbury cinemagoers.' He wondered what had happened to the public petition against the closure and whether this had fallen on deaf ears.

Mr Richardson felt that if the petition had been taken more seriously ABC might have been persuaded to carry on showing occasional films between bingo sessions, but instead they had fairly promptly sold up to Star. He also asked whether any real pressure had been brought to bear in the matter of the restrictive clause affecting film shows at the City Hall, feeling that an organisation of the stature and reputation of Rank should not fear a little competition in the city.

Indeed, Mr Richardson wondered if there really would be any 'competition' as such if the City Hall was used for one off showings of films aimed at cinema aficionados, as opposed to the rather more conventional fare generally offered at the Odeon. His idea of a small community/ sponsored 'specialist' cinema has nowadays perhaps materialised to some extent with the Salisbury Arts Centre in Bedwin Street but, as we will read later, Alan's part in the history of the Odeon was not yet finished.

VETERAN OF THE CINEMA DIES IN HOSPITAL

MR. G. A. HOWES, who spent more than 50 years in the cinema industry, died in hospital at Southampton on Thursday, aged 66. He leaves a widow.

Mr George A 'Ted' Howes, who spent more than 50 years in the cinema industry, died in hospital in Southampton on 30 April 1970, aged 66. He had managed three Salisbury cinemas and ended his career in charge of the Odeon before retiring to live in a flat in The Friary. During his working life Mr Howes received a number of awards and certificates. He was particularly proud of two Showmanship Stars which he received in connection with the publicity he arranged for the films A Queen Is Crowned and The Young Savages. He met many leading film actors and actresses, including Jack Hawkins, John Mills, Laurence Olivier, Trevor Howard, Valerie Dobson and Petula Clark, and saw many changes.

".... Some of the patients had never seen a film before I started doing the ward rounds at the Infirmary ...."

His favourite part of working in the industry had been 'The chance of meeting people, and the great variety of the operations. Special performances, continuous performances, stage shows and now bingo are just a few.'

In June 1970 a request from the distributors of the controversial film adaptation of James Joyce's Ulysses, that WCC should reconsider its decision not to approve the exhibition of this film in Wiltshire, was turned down by the Public Protection Committee. The Committee decided to adhere to its original decision made in September 1967 and confirmed a year later that the film should not be shown in public cinemas in the county in its complete form. Ulysses was not granted a certificate by the BBFC until significant changes had been made to its dialogue.

Meanwhile, the Salisbury Times reported on an interesting project organised by Mr Reginald Broom, who 'In odd moments during his demanding job as Group Engineer at Salisbury Infirmary...negotiates for the best in celluloid from London's bigger film tycoons...to provide amusement for long - term hospital patients.' This voluntary activity had started 30 years previously and Mr Broom had no intention of giving it up. 'The film shows break up the dreary hospital routine for patients, as well as providing a useful meeting point for them' he said.

Mr Broom prided himself on getting the best of the current productions as soon as they became available for private showing. Recently he had shown Thoroughly Modern Miss Millie, starring Julie Andrews, and Lee Marvin fans would soon be able to enjoy The Dirty Dozen. This was all achieved 'on a minute grant from the Hospital Management Committee, a sense of a bargain, and a voluntary collection made by patients.' MGM, Rank, 20th Century Fox and United Artists all supplied Mr Broom with films but he recalled that it hadn't always been so well organised: 'When I started, anything would do. Some of the patients had never seen a film before I started doing the ward rounds at the Infirmary.'

In the late 1940s Mr Broom showed pre - war

Hospital projectionist Mr Reginald Broom

Rank releases and then did a deal with MGM, whereby he was allowed their films if he put on village showings as well. 'Then I got tempted' he remembered, 'difficult negotiations with 20th Century Fox produced Carousel. I had to buy my own Cinemascope lens to show it, though after that I was always equipped to handle the big screen productions.' A hut at Odstock Hospital was converted into a small cinema and The King And I and Carmen Jones followed Carousel. By 1970 Mr Broom was renting one film a week from the distributors and using two 16mm sound projectors with the aid of his assistant, Miss Mildred Mitchell, he showed the films on a rota at Newbridge, Odstock and Harnwood Hospitals.

Apart from his film interests, Mr Broom was also well known in the world of local sport. He had been a football manager for 48 years in total including spells with Salisbury Corinthians and then with Salisbury Football Club for the first 18 years of its existence - he was a founder member of the club in 1947. He was also chairman of the Western Football League. During his time as manager, Salisbury won all of the competitions they entered at least once, with the exceptions of the national FA Cup and FA Amateur Cup. Mr Broom was manager on the occasion of a record that is unlikely to ever be broken, when 8,902 spectators packed in to Salisbury's much - missed Victoria Park home for a Western League Division 2 match against Weymouth.

January 1972 brought disappointing news for the Myles Byrne Organisation, the new owners of the Amesbury Plaza, as Amesbury RDC turned down a request for financial assistance. RDC members heard a letter had been received from Mr Byrne indicating that his organisation might not be able to operate the cinema without local authority backing, and requesting an early meeting to explain the situation. The Council responded that there was no point in having a meeting as, although it wished to see the cinema continue, it was not its intention to provide any financial aid.

In March 1972 the Salisbury Film Society (SFS), formed a little more than a year previously, reminded Salisbury Times readers that there was now only one cinema in Salisbury but that there were students at four different colleges in the city, as well as citizens that would welcome a more 'intelligent' form of cinema entertainment than that being offered at the Odeon. With a growing membership, attendance at the society's meetings regularly numbered between 350 and 500 and a large screen and loudspeaker system had been obtained for 'one - off' showings of films in various venues. However, it was felt that a substantial long range plan needed to be put in place in order to achieve the society's aims.

The society had approached the BFI, who had agreed in principle that a specialist film theatre could be established in the area and that, if suitable premises could be found, up to £12,000 could be provided for equipment including two 35mm projectors, two 16mm projectors, loud-speakers and an electronically operated screen. The society had told the City Council the theatre would be operated by volunteers, possibly once a week, and the City Hall was considered highly suitable. The Council had agreed to make inquiries regarding the lifting of the covenant preventing the showing of films to a paying

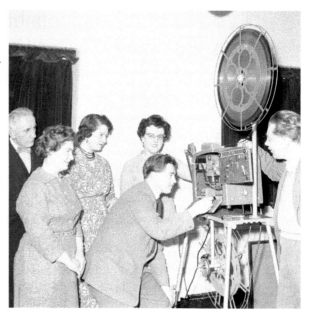
Salisbury Film Society

audience at the premises and would meet the society for more detailed discussions if a positive response was received, but nothing further transpired at this stage.

In April 1972, the subject of censorship raised its head again. At a City Council meeting Councillor Mrs Betty Sheppard told members that the authority should not act as 'judge and jury' when it came to such matters and also criticised how the Watch Committee reviewed films. In response Councillor A J Burden suggested that two or three people 'experienced in social welfare or morals' could be co - opted to the Watch Committee, saying that advice on the side effects of viewing films could be given by such persons to assist with decisions. This idea was rejected but it was agreed that two councillors should be co - opted to the Committee - Mrs M J Benson and Mrs C Till were elected.

As the SFS had already pointed out, the loss of two cinemas had obviously seriously reduced the choice of available films in the city. For example, in the Salisbury Times of 27 October 1956 no less than eight main features – as well as bingo and Pathe news – were available across the three then extant cinemas. This was in stark contrast to the corresponding week in 1972, when just two main features were available at the Odeon – one of which was Walt Disney's Fantasia, a classic of course but by now 32 years old (the other feature was a spaghetti western from 1971 – Red Sun).

"…. For a long time there has been a need in Salisbury for a more varied cinema entertainment …."

This was fairly typical of the Odeon offer at the time, so it was perhaps not surprising it continued to struggle, despite the significant amounts invested in redecoration and reseating in 1966. In October 1972 it was reported that major structural changes were to be made to the building. In line with many other cinemas at the time, the Odeon was to be converted to a three screen theatre.

Two images of the three screen conversion

The existing screen in the circle area would be retained as Screen 1 and would remain open during the six - week construction period. The new Screens 2 and 3 would be constructed under the former circle. In order to achieve this, a main dividing wall would be built under the circle, completely enclosing the former rear stalls, with a further central wall then dividing this area. New 35mm projection boxes would be fitted and brand new armchair style seating provided.

The cinema could then show both major general releases and the pictures of a more specialised nature craved by the SFS and others. Odeon manager George Chantrey told the Salisbury Times that to date he had not been informed of any proposed price increases and could not foresee any problems with a three - screen booking system – advance booking would be possible for Screens 2 and 3. Mr Chantrey was confident the conversion would bring more business: 'It has been proved so in other conversions. For a long time there has been a need in Salisbury for more varied cinema entertainment. People's tastes are so different that one film a week is not enough.'

On 26 November the Odeon re - opened as a three screen cinema. Screen 1 now comprised 554 seats, with Screen 2 and 3 providing 120 seats each. Although this resulted in an overall reduction from 1,332 seats, the works (which cost £35,000) would ultimately achieve the aim of boosting flagging audiences by providing more viewing options. At a special press preview two days previously Mr John Bell, the Operational Controller for Rank, explained some of the advantages of the new set - up. New film releases would arrive in Salisbury sooner while specialised films, which had often been passed over because of the risk of low audiences, could be shown in the smaller theatres, which would also be available for private hire.

At the public re-opening ceremony the Mayor of Salisbury, Councillor Mrs H E Barker, cut a reel of film that had been strung across the foyer. To add to the 'triple' nature of the occasion, 13 - year old Pewsey triplets Joan, Jennifer and Julie Bewley presented bouquets to the Mayor and to Mrs Colquhoun, the wife of Salisbury's Town Clerk.

To complement the provision of more choice at the Odeon, the SFS continued with its one - off showings of films, particularly those with a perhaps more 'Arthouse' appeal. For instance, Luchino Visconti's Death In Venice was shown at the Playhouse in February 1973. At the society AGM the following month Barry Seabourne stood down as Director, explaining 'The feeling has been growing that I have been doing too much… it seems that when you are trying to get something off the ground a lot of work falls on one person.'

Conscious of the growing interest in the provision of a dedicated Arts Centre in the city, Mr Seabourne felt the need for the society might become redundant. For the time being however it was in a healthy position with 685 members (including 269 study group members), making it one of the biggest film clubs in the country not connected with a university.

Showings of Sam Peckinpah's Straw Dogs were banned in Salisbury in 1973 – the ban was upheld in 1974 but eventually lifted as the film was shown in February 1975. The playgrounds of Salisbury schools (particularly boys') in the 1970s were awash with rumours of the reasons why various films had either received an X certificate, or been completely banned in the city 'because of the cathedral'.

Often exaggerated from tales passed on by elder siblings and set out in lurid detail, these reasons might include devil worship/possession/ exorcism, extreme violence (including in sporting settings) sometimes leading to torture and death, and glimpses of female anatomy or odd sexual practices – the latter including the unorthodox use of butter. Whether the original source for the plots, or quick-buck cash-ins, paperbacks relating to these films were a prized possession, alongside the works of Sven Hassel, Richard Allen and Timothy Lea.

As a case in point, Ken Russell's controversial The Devils, concerning the nuns of Loudon, was banned from the Odeon at a City Council meeting in June 1973. The film had already been shown at the Amesbury Plaza, but the Salisbury ban was imposed on the grounds that the film contained matter which, if exhibited, would offend against good taste or decency. Interestingly, a previous ban on Stanley Kubrick's equally controversial A Clockwork Orange was lifted at the same meeting, where members took note of the recommendation of four Councillors who had attended a special viewing of the film.

In a letter to the Salisbury Times, Geoffrey Maltby of Amesbury pondered on the reasoning behind these decisions: 'Having seen both films at the Plaza, Amesbury, I know which one offended my taste and it was certainly not The Devils. Could it be that this film, with its anti-religious theme offended the City Fathers and the Church more than the sex crimes of A Clockwork Orange, which is considered fit for public showing? No ban can be good, but this would be a strange decision for the rejection of The Devils. Or perhaps it only occurs to Godless people like my - self.'

Councillor and Mrs George Shingler, the Mayor and Mayoress of Salisbury, were given what the Salisbury Times described as a 'Film Star' welcome to the Odeon Cinema Saturday Club in December 1973. The visit was to launch the Mayor's Christmas Appeal Fund for elderly and needy citizens. Odeon manager Philip Cross felt that his young club members should be aware of the hardships facing these people at Christmas, and of ways in which they could help.

During the interval of the Super Saturday Show, which featured competitions and games as well as a film show, the Mayor received the first donations towards his Appeal. 11 - year old Club member James Burtt, of Dinton, presented the Mayor with a Toss-A-Cross game, and Brenda Higgins of Carmelite Way handed over the Mayor's personal gift – a dozen Christmas puddings. Mr Cross invited the Mayor and Mayoress to become honorary members of the Saturday Club and there was a big cheer as Councillor Shingler showed off his new badge, pinned alongside the Mayoral chain.

"…. Triple screening seems to be the answer to the problem of falling attendances at cinemas all over the country …."

In an interview with the Salisbury Times published that same month, Philip Cross looked back on his first year at the Odeon and the decision to convert to a three screen cinema, as well as his ongoing plans. Mr Cross was born in Devon. After his schooldays and national service he joined the Rank organisation in 1953, as a trainee manager at the Derby Gaumont. He subsequently worked in Oldham, Leicester, Loughborough, Shirley (in Southampton – the Shirley Odeon, one of the largest cinemas in the country) and Walsall, before moving to Salisbury.

Mr Cross was in no doubt that the triple screen project had been a success – although precise figures were not available, during the 12 months since the conversion there had been an increase of 27% of people using the cinema. 'Triple screening seems to be the answer to the problem of falling attendances at cinemas all over the country,' he said 'the two key words are flexibility and choice. Generally speaking Screen 1 is used for pictures on national release, Screen 2, with its continuous performances, caters for adult or for family material, and Screen 3, while not pretending to be an arts house, shows a number of higher calibre films, but these are just guidelines, there is no rigid ruling about which films are shown where.'

The change in format had been accompanied by a fresh approach to encouraging more visitors to the Odeon. One of Mr Cross' first innovations had been the introduction of a film information service: 'My idea is for the cinema to be at the centre of things. I'm all in favour of personal contact with people who want to find out about the films we are showing, and suggest the films they want to see. So far, quite a few people have approached me but I would like to hear from a lot more.'

However, another idea had not yet proved quite as successful: 'I'm rather surprised that we have so few pensioners making use of the special rates offered to them for afternoon shows. For only five pence they can see the film of their choice on any weekday up to four o'clock and I would have thought this would be very popular.'

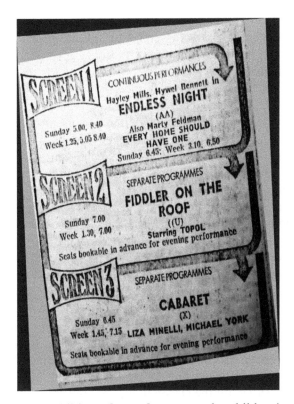

The addition of new features to the children's Saturday Club had prompted a steady, if slow, rise in membership. Other indications of the public's awareness of the cinema had been the high attendances for the previous month's late night preview of A Touch Of Class, and the 1000 entries received for a recent competition to win a year's supply of free cinema tickets.

On the basis of attendances, Salisbury's favourite films of 1973 had been: On Screen 1 a re - run classic (Snow White and The Seven Dwarves being almost a complete sell out over a fortnight) and the latest in the ever popular Bond series (Live And Let Die on a five week run); On Screen 2 That'll Be The Day (which returned to the cinema on three occasions due to public demand); and on Screen 3 a re-run of Far From The Madding Crowd (filmed in Wiltshire and Dorset and playing to two weeks of full houses). A study of all the films shown indicated that the best - selling genre in Salisbury was comedy followed by 'adult' themes, artistic films, horror and musicals.

Mr Cross hoped the popularity of the cinema would grow over the next year. 'I would like to see it used as more than just a cinema,' he said 'there are lots of ways in which it could help people and organisations: staging meetings, fashion displays or parties with film shows for instance. The building could be utilised in several ways, but I can only help if people get in touch with me.'

A film star of sorts visited the city in January 1974 as Robin Hood, in the guise of a fox, arrived at the front of Oakeshotts food shop in Silver Street, in an open - topped, green double - decker bus. To the delight of around 100 children – many perched on their father's shoulders. Robin, armed with his bow and arrows, and bad Prince John, with his crown and a frown, distributed sweets before squeezing into the store – although poor Little John had to wait outside as he was too large to get through the door! The pair collected bags of goodies from the shop manager Frank Green, which they later distributed to young patients in the Dorset Ward at Odstock Hospital, under the supervision of Sister Taylor. The event was aimed at bringing some cheer to the hospitalised children, whilst also promoting the animated Disney film of the Robin Hood legend, scheduled for the Odeon in the near future.

Under the management of Reggie Salberg, the Playhouse located in the old Picture House had grown into a theatre with a national reputation. However, the building was in a fairly sorry state when it had first been used as a theatre more than 20 years previously. Each year the building was granted its licence more or less on the understanding that each time would be the last year it would be needed. Poor ventilation, uncomfortable seats, inadequate cloakroom facilities, an ill equipped stage, primitive conditions backstage, support functions struggling in condemned cottages and nearby sheds for workshops were the cause of the problems. In an interview Mr Salberg commented 'This building has been condemned ever since I've been here. It's only fit for human habitation by theatre managers.'

In April 1974 at the Theatregoers' Ball an appeal for a new building was launched. Mr Salberg wanted the new Playhouse 'to be built by a thousand people' and for 'the small men' to play their part. £750,000 was raised and the new building, the Playhouse that remains today, was opened by Sir Alec Guinness on 30 November 1976 – several months ahead of schedule.

The appeal fundraising had included, on 2 November 1975, a nostalgic one - off return to the showing of films at the old Playhouse. A series of BBC films, previously shown on television, was screened, including some with local interest: The Spire (showing the annual climb and maintenance check by Salisbury Cathedral Clerk of The Works Roy Spring); The Village On The Wall (concerning the fascinating murals at Woodgreen Village Hall); Eric Ashby's film about Cranborne Chase; Summer In Arcadia (about Cecil Beaton's home, Reddish House) and Treble Chance (about the competition for three places in the Salisbury Cathedral choir).

The demolition starts....

Despite its physical condition, the old Playhouse would be fondly remembered and there was a great demand for seats for the very last production in October 1976 - an 'Old Tyme Music Hall'. Various potential uses of the building were explored: The lease of the building could perhaps be used for a short term warehouse use or could become a joint leisure complex with the City Hall – or it could be demolished and the site redeveloped.

A survey of the building was to take place but as the old Playhouse was labelled as a 'building of importance' the design of any replacement would be critical and the existing frontage would have to be preserved. Despite a petition signed by over 300 local people, who wanted appeal money to be spent on repairing the old building, it was eventually deemed to be unsafe and was finally demolished in February 1979. The Methodist chapel that became a picture house and a theatre is long gone, but lives on in the name of Chapel Place. The building now on the site was most recently occupied by Baileys Beds.

.... over 350 films had been shown since the conversion of the cinema, a mobile bar had been introduced to Screen 2 ....

At the May 1974 AGM of the SFS members were shown What Colour Is The Wind, the award winning documentary about blind children at a Sunshine Home made by Henry Herbert (i.e. the Earl of Pembroke – a Patron of the society). Chairman the Reverend Barry Rogerson reported that with more than 460 members and its own projector well on the way to being paid for the society was in a healthy state, and could look forward to another good year. The society's new season would start in September with The Graduate, and would continue with Don Camillo, The Discreet Charm Of The Bourgeoisie and Alice's Restaurant, as well as a strong programme of supporting films and a children's Christmas show.

The Odeon advertising 3 films

Philip Cross was to prove innovative and seemingly inexhaustible in his ideas for promoting the Odeon – for example special ballet and opera seasons were introduced in the summers of 1974 and 1975. However, despite the claimed improvements in quality and choice at the three - screen cinema, there was still some dissatisfaction amongst the punters. In August

1974 Mr P D Wood of Palmer Road (claiming to write 'on behalf of hundreds') didn't beat about the bush when making his point in a letter to the Salisbury Times:

LOST
The Sting, Serpico, The Scarecrow, Zardog, Percy's Progress, The Last Detail, S.P.Y.S., Blazing Saddles, Chinatown, Mahler, The Exorcist, Papillon, The Conversation, Man With The Golden Gun etc. etc.

IF FOUND
Please send to The Odeon, Salisbury, (with three screens to show all the latest and best in cinema entertainment).

REWARD
Full houses again

The second anniversary of the opening of the three - screen Odeon was marked in November 1974, with around 20 people whose birthdays or anniversaries fell on the date being personally invited to the cinema as guests of Philip Cross. Mr and Mrs Dennis Hamnett were selected to represent the patrons, and were presented with a bouquet and a one - month free film pass. Mr Cross reported that well over 350 films had been shown since the conversion of the cinema, a mobile bar had been introduced to Screens 2 and 3, the film information service had become well established and the number of senior citizens using the reduced price scheme had worked well.

In March 1975 the SFS was short - listed for the title of Film Society of the Year, awarded by the British Federation of Film Societies. The society continued to present an interesting programme – that month saw a schedule of The Goons' Running, Jumping and Standing Still Film alongside a Polish comedy at the City Hall, and then a presentation of three films at South Wilts Grammar School by freelance director Graham Hurley, including Life by Misadventure, about the work of the Burns Unit at Odstock Hospital.

Page 77

During the mid -1970s the SFS also showed foreign language films alongside titles such as Ulysses, Harold and Maude, Don't Look Now, Nosferatu and Last Tango In Paris. The City Hall was now used as a regular venue, with the policy of entry being allowed by SFS membership card only seemingly overcoming the 'no fee paying film customers' covenant that still bound the premises.

HALF A CENTURY OF SERVICE

REGULAR filmgoers to Salisbury Odeon will miss the friendly face of mobile manager Mr Bill Case, who has retired after an association with the cinema world which has lasted more than 50 years.

Salisbury based Mobile Odeon Manager Bill Case retired in April 1975, after 50 years of association with the cinema industry. Mr Case was born in Newton Abbott, and in 1906 his father Alf was the first man to show moving pictures in the West Country. The family moved to London where Bill's first job was operating sound effects in the silent era. He joined the Rank Organisation as a projectionist in 1932, working in Stroud, Swindon, Dorchester, Exeter, Bridgwater and Taunton before taking over as assistant manager at Taunton Gaumont in 1938. He was soon promoted to become manager in Monmouth, but his career was interrupted by World War II, during which he served full - time with the Auxiliary Fire Service in South Wales.

After the war Mr Case took up position at the Salisbury Picture House, before moving on to Winchester, then returning to what was by now the Salisbury Odeon in 1954. Appointed as a Mobile Manager in 1970, Mr Case worked all over the south of England. During his career he had met many stars, including Richard Attenborough, Sheila Sim and Petula Clark. At a special lunch at the Yew Tree Inn at Odstock, Mr Case was presented with a TV set by Rank Leisure Services, an automatic tea maker by the local circuit of cinema managers and a wristwatch from his colleagues at the Odeon. Currently living in Tollgate Road, Mr Case and his wife Gladys were intending to retire to Teignmouth.

A selection of films from 1975

Judging by letters to the Salisbury Times, the Odeon was still not keeping all its patrons happy during this period. Dr G D Watts of Southampton University complained about the treatment he and others had received in the spring of 1975: 'The cinema chose to show what turned out to be a very popular film on the small screen three. This in itself would not have been serious if it were not for the fact that booking facilities for this screen have now been withdrawn.' Dr Watts did not name the film concerned but, based on what was billed during the preceding weeks, it seems likely it was Bob Fosse's Cabaret '...a second feature is only shown twice...it means that it is virtually impossible to get into the cinema at 7pm,' he continued '...no one wants to travel miles only to be turned away.' In response Philip Cross stated that the demand for the Easter programme of films had been greater than anticipated, even when allowing for screening on a continuous basis. Advance booking had only previously been used by a few people but would be reintroduced for certain films.

Then, in June 1975, M E Constant of Middle Woodford received a flurry of support after expressing depression about the number of X certificate films being shown, comparing the cinema experience to the old fashioned 'What The Butler Saw' machines. Whilst acknowledging that 'violence and sex have been an integral part of the greatest plays and literature' it nevertheless was felt offensive when shown explicitly.

.... All this led to a joint 'publicity campaign' with Philip Cross, with Christians throughout the city encouraged to 'take a pew' ....

Steven Kelly of Castle Road had some sympathy with these views but felt the continued showing of X rated films was inevitable given the number of Salisbury cinemagoers they attracted in comparison to U and A certificate offerings – cinemagoers who mostly '...know exactly what they are going to see and what to expect.' High Street resident Antony Miles realised '...the local manager of the Odeon has a duty to make his cinema pay...' but '...must surely have been in the business long enough to know that cheaply made X films are a most unsatisfactory way of making money for all concerned; not only this, but there must be many parents who would hesitate to take their children near some of the rather sordid and suggestive posters on display outside the cinema.' Mrs Margaret Forsyth of Friary Lane recommended that complaints should be sent in writing to Sir John Davis, the chairman of Rank. She also felt the MP Michael Hamilton and Bishop George Reindorp could '...help us fight against these evil films...'

Free tickets were again offered for the third anniversary of the triple-screening of the Odeon – to those whose birthday or wedding anniversary fell on 26 November. On the night itself Philip Cross' son David dressed as John Halle (in a costume borrowed from Salisbury Playhouse) to unveil a plaque commemorating the building as one of Salisbury's oldest. Over the winter Philip Cross continued to plug the 10p a ticket offer for Senior Citizens, even suggesting to the Salisbury Times in February 1976 that multiple weekly visits to the cinema, lasting up to three hours a time, might assist in reducing home heating bills!

Mr Cross pushed Salisbury almost to the forefront of national cinema in April 1976. To mark the 25th anniversary of the Children's Film Foundation (CFF) a premiere of the Foundation's film The Man From Nowhere was held at the Odeon in Leicester Square on the 22nd of the month, in the presence of the Duchess of Kent. Just two days later the Southern Regional premiere was held in Salisbury with full 'first night' trimmings (despite the 10am showing). Guests included the Countess of Pembroke with

Philip Cross

her three daughters, The Mayor and Mayoress of Salisbury (Mr & Mrs A Stocken), the Chairman of SDC Mr Paul, and Mrs Paul, Gabrielle Hamilton and Sarah Hollis - Brown, who starred in the film, and The Barron Knights. Over the three weeks following the premiere the cinema scheduled the showing of further CFF films: Hoverbug, Robin Hood Junior and Junket 89.

Stanley Kubrick's Barry Lyndon returned for further screening at the Odeon in September 1976, as an additional attraction to the city's Festival of The Arts. Among those who had viewed the film during its previous run were the Countess of Pembroke and the Marchioness of Bath, both of whose homes had been used in the film (respectively Wilton House and Longleat).

The fourth anniversary of the Odeon triple screening, in November 1976, saw Philip Cross presenting (on behalf of Roger Moore) a personally signed and framed photograph to Susan Picknett of Laverstock, a Salisbury Times and Journal competition winner who attended the event with her friend Karen Knowles. A specially designed cake was displayed before being taken to the children's ward at Odstock Hospital. The Odeon hosted another regional premiere of a CFF film, Fern The Red Deer, on the morning of 23 April 1977, just one day after its London royal premiere. The guest of honour in Salisbury was Mark Eden, one of the stars of the film.

Milos Forman's Academy Award winning One Flew Over The Cuckoo's Nest, based on a novel by Ken Kesey, remains one of the most acclaimed films of the 1970s. A member of the local clergy was one of many who picked up on the allegory supposed by some to be contained in the story. Ian Stratton, Curate of Sarum St Francis, told the Salisbury Times that in March 1977 he had left a Bible Society conference feeling 'heavy hearted' and had decided to visit the cinema 'to cheer him - self up.'

Mr Stratton immediately saw a parallel between Christ and the hero of 'Cuckoo's Nest' Randle McMurphy, played by Jack Nicholson. He praised the film as 'a powerful illustration of liberation through one man taking the burdens of others. I would recommend this film as an eye - opener for Good Friday and Easter. The action explores what it means to be a person.' Four members of St Francis Church who had also seen the film recorded a version of the story for use in a Sunday service – George Graham, an Irish student at the Salisbury & Wells Theological College, read the part of McMurphy.

All this led to a joint 'publicity campaign' with Philip Cross, with Christians throughout the city encouraged to 'take a pew' at the cinema, but not everyone was happy. Stella Mundy of Elm

Grove wrote to the paper expressing a 'layman's view' of the film. She thought it was an 'appalling film to be shown in England' and any member of the clergy supporting it showed 'a very bad advertisement of the Church.'

Ms Mundy's particular concern was with the unsympathetic portrayal of 'mental hospitals' (to employ the language of the day). As a former professional in the field she was disappointed with the depiction of medical and personal treatment – 'a very far-fetched exaggeration of conditions…I saw a film where authority had no respect from its audience either in knowledge or understanding.' In summary she concluded 'In an age when everyone is fighting against authority, and leadership is poor, we don't need that over - emphasis. We need plays to show obedience and discipline to good leadership, with order coming out of chaos - that is the Biblical message from Genesis to Revelation.'

Following a successful first attempt in 1976, the Odeon put on a Disney summer festival through the whole summer school holidays of the following year, featuring Bambi, Freaky Friday, Cinderella, The Shaggy DA and The Jungle Book. Philip Cross invited anyone celebrating a birthday during the festival to consider using a screening as a venue for a party. The death of Elvis Presley in August 1977 provoked a spike in sales of his records, including at the various outlets in Salisbury. There was also a flurry of letters, phone calls and personal visits to the Odeon requesting that his films be shown. In response the cinema arranged a seven day double header featuring GI Blues and Blue Hawaii in the October.

That same month, A Bridge Too Far – Richard Attenborough's epic film of the Battle of Arnhem in 1944 - came to the Odeon. To celebrate its opening night at the cinema, Philip Cross had offered special tickets for any veterans of the battle if they contacted the cinema – Mr R Penny of Salisbury, Mr H Goodman of Wishford, Mr J Fry of Codford, Mr J J Bosley of Warminster and Chief Inspector R Rose of Devizes answered the call. Following this success Mr Cross put out a call to local diving and underwater sports enthusiasts with interesting stories, in connection with the screening of The Deep in January 1978.

"…. So far as I'm concerned it is people like Muriel who are the backbone of the cinema business …."

In April 1978, the Salisbury Times reported on a scheme, subsidised by Southern Arts, aimed at allowing local villagers to stage feature film shows during the summer. The idea, said Jessica Langford of St Edmunds Arts Centre, was to make films available to people living in rural areas, who found it very difficult to get to the local cinema.

Ms Langford hoped that each show would be something of a community event, with villagers selecting their own film from a choice of 15 and carrying out the organisation and publicity. A similar scheme had been operated in Dorset over the winter and had proved a great success. The local scheme would be limited to 12 villages within a 15 - mile radius of Salisbury and Ms Langford was approaching parish councils to see who might be interested. It is believed that Downton, the Langfords, Tisbury, Codford and possibly Amesbury pursued the project.

To coincide with the opening of Close Encounters Of The Third Kind at The Odeon, in April 1978, a Saturday morning event was held at the cinema. Ian Marygold and Barry Gooding of the UFO INFO Exchange were available to discuss UFOs and similar phenomena. There was also a display of UFO photographs and related items, such as press reports of sightings.

With all the promotional work carried out by Philip Cross and his team, it was perhaps no surprise that the Odeon had reported high ticket sales over recent months, with One Flew Over The Cuckoo's Nest, The Spy Who Loved Me, A Bridge Too Far, Sinbad And The Eye Of The Tiger and The Pink Panther Strikes Again proving particularly popular. The first week of 'Close Encounters…' coinciding with screenings of The Stud and Annie Hall, 'set the 'Automaticket' machines in almost perpetual motion' as the cinema recorded its highest audience figures since the triple screens opened in 1972.

In May 1978 the Salisbury Times interviewed Muriel Eldridge, explaining that 'Countless cinemagoers at Salisbury have been met and helped by a cheery lady who has taken their tickets and shown them to their seat.' Head

The Lawman at the Odeon, 1972

usherette Mrs Eldridge had been working in cinema for 34 years and told the paper 'I love it. It is wonderful.' Born in Scots Lane, Mrs Eldridge had first worked at the Wilton Royal Carpet Factory before joining the staff at the New Picture House, where she stayed for 15 years before then moving to the then Gaumont in 1959. Philip Cross said 'So far as I'm concerned it is people like Muriel who are the backbone of the cinema business. It is amazing how many people who have been away from the district for some time come back and are delighted to see the friendly face of Muriel still here.'

Mrs Eldridge, who now lived in Pinewood Close, enjoyed the job 'very much indeed. I wouldn't go anywhere else' - what she liked best was 'The atmosphere, the management and the lovely lot of girls on the staff.' These younger girls were grateful for her advice and support as helper and confidante to the extent that they called her 'Mother'. Mrs Eldridge had not actually been able to see many films having been 'too much here, there and everywhere' but her favourite was Guess Who's Coming to Dinner. Her service had been recognised by Rank when she was awarded a company 'star' for courtesy and service to the patrons. She had also received many personal gifts from those patrons. This recognition continued as, on hearing of the Times article, the theatre director of Rank arranged for a bouquet with a personal letter of thanks and good wishes to be presented to Mrs Eldridge.

That same month, Alison Hartley of Pauls Dene Road had reason to smile as she was announced as the winner of the 'David's Disney Delight' competition organised by the Odeon in conjunction with the Salisbury Times and Journal. Her winning entry read 'My mum deserves a VIP night out because she gives so much and takes so little, being a super Mum, Nurse and Guider.' The prize was for the family, as the special guests of Philip Cross, to be taken by courtesy car to the cinema, where Mrs Hartley would be presented with a bouquet at a champagne reception, for a screening of a Disney double - bill of Candleshoe (starring David Niven) and Alice In Wonderland.

There was still some concern about the nature of the films being shown at the Odeon and more generally. Margaret Forsyth again wrote to the Salisbury Times on the subject in June 1978: 'The Chief Constable of North Wales has stated that the nationwide increase in crime can be directly linked with violent films. Many of us heartily agree with him.'

'As Salisbury District Council is the licensing authority that permits all these films to be shown in Salisbury, I have written this week to my local councillor, suggesting that it be made compulsory for every councillor to view one X film per month. There is plenty of choice – four X films this week and the AA film is more horror. When the Odeon was converted to a three - screen cinema there was great publicity that the new arrangement would cater for all the family. The Council licensing authority should now tell the Odeon management that only one X film per week will be permitted.'

'There is a lot of comment on who is responsible for the local vandalism, muggings, hooliganism and damage to property – and in this case, I suggest that it is our Salisbury District Council. As ratepayers and taxpayers, we are called upon to bear the cost of vandalism and destruction and it is time now that our councillors acted to run this city properly, to protect property and to protect and help its citizens, and most important of all, to help our over-worked police.'

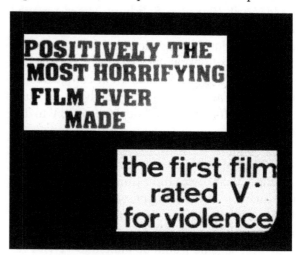

Nationwide increase in crime linked with violent films in the 1970s?

Notwithstanding this, and judging by ticket sales, the film offer at the Odeon was generally well supported. Philip Cross' promotional skills were acknowledged when the Salisbury Publicity Association held a meeting at the cinema in July 1978. Chairman Peter Lightfoot and members of the Association were greeted front of house by Mr Cross, accompanied by 'Spiderman'. Mr Cross then gave a talk on 'Publicity Pointers', explaining among other things how the superhero would be attending local village fetes and flower shows – an example of what would now be called 'outreach'. By coincidence four patrons dressed as cavaliers arrived at the cinema later that same day to buy tickets for The Four Musketeers.

Mr Cross also set out the arrangements for a motorcade to launch his latest Disney festival later that month. Featuring the stars of Herbie and Pinocchio, the motorcade would rendezvous with the Army on Salisbury Plain then travel to the Odeon, arriving there at 10.45am for a special children's matinee. During the planning of this event Mr Cross had met with Gus A Zelnick, the chairman and director of Walt Disney Productions, at the Birmingham Odeon. Mr Zelnick was very interested to hear about the unusual foyer and history of the Salisbury Odeon building.

".... Today, the grip of television is fading and the people are after sheer escapism...."

Mr Cross would be awarded a Rank Showmanship Star for his promotional work with Spiderman. This latest in a string of similar awards was presented to him in early 1979, by Ramon Roberts, the operations manager for Rank Theatres in the south west. Mr Cross also won second prize in a national competition for promotional work awarded by the film company Columbia.

In September 1978 the Salisbury Times film critic upset Graham Ford of Nunton when, reviewing the blockbusting Saturday Night Fever, he said John Travolta 'somehow finds the enthusiasm to gyrate through some of the most unremarkable records ever made.' Mr Ford thought 'obviously the critic hasn't got a great deal of what is known as taste. Maybe he doesn't realise that the soundtrack album has been number 1 in the charts for the past 17 weeks? Or am I wrong? Perhaps the critic knows good music when he hears it, and the rest of us (a few billion all over the world) don't.'

YEAR OF THE CHILD FILM SHOW

A LARGE Snoopy dog and giant Polar bear were seen in Salisbury on Saturday— but no one was alarmed because they were part of an Odeon cinema premier presentation.

Nearly 400 people turned up to see "Deep Water's" a Children's Film Foundation feature, to mark The Year of the Child.

Later that month Philip Cross reached the milestone of 25 years of service with Rank. Mr Cross felt nothing much had changed during those years: 'Today, the grip of television is fading and the people are after sheer escapism. This is what they want and this is what the cinema is giving them.' Although he enjoyed his work Mr Cross

had one minor grumble – patrons seemed to find him unapproachable as he stood in the foyer wearing his dinner jacket. 'I wish people would ask me questions,' he said 'I sometimes think they are reluctant to. I get some telephone calls and letters but I would like many more. I am happy to give them information and perhaps help them to select films.'

An unusual (for the Odeon) film was shown in October 1978 - The Silent Witness, about the Shroud of Turin. Now regularly using the Reggie Salberg Studio at the Playhouse, the SFS was also continuing to present alternatives to the mainstream fare. That same month its Luis Bunuel festival opened with Nazarin, with three more films scheduled monthly into the new - year. Committee member Tony Martin told the Salisbury Times it was hoped the society's new base would encourage more people to join, which in turn would lead to the hire of more films.

Having attended many premieres and met many stars over the years, Philip Cross fulfilled a lifetime ambition by visiting Hollywood in April 1979. The trip involved spending time in San Francisco and Las Vegas with a trip to the Grand Canyon, as well as visits to Disneyland and the Universal and 20th Century Fox studios, and a three night stay on the Queen Mary.

In May 1979 the Odeon pulled out the stops to celebrate The Year Of The Child. Spiderman, a large Snoopy and a giant polar bear were among those greeting 50 special guests and 400 patrons for the premiere of Deep Waters, the latest offering from the CFF. The guests included the Countess of Pembroke's daughters Lady Emma, Lady Flora and Lady Sophia and the Mayor and Mayoress of Salisbury, Mr & Mrs Arthur Lawrence, and their daughter.

June 1979 saw The Cat From Outer Space, Sgt Pepper's Lonely Hearts Club Band and Watership Down achieving the latest record breaking week for admissions at the Odeon. Then in July a 'Hunt The Manager' competition was the latest publicity idea, with a photograph of Philip Cross being 'hidden' in the Old George Mall. First prize went to 15 - year old Jennie

Brown of Laverstock, who was with her 12 - year old sister Katie. Jennie was presented with two tickets for the return of Saturday Night Fever to the Odeon, as well as the LP of the soundtrack. Among the other successful entrants were Martin Beckwith, Paul Miles, Toni Eustace, a Mrs Francis, Mrs T Wakeman and a Miss Karins.

Philip Cross, Spiderman, a Star Wars Storm-trooper and the spacesuit used in Moonraker appeared at the August Bank Holiday Show in 1979, held at Hudson's Field in support of the Mayor's Appeal. The screening of Moonraker, the latest James Bond film, was launched with a celebration of stalwart patrons and employees of the Odeon, including some who had attended on the opening night of the cinema in 1931. A private reception was held for the guests including Graham Levy of Durrington, Reg Pennells of Barford St Martin, George and Ted Yeates of Upavon, and Mrs M Alexandra and Miss D J Newman of Essex Square, to exchange memories. As the 'most regular' visitor to the cinema over the years, Mrs C Dominy of The Avenue was presented with a month's free tickets. Also in attendance was Fred Martin of Lovett Green, who was the original doorman at the cinema.

A potential further alternative to the Odeon had a successful launch in September 1979, as St Edmunds Arts Centre (funded by the Southern Arts Association) staged a drive - in movie show at Salisbury Cattle Market, then off Ashley Road where Waitrose and the adjacent business premises are now sited. Popcorn and soft drinks were on sale as 60 car loads attended the American style event, apparently the first of its kind to be held in southern England. A 20 x 12 feet screen was erected, with excellent picture and sound quality, and the patrons enjoyed a three - hour programme comprising The Dirty Dozen supported by Laurel and Hardy and Buster Keaton comedies.

The additional options for viewing provided by the SFS were also continuing to prove popular. In the light of so many members having turned up for recent events, the last two films of the season (Le Jour Se Leve and Casablanca, both scheduled for December 1979) would receive two screenings each. However, although popular with the punters, the society was having difficulties behind the scenes. Secretary Mrs Sally Collier feared the

The neon Odeon sign lit up at dusk

society might fold if more members did not get involved with its administration. There was a significant amount of 'disinterest' in taking on such responsibilities and Mrs Collier said 'We have tried to get members to join the committee, but they don't want to know. They are prepared to watch films, and complain when things go wrong, other than that they are just not interested in doing any donkey work.' The SFS appears to have come to a natural end around this time as the Arts Centre began to provide more regular film screenings.

In October 1979 Rank created Philip Cross a Knight of the Grand Order of Showmen. This was a special award indeed, with only six other members. The 'knighthood' was awarded in recognition of Mr Cross' contribution to the object of the Order: To encourage pride in a high standard of effective showmanship and to be a reward for outstanding ability and effort.

A special event was held at the Odeon on 18 October 1979 to mark the 500th anniversary of the death of John Halle, the original creator of the

.... Reverend Taylor 'deplored' the film, which portrayed a lead character treated as a 'Messiah by 1st Century fanatics ....

The ever popular Odeon manager Philip Cross in great form at a civic event! Mr. Cross won many awards for his promotional work at the Odeon including the Rank Showmanship Star!

medieval building that still formed part of the cinema. The Wessex Tourist Group arranged a mini - exhibition illustrating the life of John Halle and his contemporaries in the Salisbury area, as well as pictures on the subject provided by local school children. Gary Nunn, the presentations manager at the Arts Centre, wore a medieval minstrel's costume and four suitably attired wenches were on hand as medieval music was played on the balcony. Hugh Thomas and Philip Cross (acting as 'John Halle') welcomed guests including Mrs Marc Sinden, whose husband was currently appearing at the Playhouse, Alan Richardson, Mr R J Pullin – the general manager at the late Lord Mountbatten's Broadlands home - and representatives of the tourist authorities and the media.

There was still however some civic concern over the content of some films. At the November 1979 meeting of the SDC Amenities and Tourism Sub - Committee, Councillor Mrs Amy Hall spoke of the 'bad language, filth and dirty sex' depicted in both film and television. The meeting was specifically debating Monty Python's Life of Brian and Mrs Hall referred to a letter received from the Reverend G L Taylor of the Elim Pentecostal Church. Reverend Taylor 'deplored' the film, which portrayed a lead character

treated as a 'Messiah' by 1st Century fanatics. In his view this character, Brian, used the 'foulest obscenities' and performed 'pseudo-miracles'.

Because the film had received an AA Certificate, children would be able to see it. Reverend Taylor thought this rating should be raised to at least X and pleaded with the Sub - Committee to arrange a special viewing panel, to decide whether the film should be shown in Salisbury. Whilst admitting that any 'ban' might provide more publicity for the Pythons, Councillor Mrs Hall said such films were responsible for the lowering of moral standards and the 'bruising of the minds of young people', and fully supported the Reverend's views. However, Councillor Bill Oglethorpe said 'It would be wrong for us to set ourselves up as censors' and the Sub - Committee resolved to accept the film's AA classification and its showing at the Odeon.

The decade was rounded off by the latest in Philip Cross' publicity events, this time for a Disney double header of The London Connection with the classic The Aristocats. Hundreds of pre - school age children and parents made their way to the venue on a Tuesday morning, to meet Scat Cat and his Band from the latter film. Five lucky participants were awarded pairs of tickets for the films, which played over Christmas: Natasha and Kevin Coleman of Blandford, Samuel and Jamie Singleton of Harnham Road, Mrs J Formosa of Amesbury, Mrs P Newton of Winterbourne Dauntsey and C Riman of Wimborne.

Page 85

Sir William Golding at the Odeon cinema in 1965

CHAPTER FIVE:
HOW THE ODEON WAS WON
(The 1980s and Beyond)

The 1980s began with a serious slump in the British film industry, with fewer films being made in 1980 and 1981 than in any year since 1914. The incoming Conservative government removed the special support that had been available for the industry, tax rules were tightened and the quota system was suspended in 1983. The Rank Organisation also withdrew from film production, which further reduced funding opportunities.

Through the second half of the decade, film production declined further, with only 30 films produced in 1989. Several filmmakers switched to production of drama for television. National cinema attendance numbers continued to drop annually until 1984, at which point the all - time low point of 54 million was reached. Numbers have since that time increased again, although still to only a fraction of their 1940s and 1950s peak.

On 1 November 1982 the BBFC ratings system for film certification was completely overhauled, with only the U certificate remaining unchanged (though its description was slightly modified). The A certificate was replaced by PG and the age for AA raised and the certificate renamed 15. The X certificate level was unchanged but renamed 18 with the aim of softening the purely 'sexual' connotations the 'X' had garnered. A new R18 certificate was introduced for sexually explicit films. In order to show R18 films, cinemas would have to be licensed members - only clubs - previously, a loophole had allowed such clubs to show such films unrated.

The full certification list now read: U (Universal – Suitable for all); PG (Parental Guidance – General viewing, but some scenes may be unsuitable for young children); 15 (Suitable only for persons of 15 years and older);

The Odeon in the 1980s

18 (Suitable only for persons of 18 years and older); R18 (Restricted 18 – To be shown only in licensed cinemas to persons of not less than 18 years).

There would be two further changes to film certification during the 1980s. Firstly, the Video Recordings Act 1984 gave the BBFC the legal responsibility to rate all videos. The current certificates for films were all used with some modifications. Then in 1989, due to industry pressure regarding the new Batman film, a certificate was introduced for cinema films suitable for persons of 12 years and older.

Despite the national decline, with a 50th anniversary to look forward to, the Salisbury Odeon entered the new decade in an apparently very healthy state. The choice offered by the three screen conversion in 1972, combined with the promotional work carried out by the seemingly tireless Philip Cross had led to record breaking attendances again and again. However, the middle of the decade would see the biggest ever challenge to the future of cinema in Salisbury.

Away from the Odeon, St Edmunds Arts Centre was by now providing a regular alternative for cinema buffs. February and March 1980 saw an Orson Welles' season at the venue, comprising Citizen Kane, F For Fake, The Magnificent Ambersons and Immortal Story. The following March saw an 'Introducing Alternative Cinema' festival screening films from Man With A Movie Camera (1929) to a Short Film Series (1976-1980).

Margaret Thatcher at Wilton Carpet Factory 1980

A future Academy Award nominee was involved in a spot of mild controversy in the city in February 1980. Letters to the Salisbury Times expressed 'abhorrence and disgust' over a protest during Prime Minister Margaret Thatcher's visit to the SDC offices, calling the participants 'ill assorted' and a 'mob'. In response, three pupils from Bishop Wordsworth's School claimed they were in fact part of a specific and organised group objecting to cuts in education and transport concessions for students. The boys claimed that '10% of the pushing was caused by pensioners trying to get a glimpse of Mrs Thatcher [and] the other 90% by the television cameramen.'

Among the signatories to this response was 17-year old Ralph Fiennes. The Prime Minister had

some sympathy with the protestors' rights, if not their opinions. Asked about the incident during her later walkabout in Salisbury, she responded 'I am rather glad to see demonstrations because I am glad we live in a free society.'

Meanwhile Philip Cross was advertising for a team of four 'girls' (such gender targeting still being a common practice at the time) to assist at Odeon promotional events, commencing with a nostalgia night for the showing of Yanks. The team would be given special t - shirts and would be involved in activities such as presenting special guests with bouquets – and there would of course be the opportunity to see the latest films for free. Almost as an afterthought, Mr Cross did suggest that 'boys' might wish to write in for the jobs as well and he '…could then select [just] one to join the team'.

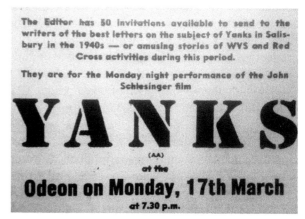

The Editor has 50 invitations available to send to the writers of the best letters on the subject of Yanks in Salisbury in the 1940s — or amusing stories of WVS and Red Cross activities during this period.

They are for the Monday night performance of the John Schlesinger film

YANKS
(AA)
at the
Odeon on Monday, 17th March
at 7.30 p.m.

Not everyone was happy with the range of 'choice' offered at the Odeon. 12 - year old Stephen Hall of Winding Way wrote to the Salisbury Times in March 1980, pointing out that for two consecutive weeks all the films being shown were either AA or X rated, meaning he could not 'support our local cinema' in the way that was always being requested.

Philip Cross was regularly invited to special film events in London. In July 1980 he asked Jill Goddard, who had been working as an usherette and receptionist at the Odeon for 16 years, if she would like to join him at a private showing of The Sea Wolves. His reason for asking was that he knew Jill was a lifelong fan of the star of the film, Gregory Peck, who would also be in attendance. Imagine her delight when, on being introduced to her, the screen idol told Jill she had a 'radiant' smile – and then kissed her!

"…. there is never smoke without fire, and changes have a habit of occurring without much warning to the public …."

The 1980 August Bank Holiday saw a Harnham born actor returning to the city. Anthony Daniels, famous for his role as C3P0 in Star Wars, was the Mayor's special guest at the Family Fayre held at Hudson's Field in support of the diagnostic day unit at Salisbury General Infirmary. Alongside a cardboard cut - out of his Star Wars character, an Imperial Stormtrooper and Philip Cross, Mr Daniels (who had left Salisbury at the age of one) arrived in a Ford Mustang. Having been presented with a framed picture of the Poultry Cross by the Mayor (Douglas Stephenson), Mr Daniels spent three hours signing autograph books and Star Wars ephemera.

In a lengthy letter to the Salisbury Times, published in October 1980, Alan Richardson (now returned to the city of his birth) provided a prescient warning to cinema fans in Salisbury. Reports had appeared in the national and trade press stating that the Rank Organisation was 'possibly thinking of selling a substantial number of cinemas, either to other cinema circuits…or to property developers.' Rank's only response to the rumours was that there was 'no immediate intention of selling off a large portion of their cinema circuit, and that only those cinemas that are in a 'poor earning area' are likely to be sold in the near future.'

Mr Richardson's concern was that 'there is never smoke without fire, and changes have a habit of occurring without much warning to the public.' He reminded readers that although three screens were still open, afternoon performances had ceased at the Salisbury Odeon a year previously without public consultation and, more recently, Saturday morning children's shows had ceased 'virtually overnight.' The fear was that 'Salisbury cinemagoers might wake up one day and find the doors to their delightful cinema barred and shut, and the superb building left closed and empty for months, the victim of damp and vandalism, while its future was being discussed.'

Alan Richardson felt the continuing management of Philip Cross – 'one of the Rank Organisation's top showman managers' stood the Odeon in good stead but, nevertheless, 'the stark facts of financial viability stare all managements in the face during these hard times.' Alan noted that Salisbury Playhouse looked outside of the city for the bulk of its audience, national pop promoters generally avoided the city and even local balls and dances struggled to break even. Television, cosy pubs, inflation and apathy were all factors affecting patronage and the Salisbury public would have to make their minds up about whether they still wanted the amenity of a city - centre cinema.

Addressing the local Rotarians lunch the following month, Philip Cross sounded a more optimistic note. He was confident that the 'huge commercial threat' of TV could be overcome and listed some of the innovations of modern cinema including drive - ins, creation of a 'pub' atmosphere, a wrap - around screen the height of a six storey building and the redevelopment of 3D and laser technology. He later told the Salisbury Times he expected 1981 to be 'a major film year', with record breaking and high profile films such as The Blue Lagoon, The Fog, Smokey and The Bandit Ride Again and the new Bond – For Your Eyes Only – coming on stream.

In December 1980 Mr Cross started to make plans for celebrating the following year's 50th anniversary of the opening of the Gaumont / Odeon. He was particularly hoping to track down Miss Nancy Mosselmans, who had presented a bouquet to Lady Pembroke on the Gala opening night. There were also plans to show a night of Mickey Mouse films, in recognition of Mickey Mouse's Birthday Party having been shown on the cinema's first night.

The subject matter of certain films continued to attract concern. Reviewing the Odeon programme for the Salisbury Times in May 1981, Sandra Jones (commenting on Flesh Gordon and Let's Make A Dirty Movie) noted that women in films were often portrayed as 'an insatiable nympho'. In a letter to the paper Sandra Owen, of Salisbury Women's Group, felt this point should have been addressed in more detail. Many women were seriously concerned about the casual acceptance of this type - casting which, Ms Owen said 'continually re - emphasise the male ideas that 'women are easy game', 'they are there for the taking', 'like a bit of rough and tumble'.'

Whilst the treatment of women as sex objects was bad enough in itself, Ms Owen felt there was 'an even more sinister undertone' as 'the implication in so many recent films – Dressed To Kill, Monster and When A Stranger Calls – merely seem to perpetuate the idea of male violence towards women.' Ms Owen hoped Philip Cross would appreciate how offensive such films were to women and would think more carefully about the films to be shown at the Odeon in the future.

The Salisbury Hospital Fete Queen, Sue Jones, was invited to step down from her horse - drawn carriage to join VIP guests at the Odeon in June 1981, for a Gala performance of Chariots Of Fire. Other invitees included the film's producer David Puttnam and star Ian Charleson, The Mayor and Mayoress of Salisbury (Derrick and Vida Alford), SDC Chairman Douglas Stephenson and his wife Margaret, Lord Pembroke and local film writer and author James Leasor. This event was such a success that Philip Cross wrote to the Salisbury Times to thank those involved – Runner Ian Ray, Miss Sue Coxon 'and her young ladies', Mrs Christine Powell, the Venture Scouts and Guides, the Salisbury District Scout Band, Salisbury City Cruisers and their cavalcade of custom cars, the Mayor and Mayoress and the cinema staff.

The Golden Jubilee of the opening of the Odeon (as the Gaumont Palace) was marked with a Gala screening of Escape To Victory on 7 September 1981, 50 years to the day since the cinema opening and just four days after the film's London premiere. To also mark the occasion, a special programme was produced and Alan Richardson's The Cinema Theatres of Salisbury was published in a limited edition of 500 copies.

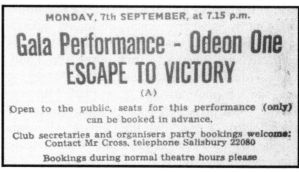

MONDAY, 7th SEPTEMBER, at 7.15 p.m.
Gala Performance - Odeon One
ESCAPE TO VICTORY
(A)
Open to the public, seats for this performance (only) can be booked in advance.
Club secretaries and organisers party bookings welcome: Contact Mr Cross, telephone Salisbury 22080
Bookings during normal theatre hours please

The celebrations had in fact begun the week before, when Mr Richardson and Philip Cross entertained 50 members and guests of the Cinema Theatre Association of Great Britain, with a tour starting at the Odeon. Among the local guests was Jim Smith, now famous as the author and illustrator of the Frog Band children's books, who started his working life on the projection staff at the old Regal. Now of course in use as a bingo hall, this was the next theatre on the tour and Mr Smith took great delight in showing the visitors the old projection room and the areas he had to keep clean and sparkling as a young member of staff. The group then visited the Playhouse and the City Hall, where staff were again co-operative in allowing access to the old cinema areas of the building.

The Odeon Gala night included the Solent Strutters majorettes, the Salisbury Scout Band under Mr Bert Whatum, the Anniversary Princess (courtesy of ADNews and Turner's of Catherine Street – and her Royal Chair, courtesy of Southon's), special music by Peter Stanger at the organ, floral displays, a wine reception (hosted by Otto's of Southampton) and an anniversary cake made in the shape of a cinema screen by Celia Cannell, who had made a wedding cake for Princess Anne and, more recently, the cake replica of St Paul's Cathedral given to the Mayor's Appeal courtesy of the Princess of Wales.

".... As manager of this lovely theatre I try to involve it in as many ways as possible with the community ...."

Guests again included the Mayor and Mayoress of Salisbury and the Chairman of SDC and his wife, as well as the president of Salisbury and District Chamber of Commerce, Mr Les Parratt and his wife, Mr H A Chrichton - Miller (the managing director of Rank) and his wife, Mr Ray Roberts (Rank's operational executive), the actor John Quayle, Mrs Joan Leasor (on behalf of her husband James), authors Richard Davies and Alan Richardson and a number of people celebrating their birthday that day, as well as patrons and staff from the original first night (including original usherette Kay Parrott) and representatives of voluntary organisations. Local sports groups and organisations and Salisbury Journal readers were offered discounted tickets. Mr Stuart Lucas of Ayleswade Road attended with his wife – he had lent an original opening night programme to the cinema to be copied and displayed.

Congratulatory telegrams from all over the World were read out to the audience, including from Roger Moore, Michael Caine, Lord Pembroke, Lord and Lady Romsey, impresario Robert Stigwood, Bobby Moore and David Puttnam. Speeches were kept to a minimum but Mr Chrichton - Miller sounded a positive note when he referred to the subject of cinema closures and conjectured on whether the Odeon would be around for another 50 years. Mr Crichton - Miller said the Odeon was 'profitable...and more profitable this year than last.' 16 - year old Jane Usher of Alderbury was named as the Anniversary Princess and, 'resplendent in a silver cat suit with silver tiara', was presented with a silver rose bowl by Mr Chrichton -Miller. On their arrival at the Odeon the other main guests were presented with bouquets by nine-year olds Timothy Martin and Hayley Knight.

SDC Chairman Douglas Stephenson was presented with a cheque for £97.30 from Mrs Ann Cutler, raised from a sponsored walk by members of the Salisbury Area Keep Fit Association, for the diagnostic day unit at the Infirmary. The Robert Stigwood Organisation donated tickets for the southern premiere of Jesus Christ Superstar at the Southampton Gaumont for Mayor Alford and Mr Stephenson and their wives.

Summing up the achievements of the cinema, Philip Cross told the local press 'I have been lucky in that my career has allowed me to develop my two main interests, meeting people and my love of all forms of show - business. As manager of this lovely theatre I try to involve it in as many ways as possible with the community. For example many hundreds of pounds have been collected for charities at the theatre, including the Mayoral Appeals.'

'A large number of film personalities and characters have appeared in recent years, including Salisbury born Anthony Daniels from Star Wars; Stormtroopers and Darth Vader have created a stir both in and around the theatre. Disneyland stars and famous cars such as Herbie and the recent Condor - Car have been brought to the city to the delight of local youngsters, and to herald their films of course.'

Page 91

Two film addicts who attended the opening night of the Odeon Cinema in Salisbury in 1931 were also at the cinema for the 50th anniversary party. On the left is Mr. Arthur Laishley, and with him is Mr. Arthur Maidment. Odeon manager Philip Cross stands proudly by the special golden jubilee cake.

'Most of Salisbury's Mayors have attended functions at the theatre. Indeed, one youngster went home and told his mother he had met the King at the Odeon (in fact the then Mayor complete with his chain!) We have come a long way since the Countess of Pembroke opened the 'wonder theatre' on 7 September 1931. With our three screens we are able to offer a much wider range of films and choice, and still retain the unique 500 year old foyer and matching décor in Odeon 1. This is much loved by patrons and tourists alike. I am also proud to receive so many requests to take part in panels, judging beauty queens, advice on staging charity functions and many similar things – it is nice to know that the Odeon is at the hub of so much local activity.'

When asked about Salisbury's favourite films, Mr Cross replied 'A difficult one that. Tess, Yanks and Chariots Of Fire are popular, as are most comedies and escapist films. The one film that I have lost count of return visits is Blazing Saddles, and it always makes good box office. We are very lucky to be in the stream of some really outstanding films at the moment, and there would appear to be quite a number in the pipeline, all good news as we start on the next 50 years.'

In his book, Alan Richardson estimated that since opening on 7 September 1931 the Gaumont/Odeon had opened its doors on 17,300 days screening around 4,000 feature films to a combined audience of well over 20 million! However, cinemas were by now generally finding it harder and harder to stay open, with competition from television and the high costs of operation, and whereas there had been 5,000 cinemas across the nation between 1935 and 1950 there were now less than 1,000, with continuing regular closures.

Mr Richardson repeated his pleas of almost a year earlier: 'Salisbury can only continue to deserve a cinema if it is prepared to support it, and it will only get the films it wants by going along and seeing those films. The lack of support for films of real quality in Salisbury is terrifyingly low, with rare exceptions. Thus it is only by partly catering for those whose tastes are for the more violent and sexually explicit films that the cinema manages to keep going at all. No matter how good the movie may be on the television screen at home there is still no substitute for a good night out at the cinema, so do support your local cinema, otherwise one day it will simply disappear without any warning at all!'

Later in September 1981, Frederick Charles May died at Newbridge Hospital in Salisbury, aged 77. Mr May had worked as a cinema projectionist for 50 years before ill - health forced him to retire aged 64. Fred May was born in Southampton and at 14-years old started working in the projection box at the Gaiety in that city's High Street, before moving on to the Broadway in Portswood. He came to the Salisbury Regal when it opened in 1937 and stayed until his retirement. Mr May was for many years a committee member of Castle Street Social Club and lived in Warwick Close.

December 1981 brought shock news as Philip Cross announced he was leaving the Odeon in the forthcoming January, to embark on a new career in public relations and entertainment in Perth, Australia. As well as raising the profile and viability of the cinema with his seemingly infinite capacity for ideas and organisation, Mr Cross had become a noted figure in Salisbury as a one - time chairman of Salisbury Publicity Association, a Rotarian, a great contributor to Mayoral Appeals and a former vice - chairman of the city's Britain In Bloom committee. Known as 'Uncle Phil' to many younger film fans, he was also an honorary member of the Salisbury Journal Trumper Club.

Mr Cross, who lived in Richards Way with his wife Marion and their children Anthony, David and Karen, said 'I am sorry to leave this unique and lovely theatre and the many friends I have made during the years in Salisbury. However, I look forward to the challenge of a new career in another country and I wish my successor every possible success.'

There was one more prize for Mr Cross before he emigrated, as he was awarded a 'gold medal' for his earlier promotion of Chariots Of Fire. In keeping with the film's Olympic theme, producer David Puttnam had offered gold, silver and bronze awards and the top prize, which also included a trip to Paris, was presented by Rank's director of operations, David Spruce. Typically, Philip Cross signed off his time at the Odeon by giving the credit for the award to 'the many people who helped in staging the Gala night in Salisbury.'

In the spring and summer of 1982 the projectionist at the Amesbury Plaza, 21 - year old Alistair Lock, who lived in the town, used the venue to create his own film, in which he played all the parts and even appeared on the Plaza screen. Behind The Screens, filmed in both colour and black and white, formed part of Alistair's five - year course in advanced film making at Salisbury College of Art and provided a glimpse of how the cinema operated, including footage of recent anniversary celebrations.

Apart from the weekly generic listing advertisements and preview/reviews, there was a noticeable reduction in press coverage of what was happening at the Odeon after the departure of Philip Cross. His replacement, Ian Wild, did however tell the Salisbury Times in July 1982 that after six months in the job he was still getting used to 'rattling around like a pea in a drum' in the various cavernous areas behind the front of house and screens. At the time he was particularly open to suggestions for new uses for the oak panelled former restaurant, with its massive antique fireplaces, which had been unoccupied since Top Rank ceased its bingo operation there in 1969. Among the many responses received was

Philip Cross who emigrated to Australia in 1981

a proposal from the Salisbury Bridge Club, who started using the room for four evenings a week from the October.

In August 1982, Mrs M A Lavender of Middle Woodford was moved to write to the Salisbury Times, complaining about bad language used in the hit film Fame. Having enjoyed the TV series of the same name, Mrs Lavender had taken her 15 - year old daughter and some friends to the Odeon, only to be shocked as the film version was 'utterly foul - mouthed. It is always bad enough hearing bad language from adults, but to hear it from young people, aged 15 and 16, is really awful.' The party was also disappointed that the theme tune of the film was different to the version in the UK charts. 'Altogether an extremely disappointing experience and certainly not worth wasting £2 on a cinema visit' concluded Mrs Lavender.

In response to the main concerns, Rupert Ackroyd of Rank told the paper 'We obviously don't want anybody to be upset when they come to the cinema, but people should take notice of the AA certificate saying that you should be over 14. Once the film has been passed by the British Board of Film Censors, we cannot start re - censoring it.' 15 - year old Louisa Giorgi, of Cherry Close, shared Mr Ackroyd's views: 'My [also 15 - year old] friends and I thoroughly enjoyed our visit to Fame and did not find it at all disappointing. It was well worth the £2 we spent. As it is an AA, Mrs Lavender should not have expected it to be on the level of a Walt Disney film.'

From January 1983 the weekly programme changeover for most cinemas (including the Odeon and the Plaza) was changed from Saturday to Thursday. This change was mainly aimed at reducing the costs of distributing films, but it had also been found that cinemas already changing programmes on Thursday tended to do better business at the weekends. It was also hoped that holidaymakers would take advantage of the greater choice offered by a midweek change.

The perennial subject of sex and violence at the movies cropped up again in February 1983. The Salisbury Journal reported that during the programme for the family - friendly ET The Extra Terrestrial, trailers were shown for First Blood '...full of hints about violence and guns' and The French Lieutenant's Woman 'which consisted almost entirely of passionate embraces.' The latter apparently frightened the six - year old boy accompanying the reporter, as he thought the characters were fighting. The reporter recognised the difficulty for cinema managers, as film programme reels were distributed inclusive of trailers. They were however impressed by Odeon manager Ian Wild's response to their concerns, as he agreed to cut the First Blood trailer, despite it having a U certificate.

In September 1983 managing director Myles Byrne decided to open up the Amesbury Plaza for daytime meetings, conferences and sales. Mr Byrne told the Salisbury Journal 'These days one cannot allow a building in the middle of a town like Amesbury to stand idle, only being used for a few hours each evening.'

On 15 March 1984 the Salisbury Journal carried shocking front-page news for local film fans.

THE LAST BIG PICTURE SHOW ..?

SALISBURY'S only cinema could soon fall victim to a multi-million £ development linking New Canal and the Old George Mall.

Under the banner headline 'The Last Big Picture Show?' it was reported that Rank, the owners of the Odeon, had confirmed talks were under way with a development company over the sale of the cinema. The adjoining Southern Electricity and Southern Gas premises would also be tied up in any redevelopment – said to be compliant with SDCs then draft Local Plan, which had outlined the possibility of extending the Old George Mall to create small shopping units.

At this point there was 'no question of losing the historic features of the Hall of John Halle currently housing the Odeon, which would have to be retained and incorporated in any new scheme.' Did this however mean the cinema itself would be safe... or merely the historic elements of the building? There was doubt in the mind of some locals, including Alan Richardson, who had of course forewarned of the possibility of closure and loss of the cinema.

A few weeks later Mr Richardson was telling the local press he was 'amazed at the apathy of local residents.' His concerns had received support from the Dean of Salisbury, the Very Reverend Sidney Evans, but otherwise 'not a thing has been said by anyone since details of the scheme were first made known.' Alan's concerns were that without the cinema, the city would become a 'cultural desert' at night (which would be of concern to both residents and visitors) and 'serious social behaviour problems could result [amongst 16 - 20 year olds] if this essential amenity is lost.'

Others reacted by considering how the cinema could be revamped but still used for the arts. Trevor Locke of Old Meadows Walk wrote to the Journal with his ideas, including retaining a smaller cinema, and adding a lecture room, recital

"…. The impression getting around is that demolition of the cinema is a fait accompli. It is not doomed yet …."

hall, stage and coffee shop. His interesting idea was for an 'Arts Centre'. This proposal provoked some reaction from the public with Jane Whittle of Redlynch and Roger Stephens of Estcourt Road both writing to the Journal in less than supportive tones. Mr Stephens in particular couldn't understand why this would be appropriate, given the eight years of successful and varied programmes thus far achieved by the already established St Edmund's Arts Centre, which of course still operates today. At the same time, Alan Richardson's concerns had elicited letters of support for his cause, from Lionel Hawes of Odstock and S G Sleeman.

That there were negotiations over proposals to redevelop the site was well - known, but the exact details were not yet in the public domain. However, Alan Richardson was working hard in the background. In October 1984 it was announced by the Heritage Sponsorship Division of the Historic Buildings and Monuments Commission that, following submission of a dossier compiled by Mr Richardson, the main cinema element of the Odeon building had been designated as a Grade II listed building. With the Medieval Hall of John Halle already Grade I listed, this provided SDC, as the Local Planning Authority, with further controls on how the site could redeveloped - but wedded with further responsibilities regarding its protection.

Mr Richardson was delighted, saying 'I have always considered the cinema to be a unique piece of architecture because of the way the auditorium has been built to fit in with a medieval entrance. I wouldn't like to say it was the only cinema outside London that was listed, but it's certainly one of the very few and the only one in the south and west.'

Notwithstanding this, SDC District Planning Officer Peter Young pointed out that, whilst listed building consent would have to be granted by the SoS for any demolition of the building, this was no guarantee that its use as a cinema would continue. Mr Young confirmed that discussions were still taking place with Rank and the prospective purchasers of the site and although

the Council might be able to exercise compulsory purchase powers to protect the building 'that would have to be backed up by a willingness to take the cinema on itself, and the Council would have to consider that very carefully.'

The details of the development proposals for the Odeon site finally became public with the submission, by Bath and Bristol Estates Ltd, of a planning application for a retail development linking New Canal via an arcade through to Old George Mall, accompanied by an application for listed building consent for the works necessary to accommodate this. Whilst the listed elements of the building would be retained, the cinema use would be lost.

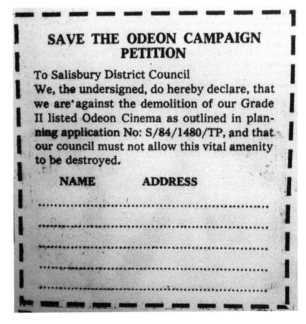

SAVE THE ODEON CAMPAIGN PETITION

To Salisbury District Council
We, the undersigned, do hereby declare, that we are against the demolition of our Grade II listed Odeon Cinema as outlined in planning application No: S/84/1480/TP, and that our council must not allow this vital amenity to be destroyed.

NAME   ADDRESS

This prompted a 'formalisation' of Alan Richardson's campaigning as the Save The Odeon group – in which he was initially joined by Laura Bell and Paul Humphries - scheduled its first meeting at the Royal British Legion Hall on 15 November 1984, to be preceded by leafletting outside the cinema and in the Market Square. Mr Richardson told the Salisbury Journal 'The impression getting around is that demolition of the cinema is a fait accompli. It is not doomed yet.'

'Our message is 'get back to the drawing room and think again.' Let's emphasise that this cinema is paying its way. And let's emphasise also that there is a great upsurge in cinema attendances in the USA, Canada and Australia. If it's happening there it's going to happen here.' A letter from Mrs Rosemary Pyke of Redlynch was published in the same edition of the Journal, effectively supporting the campaign, alongside one from local historian and tour guide Don Cross expressing hope that any redevelopment would still allow access for viewing the historic parts of the building.

Unfortunately the same edition also included a report entitled 'Final Curtain for the Plaza'. The decision to close, with the loss of five jobs, followed a drastic slump in audience numbers at the Amesbury cinema. The owners of the site, Moladean Ltd, were negotiating with possible purchasers but the Journal pointed out that the loss of both the Odeon and the Plaza could result in a 45 - mile round trip to Southampton for local film fans.

Myles Byrne, of the Plaza, told the paper 'Until about a year ago, audience figures were healthy. Now this decision has been forced on me. We know that cinema trade is down in general all over the country but we still don't understand it.' He thought that two probable reasons were the boom in the video trade and the delay in obtaining copies of films from renters who favoured the more popular Odeon circuit (i.e. in Salisbury). 'The independent cinema always has a hard fight when there is a circuit one close by. Although there is a trade agreement that we should be allowed to play a week after Salisbury, we have had to wait for copies many times, while the Odeon enjoyed a six - week run which took all our business.' Mr Byrne paid tribute to the loyalty of his long serving employees, one of whom – Mrs Stella Thorne – had been manageress of the Plaza for 19 years.

Support for the Save The Odeon Campaign was swelling. On the morning of the 15 November meeting the Salisbury Journal published opinion pieces, as well as a letter from Audrey Martingell, Secretary of the Salisbury Local History Group, describing the development scheme as 'heinous' and 'nothing more than vandalism' and asking readers to 'oppose vehemently any such plans'. A further letter, from Simon Thorne of Portland Avenue, pointed out that the developers' claim of

the cinema not being used on a Wednesday was false as on that day of the previous week he had watched Clint Eastwood in Tightrope in a 'over three - quarters full' Screen 3.

Meanwhile SDC Councillor David Parker was calling on the authority to buy the Odeon and save it from demolition. Councillor Parker suggested that £800,000 earmarked for a refurbishment of the City Hall could be used on the 'better placed and equipped' Odeon instead and wanted the proposal put to the public. His view was that, if wishing to run with this plan, the Council's Planning Committee should first refuse the current scheme and then persuade the Halls Sub - Committee and Amenities and Tourist Committee to adopt the cinema.

The Salisbury District Trades Council had urged refusal of the plans, which had also been condemned by the local Labour Party, and MP Robert Key was behind the 'Save It' campaign calling it 'magnificent... the cinema is a very important cultural interest in Salisbury and should be retained' and raising the matter of declining numbers of cinemas in the House of Commons. Even the local music fraternity, a rival perhaps for the punter's leisure shilling, came out in support of saving the Odeon, by putting on a fundraising show at the Churchill Rooms in the Red Lion Hotel, featuring local artists Afro Dizzy Acts, Don't Feed The Animals and Candy Hill, which attracted a crowd of 170.

"…. We are going to win if we all get together and act as a town rather than just a few people …."

The public meeting was attended by around 200 people, who heard Alan Richardson proclaim 'Let our Council have the guts to throw back this scheme. Why leave the decision to the Secretary of State for Environment – to one man? Let us have the guts to make up our own minds.' Paul Humphries said 'Up until now it has been a small campaign but if we are going to win we will have to make it a major campaign and we have got to make sure everybody is behind us.'

A campaign petition had risen to 2,700 signatures but Mr Humphries asked people to take additional blank pages, posters and badges to their villages, schools and workplaces, and help with mundane tasks such as photocopying, as well as writing their own letters of objection. 'We are going to win if we all get together and act as a town rather than just a few people, and when it's all over we are going to have a victory party' he concluded. Alan Richardson then outlined the history of the campaign to date, before Laura Bell spoke of the social impact that would result from the cinema closure.

There was now news of an immediate reprieve for the Amesbury Plaza, at least for a short time until Christmas and possibly in to the New Year, depending on any planning proposals. Myles Byrne had decided to let the cinema run on following a boost in audience numbers together with 'a batch of coming attractions [including Clint Eastwood, Bo Derek and 101 Dalmations] which he considers outstanding'.

Mr Byrne did however have a stark warning for the local public. In a letter to the Journal he said 'It is always sad to see a cinema close, but this would not happen if the public supported the Odeon, Salisbury, and the Plaza, Amesbury. Ask anyone how often they go to the pictures and you find their answer 'not very often' or 'not for years'. It is no use these same people crying out when the doors are bolted, or the cinema is about to close. The Plaza has had a reprieve, and if it gets the support it could save its future closure. So it is now up to the people crying out to show that they really mean what they say about saving cinemas and return as an audience. It is, after all, now or never!'

The last two weeks of November saw more supporters of the Odeon campaign submitting letters to the Journal. Carl Tomlinson of Redlynch pointed out the loss of the cinema would see local film fans having to pay £3 for a return journey to Southampton in a 'filthy train or slow bus', and all for the sake of 'yet another' shopping arcade. Whilst agreeing that 'nostalgia is not a very good reason to save the Odeon', one - time usherette Mrs F D Purdy of Fisherton Street begged the indulgence of readers as fond memories were evoked, culminating with her younger brother sitting on Paul Robeson's knee. Mrs Purdy felt there were other, more sound, reasons for saving the cinema – 'It's an important tourist attraction. It's an amenity that we can't afford to lose. It's paying its way.'

Mrs E J Bartley of Bedwin Bridge Club was concerned about the loss of the former restaurant at the Odeon, pointing out that this was used by hers and now other groups, with very few other options available in the city. Mrs Hazel Whipple of Crane Street backed this view and suggested the old restaurant could be additionally used for lectures and exhibitions, thus increasing viability of the cinema. N M Taylor of Milford and Kevin Farwell of Pitton (and the Institute of Amateur Cinematographers) set out their objections to the proposals, with the latter also setting out the lack of technical facilities and ambience of suggested alternatives (i.e. The City Hall in comparison to the historic and purpose - designed Odeon).

'SAVE-IT' SIGNATURES TOP 13,000

THE Save the Odeon petition has more than 13,000 signatures including nearly 1,000 from the Journal's campaign alone.

Boosted by a Saturday market 'fancy dress' event, the number of petitioners rose rapidly to 8,000, then 13,000, and the Salisbury Journal made a decision to break its rules of impartiality by publishing the petition sheet on its front page. Meanwhile, across the channel, French national newspaper Liberation had gotten hold of the story and published an article in support of the 'Save It' campaign.

At this stage Rank brought forward what Peter Young of SDC called 'an options package' aimed at alleviating local concern. David Cole of Rank explained the proposal was that, if the redevelopment of the Odeon were agreed, then the company would agree to the lifting of the covenant (still held in its favour) restricting the showing of paid entry films at the City Hall. Furthermore Rank would be willing to make its 50mm projection equipment available to an alternative venue, as well as its booking facilities and 'expertise', in order that 'the best films were screened in Salisbury.'

Mr Young was cautious, saying 'the Council would need a lot more information on this proposal before making a decision.' He doubted that any of the recently refurbished City Hall

auditoria could be used for screening films 'every night of the week.' Alan Richardson was more forceful: 'The Rank Organisation has already gone on record as stating that they have no intention of looking for an alternative site in Salisbury. Let us remain firm in our desire to keep this splendid Grade II listed auditorium. Nothing else can be a substitute, let alone vague undefined promises.'

Derrick Alford holds the petition with Alan Richardson to his left

The petition was eventually handed to SDC Chairman, Derrick Alford, on the Guildhall steps on 1 December, by which time it contained 21,984 names. However, the groundswell of public opinion apparently didn't dampen Rank's determination to proceed with selling the site as later that same month it announced its agreement of a sale to BBE.

A spokesman for Rank said that 'In the past 12 months admissions to this cinema have fallen by over 35%, a far greater decline than the national average, reflecting a massive decrease in public support for the Salisbury Odeon. The theatre is loss - making and if stringent economies had not been made, much more serious losses would have been incurred. Profit has been achieved only once in the last three years.' Turning to the building itself, the spokesman said that a substantial amount of money would need to be spent to refurbish it to modern cinema standards. Trading performance showed that such a level of expenditure was simply not viable and present trends in the business left the company with no option but to plan for its disposal and re - development.

"…. As far as I am concerned Salisbury is a cinema town and I think there is potential in the city …."

When considering the sale of the site to BBE, Rank was mindful of the historic interest of the Hall of John Halle and said the developers were 'experts in the preservation of historic buildings, Rank Theatre believe they represent the best opportunity for the part of the building to be preserved and thereby allow it to seen and enjoyed by very many more people than has been the case in recent years.'

1985 was to prove a critical year for the future of cinema in Salisbury, and from January the ongoing Save The Odeon campaign shared media space with another high profile building, as a multi - million pound appeal to save the cathedral spire was launched by the Prince of Wales. During the same period former Prime Minister Ted Heath purchased, for £250,000, a 60 - year lease on the historic house Arundells in The Close.

To the delight of the 'Save It' camp early January saw the possibility of salvation from a giant cinema company. Impressed by the campaign and the numbers who had signed the petition, Cannon Classic had written to SDC expressing interest in making a bid for the Odeon. This would only be pursued if the current planning applications were refused and Rank was able to withdraw from any agreement with BBE, but at least Cannon Managing Director Barry Jenkins' comments that 'As far as I am concerned Salisbury is a cinema town and I think there is potential in the city' provided encouragement to the campaigners and perhaps cast some doubt on Rank's assessments.

January 1985 also saw an announcement from the Arts Centre that a £550 grant from Southern Arts had enabled the purchase of a new Cinema-scope screen, thereby allowing a greater variety of films to be shown at that venue.

With the Odeon planning applications due to be considered by the SDC Planning Committee, Myles Byrne had thrown another consideration into the ring: 'If the Odeon closes it leaves the Plaza as the nearest alternative for Salisbury,' he said 'and with some good films coming along it could make all the difference. But if the Odeon

stays open I don't think we can keep going for long. It's a struggle.' Mr Byrne added there had been an improvement in attendance at the Amesbury venue since it had been given a facelift and he also felt there had been a drop - off in the novelty of video home - rental. However, these factors were not enough to save the Plaza, which might have to close for good if the Odeon proposals were to be refused and that site taken over by another cinema chain.

BBE now announced it was considering potential revisions to its proposals for the Odeon, taking on board the scale and content of local concerns. With Cannon also apparently on stand-by a further group of potential purchasers arose in the form of a locally - based, privately - funded consortium, which had received backing from the BFI – on the clear understanding that the existing auditorium would be retained and put to cinema use.

THEY'RE TRYING TO CLOSE THE ODEON? THE HELL THEY WILL!

Mystery backer for 'DIY' Odeon

It was Alan Richardson who announced the consortium's interest and he followed this up with news of its potential principal financial backer. A London firm of chartered accountants had written to SDC on behalf of its (evidently very wealthy) client, 'who is concerned about the decline of Britain's cinema buildings.' The letter explained the client's particular concern over the Salisbury Odeon and confirmed that 'Should it be possible for the local authority or an appropriate local group, conceivably with the help of the British Film Institute, to take over the running of this cinema, then I am in a position to state that my Client would probably be willing to make a substantial donation towards the cost of acquisition and refurbishment.'

Alan Richardson was unable to name the mystery client but told the Salisbury Journal 'The generous backer of this scheme is anxious that a consortium of both local and London people, with the necessary managerial and creative expertise, should be formed as soon as possible. The Council must not let this fantastic opportunity to go by because if they did it would be a slap in the face for the benefactor and a slap in the face for the city. It must be unique for such a wonderful opportunity to be offered to the city.' Mr Richardson saw this as an opportunity to bring SDC, Rank and BBE to the table for high level discussions about the future of the Odeon site.

In February 1985, and following a site visit by its members, the SDC South - East Planning Sub-Committee resolved to recommend refusal of the Odeon planning applications to the main Planning Committee in line with the following concerns in a motion proposed by Councillor Bill McGrath: The proposed retail element would exceed that identified for Salisbury in the Local Plan; The County Surveyor had directed refusal because of highway safety concerns; Lack of a direct external link with the Old George Mall; Loss of the cinema as a public facility; Failure to explore all alternative uses of the building.

The motion was carried unanimously but it is interesting to note that these reasons did not refer to the impact on the heritage asset per se – not everyone was convinced of the value of this asset. Indeed Councillor Phoebe Lonsdale would not have objected to the loss of the building if a suitable use for the site could be found - 'I don't think it's a beautiful building on the outside – it's hideous' she said 'and I don't think it's very beautiful inside either.'

Alan Richardson was naturally delighted with the committee decision but warned it would be the outcome of the final battle that would be most important. BBE had now put forward an option of a revised scheme retaining a 250 seat cinema. However, Mr Richardson had concerns that redevelopment of the site would mean no cinema provision in the city for at least 18 months – 'by then the cinema - going habit would be lost, and after a few months the developers would claim lack of support, and within a few weeks the cinema would be another shop! What a terrible slap in the face it would be to that wonderfully generous benefactor who is prepared to purchase and refurbish our existing cinema if we were to so churlishly refuse that offer.'

"…. They will have to provide a feasible plan to preserve what makes this such an important historical building …."

Alan Richardson (left) meeting British Film Institute Director, Anthony Smith (centre) and two BFI members

Revised BBE applications for planning permission and listed building consent were submitted to SDC for demolition of the building (excluding the Hall of John Halle) to accommodate the construction of new shopping units, a cinema and café, with various associated works to the building and adjoining properties in New Canal and Catherine Street. BBE indicated that if the proposals were approved they would instruct a first rate interior designer to provide an 'exceptional and exciting' new cinema, which, it was suggested, Rank might even be prepared to manage on its behalf. Notwithstanding this, BBE had also lodged an appeal against the previous refusals.

The 'Save It' campaign regrouped and lobbied the local press on the revised scheme, with Alan Richardson reiterating points previously made – stressing that the previous petition had specifically spoken of the desire to retain the cinema auditorium and building as it stood and the adaptation to provide a 250 - seat cinema

would not satisfy this. Paul Humphries told the Salisbury Journal of a fear that people may be beguiled into accepting what could be a poor alternative to the existing cinema. 'We are not happy about the proposed 250 - seat cinema included in the new plans. It's ill - conceived and appears not to be viable,' he said 'we are hoping to mobilise people quickly and make them aware of the problems involved in accepting this new proposal.'

Alan Richardson had meanwhile arranged for BFI director Anthony Smith and members Ian Christie and Chris Ellicott to visit the Odeon. The BFI men apparently 'fell in love' with the cinema, with Mr Smith saying 'it would be tragic to lose it.' The Institute was apparently still only interested in supporting a bid to retain the existing cinema and not a smaller replacement. Mr Smith said of the BBE proposal for a 250 - seater 'One would assume that it would not be economically viable in a city of this size.'

The group could however see the potential viability in the existing facility. Mr Christie said 'It's absolutely magnificent and it would be a crime to lose it'. He acknowledged it would require careful restoration to achieve its full potential but there were hopeful signs that the cinema industry was making a comeback. Mr Christie also praised Rank for its 'enlightened' approach and for the enterprising manager at Salisbury, Ian Wild, who had successfully experimented with special Tuesday evening screenings. After the tour of the cinema the BFI team met with members of the potential Odeon consortium.

Anthony Smith subsequently wrote to SDC Chief Executive Fergus Colquhoun saying he was strongly impressed by the 'remarkable' décor of the Odeon. Mr Smith felt it must be one of the last surviving examples of the heyday of cinema and the building could become a 'living museum and a versatile cultural amenity'. The BFI had no interest in the business concerns of Rank and neither did it have any influence on the local authority but Mr Smith and his colleagues had two main observations: Firstly, 'From our nationwide experience of trends in film exhibition, we doubt strongly that this [the BBE 250 - seat proposal] will be of interest to any commercial operator who would require either a larger auditorium or, more likely, a multi - screen format.' Mr Smith's second point was that the Odeon offered considerable space for ancillary activities but was not being used to its full potential. The provision of bar and catering facilities together with relevant marketing activities was an essential step towards making cinemas economic.'

'It must be admitted that the challenge facing the Odeon campaign group is considerable.' Mr Smith continued 'They will have to provide a feasible plan to preserve what makes this such an important historical building and at the same time bring it up to modern technical standards, but if they succeed in doing so, thanks to the exceptional support of their would - be sponsor, they will have achieved something unique in the conservation and enhancement of our heritage.'

In a letter published by the Salisbury Journal in April 1985, Laura Bell set out the flaws with the revised BBE scheme. Apart from the objection to the loss of the cinema, none of the other reasons for refusal of the original planning applications had been overcome – and in any case the proposals would see the capacity of the cinema reduced from 710 to 250. There were parties who had indicated confidence in the viability of the existing cinema should Rank wish to dispose of it whereas by contrast a 250 - seater – in any context – would be likely to require grants to continue operating, and the BFI for one had said it would not be interested in supporting a cinema of that scale. The doubt associated with the viability of the BBE cinema meant there was no guarantee it could be maintained in the future. The upshot would then of course have been the loss of the last cinema in Salisbury - in other words the same outcome as the previously refused scheme.

The Salisbury Journal continued its support for the campaign and editor Gareth Weekes warned 'the war is far from won', noting the apparent drop-off in wider support since BBE had revealed its revised scheme. Mr Weekes saw this revision as anything but a satisfactory compromise as, not only would the cinema be too small to be viable but it would be tucked away 'at the top of several

flights of stairs' and 'a very poor substitute for the three screens of the Odeon.' After reiterating the other objections Mr Weekes warned of the developers' determination to pursue its aspirations for the site and concluded by saying 'Councillors opposed to the scheme have an uphill task, but I hope they will continue to put every possible obstacle in its way.'

EDITOR'S COMMENT

It's an uphill task to save the Odeon

by Gareth Weekes

SOMEONE said recently how pleased he was that the campaign to save the cinema in Salisbury had finally been won.

He was sadly misinformed. The war is far from won. Despite an early success, the odds are still strongly in favour of the Odeon auditorium being demolished to make way for a new shopping centre.

Many of the Odeon's supporters are silent. This suggests that they have been seduced into believing that the developers' proposed new 250-seat cinema above the shops is a satisfactory compromise.

to present a water-tight case. They are trying to ensure that whatever they propose will be a properly run, viable cinema.

And it begins to look as if they will somehow find ways around other planning objections such as traffic disruption and access to the Old George Mall.

This makes the Odeon's future look increasingly bleak. It is an appalling prospect, but the clearly expressed hopes of 22,000 people who signed the peti-

Later in April the SDC Amenities and Tourism Committee stated its support for the retention of a cinema in the city, but stressed that the Council could not be expected to make any major financial contribution to any 'rescue' operation. Other than this media coverage fell quiet for a few months as the revised planning permissions ran their course.

Out at Amesbury, the Plaza had run into a new problem as it fell - foul of fire safety legislation. Wiltshire Fire Brigade had inspected the premises in March 1985 and had reported a number of defects. A follow - up inspection carried out in May found that the situation had deteriorated despite a warning letter having been sent. SDC now wrote to the cinema warning that its licence might be revoked if the contraventions were not resolved by the time of a further inspection. Myles Byrne explained he had been recovering from a long illness but would now take the necessary action to overcome the fire safety

"…. you are left with basically two newly painted large boxes, of no particular architectural merit …."

concerns. The matter was dealt with satisfactorily but within a few months Mr Byrne was again reporting the likely closure of the cinema – although a Salisbury couple and a group of Bournemouth cinema enthusiasts had expressed an interest in buying the site.

In June 1985 BBE revealed another revision of its proposals for the Odeon site, this time incorporating a two-screen option for the cinema – one a 250 - seater and the other 115. The facility would allow the two auditoria to be combined if required and the developer invited Council members to view a film at the Odeon and then at a modern complex at the Bristol Odeon, for comparison. Council members insisted that any such trip should be paid for by SDC and not BBE.

B and B confident about a revised plan for cinema

Alan Richardson saw the fact the campaigners had compelled the developer to rethink its plans for a second time as a positive, but was still unsupportive of the scheme as a whole. He explained the consortium's proposals for the Odeon included the updating of technical equipment and seating to meet modern standards, but without the need to demolish the historic building. Take this away he said, referring to the BBE cinema - trip offer, and '…you are left with basically two newly painted large boxes, of no particular architectural merit, in Bristol.'

Paul Humphries suggested that, should the offer of the Bristol trip be taken up, Council members might like to consider how the cinemas would compare in other ways - not just the auditorium experience: Would food and drink be available (the latest Salisbury proposal had sacrificed a café for the cinema space); What

provision was made for offices and staff rooms ('One glance' would show the inadequacy of this in the Salisbury scheme); Public access to the cinema entrance (via (at night time) a deserted shopping arcade in the Salisbury scheme); Queuing, circulation and toilet facilities (all lacking in the case of Salisbury). Mr Humphries was evidently familiar with the Bristol Odeon redevelopment, calling it 'well thought out' in comparison to 'the apparently thrown together plans for Salisbury.' BBE expected to submit its third suite of planning applications in August, and in the meantime the Public Inquiry (PI) into the appeal against the first applications' refusal had been scheduled for 21 January 1986.

There was good news at last for the Plaza in June 1985 as Bournemouth Independent Cinemas Ltd stepped in at the last minute to prevent its closure. Operated by three cinema professionals, who preferred to remain anonymous, the group was also planning to purchase another of Myles Byrne's premises in Devizes. Plans for the Plaza included a 'spruce up' prior to its forthcoming 50th anniversary, to be followed by a full restoration to its former glory, and diversification into the likes of dance classes and jazz concerts.

THE PLAZA — Amesbury

'Do it at the Plaza!'
A new season of activities for the young

NEW!　Commencing Tuesday, 10th September
PLAZA UNDER 14's DISCO
Every Tuesday, 5 p.m.-7 p.m. Admission 50p

NEW!　Commencing Wednesday and Thursday, 11th and 12th September
PLAZA YOUTH THEATRE
A proper training for all young people interested in theatre. Run by professional, fully qualified theatre people. Numbers limited to 25 per group.
10-16 years, enrolment Wednesday, 11th September, 6-7.30 p.m.
16 years and over, enrolment Thursday, 12th, 6-7.30 p.m.

NEW!　Commencing Saturday, 14th September
SATURDAY PICTURES ARE BACK!
Leave your parents while they go shopping
EVERY SATURDAY 11 a.m.-1 p.m. Admission 75p
For information regarding any of the above ring Gary on Amesbury 23854

Councillor Mrs Purdy made her views on the Odeon proposals public in a letter published by the Salisbury Journal in July, citing the following facts concerning the cinema industry in general: The cinema in Cromer, Norfolk had recently reopened under new ownership; At 18 of its 78 cinemas Rank had cut its prices from £2.20 to 99p, and had seen a threefold increase in attendances; Cinema attendance generally had been up by 50% on the first six months of 1984; British films were among the best of the last four years. Mrs Purdy felt that 'To encourage families away from their armchairs and takeaways we

The first entrance hall would be used for film advertising and information both locally and nationally, together with information for attractions in general in the Salisbury area. The former stalls entrance, dressing rooms, music rooms and managers' flat to the rear of the building would be used for practical involvement by local people involved in film projects, with access from Catherine Street rather than through the cinema. An intriguing prospect overall, and it would have been interesting to see how these proposals would have been treated if submitted in the form of a planning application.

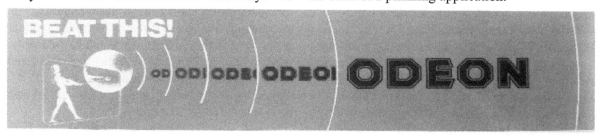

must make our cinema bright and cheap so that they will want to visit at least once a week. Once again it could be the social event it once was. Please make sure we at least retain this opportunity... get out of your armchairs and down to the Odeon before it's too late. It's in your hands. Shops or cinemas – it's your choice.'

In August it was announced that the privately financed Odeon consortium now had a name – Hexagon Enterprises Ltd. Members of the board included Romaine Hart of Mainline Pictures, who ran the Screen On The Green, Screen On The Hill and Portobello Road Electric Cinema in London, and Andrew Christie - Miller of Clarendon House near Salisbury. Hexagon had placed an alternative scheme for refurbishing the site in the public domain, by way of comments to SDC on the current BBE proposals.

In Hexagon's planned 'film centre' there were no proposals to change the extant arrangement of the three screens. The immediate aim was to maintain these with the gradual updating of projection and sound equipment and the improvement of comfort and décor. The re - opening of the restaurant and introduction of a bar would mean no structural changes. It was proposed to move the ticket kiosk to the vestibule and use the foyer as a retail sales area for film-related books, cards, magazines and posters, confectionary and ice - creams together with a video rental outlet.

The SDC South-East Planning Sub-Committee considered the BBE proposals later in the month. While there were concerns over the loss of the auditorium and the lack of safe vehicle servicing of the development, members noted that a cinema use would be retained and the refurbishment of the Hall of John Halle would be achieved – for use as a foyer to the new retail premises. Opinion was, it appears, very much divided with at least one member, Councillor Lodge, admitting his views on retaining the existing 'brick monstrosity' had been influenced by the degree of public protest. The planning applications were referred up to the full Planning Committee without a recommendation.

The full Planning Committee meeting took place on 14 August at the SDC Bourne Hill offices, where more than 50 film fans filled the public gallery to listen to a two - hour debate. The upshot was that on the casting vote of the chairman, Councillor Mrs Titt, planning permission was refused for the BBE proposals - but the campaigners were less than happy with the outcome. The applications had been refused on a single issue – the lack of safe vehicle servicing of the development – on the advice of WCC as the local highway authority.

Unlike the subjective matters of building design and retention of facilities (which the Committee evidently felt had been satisfactorily

".... the scheme is seen for what it is, a quality redevelopment of this redundant land ...."

addressed), the servicing provision was a technical issue, which could perhaps be resolved by way of a change of layout. As Alan Richardson astutely observed 'All this refusal does is to open the door for the developers to amend their servicing arrangements. Presumably if this is done, the Committee will be satisfied and the scheme can go ahead.' From the 'Save It' point of view this did not bode particularly well for the forthcoming appeal.

The day-to-day operation of the Odeon was meanwhile continuing and doubts over its viability seemed questionable as that same week saw Police Academy, Return To Oz and the latest Bond movie, A View To A Kill, attracting 'attendances that were a record for recent years' according to the Southern Evening Echo, which had also been reporting regularly on BBE vs the Campaign.

BBE had now placed their latest proposals (incorporating the two screen cinema option) fully in the public domain with a two day exhibition in the Hall of John Halle. Development manager Johnathan Lloyd hoped '... the scheme is seen for what it is, a quality redevelopment of this re-dundant land, which gives the people of Salisbury the cinema facility that they want.' 'Redundant' was surely overstating the case and BBE were no less forceful in their report on the existing building: 'it is widely accepted that if a planning application for the construction of the existing auditorium… were to be received today it would stand no chance of success…' and 'internally the Odeon is at best a copy, at worst a fake, an example of what might be described as Steak-house Gothic' and 'it is difficult to see how such a grossly mis - proportioned structure grafted on to a genuine 15th Century building can be considered worthy of a city with such obvious concern for its heritage.'

With the gloves off and no doubt one eye on the planning appeal, BBE also challenged the validity of the 'Save It' petition. A survey of 496 people who lived within 10 miles of Salisbury's Poultry Cross, carried out by Marplan on behalf of BBE, found that 71% had not signed the

petition and 62% thought the latest scheme was a good idea. In response Alan Richardson admitted that a 'few hundred' petition signatories had been tourists but this demonstrated that visitors to the city also wanted to use the cinema.

The Odeon Cinema which was referred to as a 'rat-hole'

The refusal of the latest BBE planning applications had been a close call with comments from committee members referring to the cinema being a 'rat - hole', whose future was 'in the balance'. As well as Alan Richardson, in the ensuing weeks others involved in the 'Save It' camp wrote to the Journal: Gaynor Ruderham said 'The key to successful film exhibition is sensitive programming (to account for local needs and trends), attractive pricing and effective advertising, facts which have largely escaped the notice of the national cinema chains, Rank included, whilst independent cinema owners have forged ahead.' Ms Ruderham's view was that a re - named Odeon, under new ownership, could be similarly successful, comparing it with the Playhouse and its '40 or 50 miles' of catchment area, whereas the BBE proposal would be unlikely to achieve success as it would only show mainstream movies available at other cinemas.

Laura Bell doubted whether BBE's vehicle servicing problem could be overcome given the tightly laid out and densely developed nature of the site and surrounding area. This being the case, the proposals put forward by Hexagon would provide an opportunity to retain the cinema facility and make it viable, thereby also overcoming concerns over impact on the listed building. Proposed developments at The Maltings, the old Co - Op and Goddard's garage (the last two both in Winchester Street) would provide enough retail floor - space to meet the requirements of the SDC Local Plan, without the need for further provision on the Odeon site.

Meanwhile, controversy surrounded the latest blockbuster to be shown at the Odeon. Rambo: First Blood Part II, starring Sylvester Stallone, apparently included 200 incidents of violence in its 93 - minute running time. The head of the British Safety Council, James Tye, had written to all the MPs in the country, as well as licensing authorities and the BBFC, hoping to have the film banned because of its 'mindless violence' and its being 'sadistic in the extreme.'

"I particularly liked the mindless violence!"

Mr Tye's efforts were to no avail and Odeon manager Ian Wild told the Salisbury Journal the film was very popular, saying 'It's only a 15 Certificate and the British censors are some of the strictest in the world – so it can't be all that violent.' Cinema - going students Alex Harvey and Steve Jones, both of Devizes Road, thought the film was one of the best they had ever seen,

dismissing the violence as merely 'action.' Mark Chapman, an electrician from Ashley Road, attending the cinema with his wife Anne, said 'It's not the sort of film I would take my kids to see but I thought it was very good.'

In October 1985, BBE submitted informal additional Odeon proposals to SDC, which sought to overcome the WCC highway objections by altering car and coach parking spaces in New Canal to accommodate servicing vehicles. Alan Richardson was, unsurprisingly, disparaging of these proposals: '... the developers intend to solve the problem by squeezing the existing space allocated to the country coach parking, and hijacking (there is no other word for it) the existing public parking area and using this space for the parking of two juggernauts in the middle of the road!'

Explaining how difficult it would then be to transfer goods to and from the vehicles and the new shops, Alan summarised the proposal as 'inconvenient, irresponsible and dangerous', before reminding readers of the Hexagon group's aspirations for the Odeon site. In fairly short order the County Surveyor objected to the BBE suggestion and the company decided instead to simply allow their previously refused schemes run to appeal at the forthcoming PI. Notwithstanding the servicing issue, John Lloyd said 'we are satisfied we have a good scheme for the city and are confident that an inquiry inspector will rule in our favour.'

Public support for the 'Save It' campaign was still not unanimous. In a letter published by the Salisbury Journal that month, Peter Murrell of Feversham Road explained 'I am not a regular cinemagoer and so felt unable to sign the petition to save our local Odeon. Last week, for the first time since moving to the city 18 months ago, my wife and I did visit the Odeon and it is now clear to me why it is no longer viable. The programme was short and represented very poor value for the £2.50 entrance fee. The seats were uncomfortable, the sound and picture quality were poor. It does not deserve to survive.'

On the other hand, in response, Ray Evans of Coombe Bissett wrote to the paper to say that he and his wife had visited the cinema four times in the three months they had been living in the area. 'All the films we selected were extremely good. All were well patronised and quite full for one of their special Tuesday showings, which we greatly appreciate,' he said. 'As for the seating I don't go to the cinema to sleep, and the seating for quite a big chap like myself was certainly adequate. With its unique and astonishing entrance hall we are absolutely appalled that the people of Salisbury should allow it to be destroyed [sic].'

Gaynor Ruderham also responded to Mr Murrell's concerns. Acknowledging there may be problems with physical comfort and sound and picture quality, Ms Ruderham asked who was to blame for this: 'Rank have allowed the building to decay generally in a totally irresponsible manner, and as far as I can see have spent little or nothing on updating the facilities.' Pointing out how the proposed Hexagon scheme would involve appropriate investment and upgrading, as well as a better value pricing structure, Ms Ruderham concluded 'Let me assure Mr Murrell and anyone else who is concerned about the Odeon's economic viability – this cinema is a sound financial proposition. The Odeon must be allowed to survive and under the management of people who have both the cinema and the interests of local people at heart.'

In November 1985, Ian Wild left his post as manager of the Salisbury Odeon. Born in Bradford, he was returning to his home county to run the Anvil Community Cinema, owned by Sheffield City Council. Although looking forward to the new challenge, Mr Wild was sorry to leave Salisbury, where he had made many friends. 'I love the cinema building and I hope Salisbury manages to retain it' he said. 22 - year old Cliff Baillie, born in Ayr and previously assistant manager of the Bristol Odeon, moved to Salisbury to become what was thought to be the youngest cinema manager in the country.

That month also brought the 50th anniversary of the Amesbury Plaza in November 1985. A packed week - long programme of films ranging from modern releases to classics of the cinema's early heyday (The 39 Steps and Brief Encounter) would be shown alongside late night specials (The Evil Dead and Lady Chatterley's Lover). Local children would take part in a fancy dress

parade through Amesbury, dressed as film characters, and Amesbury Town Band and local drama groups would be giving a concert at the cinema.

General Manager Gary Willis said 'it's all part of our effort to get people using the cinema again. Since moving in we have re - decorated, completely refurbished and re - opened the bar. We have started theatre workshops for adults and children, under - 14s discos and a Saturday morning cinema club. We intend to turn the cinema into an arts centre, and this birthday week is an ideal opportunity to show everybody what's happening at the Plaza.'

"How many visitors will want to visit the new proposed run-of-the-mill cinema?"

Ian Wild

Ian Wild left Salisbury at the end of what had been a highly successful economic year for the Odeon. He evidently was not supportive of his previous employers' plans for the cinema and in a subsequently published opinion piece he told the Salisbury Journal he did not think the proposed BBE cinema would be viable: 'I do not believe that what Bath and Bristol are proposing is a serious commercial cinema, but a sop to get their plans passed by the Council.' His view was that the proposed cinema would be '20 years out of date' because it would not provide café and restaurant facilities and the trend was towards more seats, not less (many people had been turned away from the sold -out Odeon in recent months). The proposal to open out both screens for major releases would remove choice from film - goers over periods of sometimes several weeks.

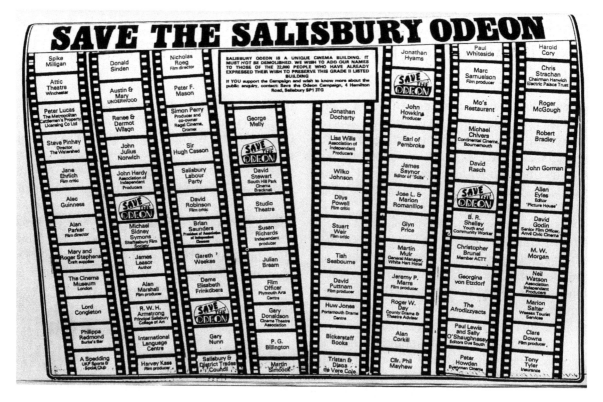

SAVE THE SALISBURY ODEON

The proposed cinema would be situated at the top of several flights of stairs accessed from a shopping arcade. Mr Wild noted this was a very popular trend in the 1960s and 1970s but he could think of no examples that had survived - citing Trowbridge as a recently closed example – because patrons were unwilling to walk through deserted shopping arcades of an evening. If Rank were selected to run the cinema on behalf of BBE, they would not be overly concerned if it failed because they would not have made any financial investment in it.

Mr Wild's experience was that the historic character of the Odeon building helped to attract visitors 'from all over the World'. He wondered 'How many visitors will want to visit the new proposed run-of-the-mill cinema?' Furthermore, BBE had suggested attendances at the existing cinema had increased by just 4.25% in the previous year, whereas Mr Wild believed the figure was more in line with the national trend of 40% (BBE later revised its figure upwards, to 24.5%, admitting the previous figure had been erroneous). Mr Wild was firmly in support of the Hexagon proposals – 'It is my belief that if these plans are realised, Salisbury could have the most exciting venue for film exhibition in Southern England.'

By the end of 1985, as well as more than 20,000 locals, the 'Save It' campaign had attracted support from many notable names: Alec Guinness, Donald Sinden, George Melly, Julian Bream, Sir Hugh Casson, Alan Parker, Nicolas Roeg, David Puttnam, Wilko Johnson, Roger McGough, John Gorman and Spike Milligan were among those listed alongside local and national businesses and organisations and personalities in a full page advert in the Salisbury Journal on 2 December, which stated 'Salisbury Odeon is a unique cinema building. It must not be demolished. We wish to add our names to those of the 22,000 people who have already expressed their wish to preserve this Grade II listed building.'

Early in the new - year Alan Richardson kept the Odeon saga and the forthcoming PI in the public eye with a letter to the Salisbury Journal: 'The writing is on the wall, crisp and clear for all to read'. The paper had previously reported the impending closure of International Stores and Texas Homecare in the city, which Alan saw as a 'clear indication that Salisbury is in the gravest danger of becoming 'over - shopped.'' Despite this '...our planners and council blindly continue with the concept that Salisbury has to compete in size and scale of its shops with such large centres

".... If there was an application to put up such a building today it would be met with derision and disbelief ...."

as Southampton, Bournemouth, Portsmouth and Fareham. He hoped 'the people of Salisbury will come in large numbers to the Inquiry and let the Inspector be made very well aware of the views of the citizens of Salisbury over this controversial issue.' The Save The Odeon Campaign was to be represented at the PI by top London lawyers and QC. The costs would be met by the still anonymous generous benefactor who was also 'still prepared to give substantial sums towards the purchase of the lease and the refurbishment of the cinema.'

Led by Mr Stephen Marks of the Planning Inspectorate, the PI opened on Tuesday 21 January 1986, at the City Hall. Opening for BBE Anthony Anderson QC attacked the design of the existing Odeon, calling it 'a windowless brick box, without any relief' that completely dominated surrounding buildings by 'rising to a maximum height of 76 feet. This makes it the second highest building in Salisbury – there are no prizes for guessing which is the highest.'

'If there was an application to put up such a building today' Mr Anderson continued, 'it would be met with derision and disbelief. It is almost twice the current [planning policy] height limit in Salisbury, and to take such a structure out of the street would be a major conservation benefit in itself.' The developer's view was that 'The new shops are important if Salisbury is to maintain its role as a regional centre in competition with other cities'. Mr Anderson told the Inspector his client was also prepared to increase the total seating capacity of the cinema element of the proposal to 500.

Notwithstanding all this, SDC's sole reason for refusal of the planning applications related to the insufficient provision of safe vehicle servicing for the proposal. Mr Anderson criticised WCC for its 'rigid' objection, stating it had demonstrated an 'unexplained inflexibility' despite repeated attempts to seek more detail of the reason for the refusal.

BBE had published a full page advertisement in the previous week's Salisbury Journal and managing director Stephen Green followed this

up with a letter to the paper explaining the benefits of the Odeon scheme. BBE had first become involved in 1984 'at a time when cinema audiences throughout the country were half their 1980 levels and a small fraction of their 1960s levels, which made a large cinema facility

Shifting Odeon 'major benefit to city' – QC

THE ODEON auditorium was branded a "windowless brick box" on the first day of the public inquiry into its future.

Developers Bath and Bristol Estates fired the opening salvos in a hearing, which will go on well into next week.

By Dick Bellringer

Counsel for Bath and Bristol, Mr Anthony Anderson QC, in attacking the auditorium, said it completely dominated surrounding buildings.

"It is a windowless brick box, without any relief, rising to a maximum height of 76ft.

"That makes it the second highest building in Salisbury — there are no prizes for guessing which is the highest.

"If there was an application to put up such a building today it would be met with derision and disbelief."

"It is almost twice the current height limit in Salisbury, and to take such a structure out of the street scene would be a major conservation benefit in itself."

Mr Anderson said, the Bath and Bristol plan provides modern shopping and a cinema combined with conservation improvements, particularly to the medieval Hall of John Halle.

"The new shops are important if Salisbury is to maintain its role as a regional centre in competition with other cities like Bournemouth, Southampton and Dorchester," he said.

And he told Department of the Environment inspector, Mr Stephen Marks, that Bath and Bristol were now prepared to increase the seating of the two screens from 110 and 250 to 150 and 350 respectively.

Mr Anderson also attacked Wiltshire County Council for its "rigid" opposition on servicing grounds, which was Salisbury District Council's only official objection to the plan.

"We have to say that the county council's role has been less than satisfactory," he said.

He said the county council had retained its position of "unexplained inflexibility," despite repeated attempts to get more detailed reasons for its objection.

● Odeon inquiry inspector, Mr Stephen Marks.

unviable in Salisbury.' Because, at the time, there has been a suggestion that a new cinema might be incorporated into a redeveloped City Hall, their initial plans for the New Canal site had not included a replacement cinema.

The reaction to that proposal had triggered the 22,000 signature petition and this, combined by the boost in audience numbers resulting from British Film Year in 1985 and blockbusters such as Ghostbusters, led BBE – alongside Rank - to risk further investment in providing two state of the art screens with a total of 500 seats at the Odeon 'many times the capacity for the current average occupancy levels.'

At the public exhibition held in August 1985 many younger visitors had expressed a desire for new, modern facilities. BBE had however also tried to please older audiences by using 'the same mock Tudor treatment as exists now so that when the lights go up you know you are in Salisbury.'

Page 109

Mr Green pointed out that, due to structural defects, the building would in any case require an investment of £250,000 to bring it into the condition as befitted its status and the removal of the fly - tower and the brick shell around the building would improve its appearance as well as the setting of adjacent listed buildings and the conservation area.

The scheme would also provide covered pedestrian links between New Canal, Catherine Street and the Old George Mall, resulting in prosperity in the conservation area and its buildings, in response to the Maltings development off Fisherton Street. In conclusion Mr Green noted the proposals had received support from many local people and groups, including the local Architects' Panel, the Royal Fine Arts Commission and the Society for the Protection of Ancient Buildings.

Writing to the Journal in response to the BBE advertisement, Terry Parkinson of Park Street pointed out that: The cinema currently housed three screens, whereas the revamped cinema would house two – and would have a reduction in overall seating provision; The heritage asset of the Hall of John Halle would be compromised internally by the introduction of a circular staircase and externally by its setting against the shopping precinct roof; The existing cinema facility would be removed in its entirety, as would part of the frontage to New Canal, all resulting in damage to the integrity of listed buildings, and; Expansion of the retail offer in Salisbury had already been approved at The Maltings, and this amid a climate of shop closures.

Meanwhile at the City Hall the PI continued with BBE lining up a range of professionals to support its case. Planning and development expert Anthony Bowhill told the Inquiry the proposals would deliver 'considerable advantages for Salisbury.' In Mr Bowhill's view, a new shopping scheme and replacement cinema, with important pedestrian links, would be delivered in a sympathetic manner, allowing the refurbishment and restoration of the listed building. Chartered architect Edward Nash said the demolition of the cinema would remove 'a massive and undesirable structure of no external quality, and wholly out of scale with that part of the city.'

Chartered surveyor David Owen told the Inspector that in his view the building showed many of the defects that would be expected in a building of the auditorium's age, where maintenance expenditure had been kept to a minimum. This left the building's owners with a very onerous liability for the foreseeable future.

Unique cinema

THERE is only one cinema in Salisbury, but there is no other like it in the country. The entrance to the Odeon on New Canal is through a medieval hall!

This was part of the house of John Halle, a wool merchant who was four times mayor. Here, in an ancient room with a fine beamed roof, gallery and stained glass windows, the association with a cinema gives the impression it might be a film set, but it really was constructed in the 15th century.

Walk in and see it, at a time when the cinema is open. It really is most unusual.

If you want to find out what films are showing before going there, you can telephone 22080.

Expanding on financial matters, Anthony O'Ferrall, managing director of Rank, explained recent trends in cinema attendance. Mr O'Ferrall said Rank was committed to film provision and had embarked on a programme of modification, despite a general downturn in audience numbers leading to an unprecedented low level in 1984. Furthermore, the company had been keen supporters of British Film Year and were encouraged by a recent resurgence in the industry. However, it had to be borne in mind that 1984 had been disastrous and he felt 'the most recent figures do not mark the end of the industry's troubles and the temptation of a false sense of security should be resisted.'

'Financial results from the Salisbury Odeon had never been satisfactory and in the past ten years profitability has been minimal' Mr O'Ferrall continued, adding that the building was a prime candidate for radical refurbishment and repair. The refurbishment of the auditorium would cost around £300,000 and the repairs to the building a further £210,000. This outlay could not be recommended to the board at Rank in the light of the financial performance of the cinema. Mr O'Ferrall further warned that if the proposed development did not proceed, then the cinema would probably close, and the BBE scheme therefore provided the best opportunity for both Rank and the cinemagoers of Salisbury.

"…. The doubtful need for shopping does not outweigh the disadvantages that this development would bring …."

Key support for the 'Save It' campaigners

During his evidence Mr O'Ferrall expressed concern over the actions of former Odeon manager Ian Wild. It had transpired that Mr Wild had provided some trading figures to the Save The Odeon campaigners. 'We do have contracts of employment with managers about the disclosure of information,' said Mr O'Ferrall, adding 'I was not at all happy that one of our ex-managers had apparently passed on confidential information to a third party without authority.' Mr O'Ferrall however confirmed he had no criticism of Mr Wild's management skills.

Despite the 'Save It' campaign, the proposals did receive some support as local interested parties were invited to speak at the PI. Salisbury Civic Society welcomed the plans for 'this underdeveloped and unattractive area'. The Society's representative - former SDC Councillor Mike Pearce - told the Inspector the BBE scheme would raise the standards of design in the city, saying 'For far too long we have had mediocre standards of architecture foisted upon us.'

Turning to the highway objections, Mr Pearce attacked the WCC stance that servicing provision should be provided 'within the chequer' (i.e. off-street). The Society felt this would be a retrograde step as 'The majority of buildings in Salisbury are serviced from the street and I think that would be adequate. To some extent this Inquiry is a test case to see whether we can resist further penetration of traffic into the heart of the town.'

Mr Pearce's view was that the most difficult question was whether or not the auditorium of the existing cinema should be preserved: 'As a building of special architectural or historic interest, its interest is limited, although it is no doubt right that it should have been included on the statutory list when these applications were made, so that its interest should be properly and thoroughly considered.'

Salisbury MP Robert Key (left) and the Mayor Tom Cowie both supported the 'Save It' campaign

Speaking against the proposal the Mayor of Salisbury, Tom Cowie, said it would be environmentally harmful to encourage more delivery vehicles of all sizes into one of Salisbury's most historic streets. 'The doubtful need for shopping does not outweigh the disadvantages that this development would bring with its attendant loss of listed buildings and the impact it would have on the built environment in this conservation area' he said, 'I am also most disturbed to realise that many of the so - called conservation and preservation societies deem it acceptable that additional shopping is so necessary in this part of the city that the partial demolition of a listed building to create an ugly gap in the street scene is not worth objecting to.'

SDC Councillors Daphne Purdy and Kay Cooper also spoke in favour of retaining the cinema as it stood, as did Barbara Hawkes of Campbell Road, who had particular concerns regarding the siting of the cinema element of the proposed scheme: 'As a single woman I would feel very uncomfortable coming out of a cinema late at night into a shopping precinct. The precinct would be nice for shoppers during the day but it would also be nice for drunks and vandals at night.'

Expert witnesses for the Save The Odeon campaign then took the stand. David Atwell, an architect and the author of Cathedrals Of The

Movies – A History of British Cinemas and Their Audiences, claimed that Rank had been swayed by a profit motive in its deal with BBE. He told the Inspector he had gained this impression from Mr O'Ferrall's evidence, in which he had said the Odeon would have been in line for refurbishment and repairs if the proposal had not come up. 'Being in the business of making profits, however interested they may have been in keeping a site, particularly one that is listed, when faced with a very profitable deal to redevelop it I can only conclude that their finer interests were overtaken by mere profit motive. I cannot doubt that otherwise the policy would have been to refurbish in the near future.'

Turning to the merits of the existing building, Mr Atwell said the Salisbury Odeon stood as 'perhaps the finest surviving tribute to the imagination of its designer, William Trent.' He found BBE's proposal to 'dress up' the two new small cinemas to be '... extraordinary... I can see no merit or justification whatever for carving up the decoration of the old cinema in such a transparent attempt to perpetuate the magic of the

original.' Mr Atwell's view was that the effect of the existing decoration was to create an interior of rare integrity and unified style: 'I believe its destruction is unjustified and should be unthinkable and I cannot see how more than a very small proportion of these features could be realistically salvaged for some sort of unsatisfactory and cosmetic re - use that would reproduce none of Trent's late romantic imagery and atmosphere.' In a forceful, if somewhat florid, way Mr Atwell concluded 'In Salisbury's Odeon the Gothic Revival finally came to rest. Let us not disturb that rest by waking up Sleeping Beauty and destroying the fairy - tale forever.'

Alan Richardson appeared next, telling the Inspector Salisbury Odeon could become one of the major cinema centres of the south of England. He outlined the history of the campaign, and the development of a business arm in Hexagon, whereby suitably experienced professionals could be recruited to operate the cinema should the campaign be in a position to purchase the site. Mr Richardson could not accept that planning matters should not be influenced by emotions: 'Cities are people first and buildings second, in this instance they have truly indicated that the Odeon is a building they want to keep.'

Simon Perry, producer of the film 1984 and owner of an independent cinema in Cromer, said Salisbury seemed to have 'a larger than usual potential audience for discerning, well - heeled people for whom the cinema could and should cater. In short, we believe that films and the buildings in which they are shown are marketing tools, which can act reciprocally. A cinema, which is an attractive social centre, which the local community has a range of specific reason for visiting, has a real potential for profit.'

Paul Drury, assistant inspector for English Heritage, spoke in favour of retaining the cinema auditorium. His view was that 'as a fantastic interpretation of a late Gothic hall, the interior of the Odeon must rank as one of the latest examples of the architectural evocation of romantic nostalgia for a chivalrous – and largely fictional – Medieval past.'

Despite the lengthy representations regarding the principles of loss of the existing cinema, the provision of retail uses on the site and the impact on the listed building and conservation area, the acceptability of the scheme hinged mainly on the

"…. the appeal should be dismissed because the scheme makes no proper provision for service traffic …."

matter of vehicular servicing of the site, as SDC's refusal had been solely concerned with the latter issue. The SDC case therefore relied on the expert advice of WCC as the local highway authority. Indeed, Oliver Williams, the Solicitor for SDC, had already told the Inspector his council would be taking a 'neutral' position at the PI.

WCC policy was that servicing of development should generally be expected to be accommodated within a site, complete with safe parking, access and exit, therefore resulting in no inconvenience or hazard to users of the public highway. Speaking for WCC on the last day of the PI, Nicholas Nardecchia told the Inspector 'the appeal should be dismissed because the scheme makes no proper provision for service traffic. The proposed arrangements will cause an unacceptable degree of congestion and danger to highway users.' There was, he said, no other case in Wiltshire of a development of this size being serviced from the public highway.

In closing for the Save The Odeon campaign, Robert Carnwath QC stated three main points to why the appeal should be dismissed: Even with the proposed increase in seating, the BBE cinema would still be too small for a city of Salisbury's size; It would not be well - sited on the first floor of a shopping arcade, and; A dual rather than triple screen would reduce the level of public service. Mr Carnwath claimed that Rank had not made every attempt to continue the use of the existing cinema. 'This is a good cinema site and it has not been established that it would not continue to be used as a cinema, even by Rank, if these proposals failed.'

Closing for BBE, Anthony Anderson claimed the WCC case had been 'grossly overrated'. Granting planning permission would be 'entirely consistent with the aim of the draft Local Plan and with the traffic policies contained within that plan.' The Save The Odeon campaign was in the Appellant's view 'long in enthusiasm and wishful thinking but short on experience, realism and relevance. It doesn't provide credible support to the claim that they can finance, operate and sustain in use the Odeon as a cinema' he said.

'Save The Odeon' campaigner Alan Richardson

SAVE THE ODEON CAMPAIGN

THE SAVE THE ODEON CAMPAIGNERS WOULD LIKE TO THANK ALL THOSE INDIVIDUALS, ORGANISATIONS & COMPANIES WHO HAVE GIVEN SUPPORT TO THE CAMPAIGN IN THE LAST 18 MONTHS. NOW THAT THE INQUIRY HAS FINISHED & ALL THE EVIDENCE HEARD, THE FATE OF THE ODEON & BATH & BRISTOL'S PROPOSED SHOPPING DEVELOPMENT IS IN THE HANDS OF THE DEPT. OF THE ENVIRONMENT. ITS DECISION WILL BE MADE KNOWN WITHIN THE NEXT FEW MONTHS.

TOGETHER, WE HOPE WE HAVE PRESENTED A STRONG ENOUGH CASE TO PREVENT DEMOLITION OF OUR CINEMA.

Mr Anderson also claimed there had been a 'significant shift in public opinion' since BBE had made changes to the cinema element of the proposals.

With the fate of the Odeon now resting with the Planning Inspector, Alan Richardson wrote to the Salisbury Journal to thank those who had supported the 'Save It' campaign. Many thousands had signed the petition against the BBE proposals, and many campaigners had worked to keep the issue in the public eye for the previous 18 months or so. Journal editor Gareth Weekes was thanked for allying the paper to the cause – 'a brave commitment to an important social issue'. Mr Richardson also thanked the many who had given their name and financial contributions to the cause, in particular the still anonymous benefactor who had agreed to bear the costs of the campaign's legal representation at the PI, which ended up being estimated at around £40,000.

Mr Richardson was also grateful that three SDC Councillors had spoken against the development at the PI, but (whilst acknowledging the PI was held during normal working hours) was disappointed by the 'sparse' public attendance. Councillor Mrs Purdy agreed with the latter point, telling the Journal 'we, and I am sure Mr Richardson, would have liked to have seen just 10 per cent of the 22,000 who signed the petition on those empty seats. I just hope that the Inspector did not get the impression that the people didn't care.'

Meanwhile, the day - to - day business continued. In April 1986 John Ferris was appointed manager of the Odeon, replacing Cliff Baillie who had moved to the Odeon in York after just five months in Salisbury. Mr Ferris had previously been a senior assistant manager at the Southampton Odeon.

Earlier that month the Amesbury Plaza had seen the sudden departure of manager Gary Willis. Cinema staff handed out leaflets in an attempt to quash rumours that the cinema was about to close. 'It's business as usual and we are having a very successful Easter week' said a spokesman. Mr Willis was now running a local cabaret show and the Salisbury Journal felt his departure was bound to be a blow, especially as he had been one of a number of enthusiasts who had rescued the cinema when it was threatened with closure previously. The group had made

'remarkable transformations to entice audiences back' and Mr Willis' 'enthusiasm in turning the Plaza into more of an entertainment centre won great respect', and the revamped cinema had been featured on both BBC and ITV television. For the time being Martin Macdonald had been installed as acting manager.

One of Mr Macdonald's first initiatives was to offer the cut-price daytime screening of films that might be of special educational interest to local schools. The admission charge would be 75p with free entry for accompanying teachers. Schools wishing to bring a group to an already scheduled general admission screening were invited to negotiate a price. 'Instead of waiting for people to come to us, we are making the effort to go out to them' said Mr Macdonald, who was anticipating interest in the forthcoming screening of Revolution, the American War of Independence epic starring Al Pacino and Donald Sutherland.

In July 1986 the Planning Inspectorate issued its decision. The appeal was dismissed – the Odeon was saved. Alan Richardson told the Salisbury Journal 'We have won. One's first reaction is one of complete elation. We have had to jump so many hurdles without falling during the battle to save our cinema. Now we have successfully surmounted the last great jump and have reached the winning post and won.'

".... The innate qualities of the Odeon cinema justify its listing as being of special architectural and historic interest ...."

Mr Richardson claimed a victory for local democracy, saying the decision 'acknowledged the great groundswell of public opinion that said, in no uncertain terms, by means of those 22,000 signatures on the petition, it did not wish to see our famous cinema demolished.' He did however sound a note of caution, saying 'Who knows, there may be more battles ahead, our lawyers are examining the 70 or more pages of the Inspector's findings. But, certainly we have won this race against the demolition of our cinema. They [Rank] have only two choices – either to close it or keep it running' Mr Richardson continued. 'My great hope is that with the current upsurge in cinema audiences across the country, they will want to make a go of it.'

SoS Nicholas Ridley had confirmed the decision saying 'the innate qualities of the Odeon cinema justify its listing as being of special architectural and historic interest. Its demolition should not be permitted unless or until it is established beyond reasonable doubt that there is no other acceptable course of action.'

ODEON DEMOLITION PLAN DEFEATED

A YEAR long campaign to save the Salisbury Odeon Cinema from becoming the site of a new shopping complex has resulted in victory for the cinema's local fans.

The decision came from Environment Secretary Nicholas Ridley after a public inquiry, held in January, heard the case of developers Bath and Bristol Estate. The developers appealed against the refusal of planning permission and listed building consent from Salisbury District Council to demolish the cinema and build shopping units.

The Environment Inspector who worked on the public inquiry consi-dered the demolition of the cinema could not be justified and that, in the event of the new shops being built, servicing facilities for them would not be adequate.

The story of the building is by no means over, though. It is now up to the Rank Organisation, who own the Odeon, to decide whether the cinema should keep running.

They have yet to make a decision but were disap-pointed at the decision of the Environment Secret-ary as the new develop-ment would have given them a chance to build a new cinema within the complex.

But for the near future, anyway, the New Canal cinema and its famous historic front will remain with both the Rank Organisation and local 'Save The Odeon' cam-paigners at least agreeing on one thing – that the films must start packing in the audiences as they did in the past.

In his decision letter Planning Inspector Stephen Marks said there were two main objections to the BBE proposals: The demolition of the cinema and the lack of vehicle servicing provision within the site. The proposal would bring significant potential benefits in the repair of the listed building, the provision of an attractive and well - designed building and the assured provision of cinema facilities. However, in the Inspector's view BBE had not 'shown that every possible effort has been made to continue its use. The building has not been offered on the open market, nor have they convinced me that there is no reasonable prospect of continued use which would justify the failure to offer it on the open market.

BBE declined to comment for the time being, but Larry Johnson of Rank said the company was disappointed: 'we were looking forward to a new cinema being available to cinemagoers in Salisbury. We believe it would have been of benefit to them to have had a proper cinema in the development and we are disappointed that we are not going to get the opportunity to run it. Now we must give the whole matter very careful consideration. But, in the meantime, the Odeon will continue trading and we have a very good line up of products.' A spokesman for Marks and Spencer, whose expansion plans in Salisbury were part of the scheme, said the company would 'continue to look at ways of expanding the store and improving the service to customers.'

Councillor Mrs Purdy welcomed the decision but warned that further action would be required to keep the cinema operating – people would have to make sure the facility was used and she issued an invitation: 'Come on now. All down the flicks today.' Robert Key MP offered Alan Richardson and his fellow campaigners his 'warmest congratulations' saying 'The implications are wide. It shows that the people of the community and not commercial pressure must decide the future shape of Salisbury. This also has national significance and I hope it will make Rank think again. There has been a cinema revival in Europe, America and Australia and this could be a turning point for cinema in this country.'

Alan Richardson wrote to the Salisbury Journal, again thanking the various supporters of the Save The Odeon campaign, but also reflecting on the saga. He named five members of the campaign group, who he singled out for their hard work and tenacity: Laura Bell, Paul Humphries, Jillian Aldridge, Gaynor Ruderham and Annie Wilkinson. He noted however that the original SDC refusals of the most recent suite of planning applications had been a close run thing, councillors having voted by 13 to 12 for refusal - and then only on the highway servicing issue and not the listed building or loss of public amenity grounds.

Mr Richardson praised those councillors who had the courage of their conviction to speak against the proposal at the PI. However, some 35 years later, it is somewhat sobering to think that if just one more councillor had been persuaded to support BBE then the 'planning' fight to save the cinema would have been far more difficult, being based on technical challenges to the legality of the decision (if any could be identified) rather than the planning merits of the development.

Not everyone was happy though. Anthony Barrington - Brown of Tisbury, considered the Journal's euphoric reporting of the appeal decision to be 'misplaced' and that support for Mr Richardson's campaign had 'done a great disservice to the community.' In Mr Barrington - Brown's opinion the Odeon was 'antiquated in every respect. The seats are disintegrating, the decoration crumbling, the projection equipment – especially the sound – worn out. The overall average seat occupancy is dismal and consequently Rank cannot afford to remedy any of its defects, nor could any purchaser.'

By contrast, had the proposed development been permitted, 'we would have had at least one, possibly two, thoroughly modern cinemas, capable of attracting rather than discouraging attendance.' Mr Barrington - Brown had heard Alan Richardson lecture 'most interestingly' on the subject of cinema history, but felt 'we need a modern, not an interestingly historical, venue for our entertainment. Until we have a modern cinema, audiences will continue to stay away. The Odeon will continue to be unprofitable, will fall further into decay and before long be closed. What use then will be a vast mausoleum, planning blighted, in our midst?'

In Mr Barrington - Brown's view 'The panic listing of the building to serve a sectional interest was an abuse of the procedure in the first place' and 'thrown out with this 'victory' is the opportunity to have restored, at no cost to the citizens… [the building]… and better access to enjoy it, together with a bigger and better M&S and more shops in the George Mall.' He believed the majority of signatories of the 22,000 to the campaign petition were 'deliberately misled into thinking that the demolition of the Odeon was to be the end of cinema in Salisbury [but] it would have been – should still be – the beginning.' Mr Barrington - Brown confirmed he made the 30 -

"…. You can't leave it. The cinema just gets into you and you miss it if you're not there …."

A line-up of past Salisbury projectionists. Ray Baker, Frankie Amos, Jack Overton, Len Sheldrake, Ernie Hopkins (read below), unknown and Dennis Lavender

mile round trip to the Odeon journey around half a dozen times a year, saying 'It takes an exceptionally good film to offset the depressing surroundings.'

Elizabeth Hull of Bourne Avenue congratulated Alan Richardson on his campaign but agreed the sound system needed improvement, and suggested Rank should follow the example of the Cannon Group, which had installed a Dolby system at the Classic in Yeovil. She also dropped a hint about the Classic's '£1 for all' ticket deals on a Monday.

Whilst he was not disappointed with the decision per se, Alec Fieber of Rampart Road was concerned about the current state of the building: 'Will somebody please tell me what they [the campaigners] are actually going to do to ensure that Salisbury has a modern, purpose - built, technically up - to - date cinema? Can anyone believe that the owner will reinstate the building to its former mock Tudor glory? Any architectural pretensions are at present completely ruined by the arbitrary, but commercially necessary division into the three auditoria.'

Mr Fieber thought many signatories to the petition mistakenly believed the BBE development would have seen the whole building demolished 'genuine historic bits and all', which was not the case. His view was that 'The Hall of John Halle should not in fact be made to suffer the indignity of remaining the entrance to a rather tatty thirties mock interior anyway' and he also bemoaned the quality of the rear exterior of the building ('the awful, vast, cooking brick and asbestos roofed shed festooned with the usual drainpipes. No one could ever pretend that there was any architectural merit to that mess'). Mr Fieber was interested to see what the preservationists had in mind for the building.

In July 1986 a stalwart of the Odeon was forced to take early retirement due to ill - health, just a few months short of 50 years of service. Chief projectionist Ernie Hopkins (aged 63) told the Salisbury Journal the cinema had been 'part of my life – a very enjoyable part' but he now found the 87 steps up to the top projection room too much to cope with. Mr Hopkins had first joined the then Gaumont Palace as a page boy. 'It was a beautiful cinema then. Wonderful chandeliers hung from the ceiling and tapestries were on the wall.'

Those were of course the days when there were three cinemas in Salisbury, and Mr Hopkins met his future wife Joyce at the then Odeon in Fisherton Street. Mrs Hopkins later moved to the New Canal Odeon and had now worked there for 27 years – apart from a four week period in a fruit and vegetable shop: 'You can't leave it. The cinema just gets into you and you miss it if you're not there.'

A little bit of Hollywood glitz came to St Michael's Church in Wilsford - Cum - Lake in August 1986, with the funeral service of British actress Hermione Baddeley. An Academy Award nominated star of the 1940s and 1950s, Ms Baddeley had later moved to Los Angeles. Her body was flown home to be interred close to that of her first husband, aristocrat and socialite David Pax Francis Tennant, whose family home was at Wilsford Manor and who had died in 1968.

Although conducted with due dignity by Ms Baddeley's brother, the Very Reverend William Baddeley (former Dean of Brisbane, Australia) and the Woodford Valley vicar Canon Peter Oades, the service had a touch of the bizarre about it. St Michael's had a limited seating capacity and so, with there being an expectation of dozens of attendees, estate workmen had spent the morning erecting an 'overflow' marquee with relay speakers on an adjacent newly - mown field. Traffic police were waiting and a bus had been chartered to meet the London train at Salisbury station, to bring mourners to Wilsford in time for the 3pm start. The minutes passed by – 3 o'clock came and went - the train didn't arrive.

Back at the church the organist gallantly filled in, while the Very Reverend Baddeley passed the time discussing the merits of Nikon cameras with the assembled photographers who, to the bemusement of local and family mourners, snapped away under the assumption that everyone was a celebrity. Salisbury Journal reporter Shaun Williams was particularly amused by one photographer's excitement at capturing 'Noel Coward' and 'Michael Redgrave' – deceased 1973 and 1985 respectively!

The London train eventually arrived 20 minutes late but just six passengers transferred to the Wilsford bus. It transpired that Ms Baddeley's film - star friends would all be attending a special memorial service in Los Angeles the following week. St Michael's therefore saw a quiet service - dozens of wreaths with the deceased's favourite hymns and poetry – followed by a low - key champagne reception before Ms Baddeley was taken to Amesbury to be interred at St Mary and St Melor church.

Amesbury Plaza manager Martin Macdonald

announced a new strategy in October 1986, aimed at tempting audiences away from the hiring of home videocassettes. For the whole winter there would be two screenings per day, with all seats reduced to £1 (whereas video hire cost £1.50). Notwithstanding this, the following month saw the submission of a planning application to convert the stalls area of the cinema to a bar and dancefloor for use as a nightclub – but retaining the 200 - seat circle for cinema use. 'The income from the cinema is not sufficient to keep the place going.' said Mr Macdonald, 'We have decided we need something to supplement the cinema's income and a nightclub seems ideal. There is no other nightclub in Amesbury – the nearest is in Salisbury. The beauty of this is it doesn't interfere with the cinema side. Films will be over by the time the club opens so there will be no problems there.'

THE PLAZA CINEMA
AMESBURY
The home of the big screen entertainment

Special Trial promotion from
FRIDAY, 10th OCTOBER

"Forget the Video's take a night out —
try The Plaza"

ALL SEATS ONLY £1

(No reductions for Senior Citizens, UB40s or children under 15)

Programmes daily at 5 p.m. and 7 p.m.

Check local press or ring Amesbury (0980) 23854
for details

THE CHEAPEST AND PROBABLY THE
BEST IN CINEMA ENTERTAINMENT

FULLY LICENSED BAR

The nightclub project was not pursued but the Plaza management did start providing lunch time meals in an effort to increase income. Further diversification saw the opening of the cinema bar for public use and concerts featuring local acts, as Simon 'Wiggy' Wigglesworth of The Badgeman recalls: 'As a 14 - year old I used to dress up in an oversized leather jacket, and me and my mates would sneak into horror films . We must have looked hilarious .... I don't think the staff would have cared at all! I did [later] play there and I do remember a really great night of industrial noise from Grey Wolves and Condom. Also Mrs Taylor's Mad [played there] - featuring Dave Ware who went onto play in Jane From Occupied Europe. The Plaza had a bar, serving

".... If there is a demand for varied and better films, I can supply them, but I have to show they make money ...."

booze during pub hours. It helped keep Martin in business as people really weren't going to the pictures much. It was my favourite pub for a while!'

The management of the Salisbury Odeon changed again in early 1987, with the appointment of Desmond Fitzgerald. Encouraged by the public support for the Save The Odeon campaign, Mr Fitzgerald hoped cinemagoers would support his ambitious plans. 'I want to offer a comprehensive programme for all sections of the public,' Mr Fitzgerald told the Salisbury Journal 'if there is a demand for varied and better films, I can supply them, but I have to show they make money.' He believed that if there was a boost to audience figures then Rank – still non - committal since the planning appeal decision – would be encouraged to invest in the cinema's future. Mr Fitzgerald's plans were very much along the lines of those suggested by 'Save It' campaigners and were supported by Alan Richardson.

The plans included: offering the franchise for the disused restaurant above the foyer, to be refurbished and opened during daytime; setting up a tasteful souvenir booth in the Hall of John Halle, which would also discourage minor vandalism, a recurring problem for this part of the cinema; installing an extra 200 seats; re-introducing Saturday morning children's shows; increasing the number of screenings, and possibly introducing late night shows; opening up the little used entrance in Catherine Street; offering better accommodation for the disabled; re - furbishing and highlighting the cinema's remarkable 1930s interior. In the spring of 1987 Mr Fitzgerald introduced afternoon screenings with concessions, creating one new full time job and extra hours for part time staff at the Odeon.

In October 1987 the Odeon offered an interesting one - off late - night double package, over and above the weekly screening programme. The recently released La Bamba told the story of rock'n'roll singer Ritchie Valens, and the Odeon had paired it with The Buddy Holly Story from 1978 – Valens and Holly having been killed in the same air crash (alongside J P Richardson - aka 'The Big Bopper'). Holly had of course appeared at the Salisbury theatre (then the Gaumont) with his group The Crickets, in March 1958.

In November 1987 Mr and Mrs Lyons of Grimstead, who had supported the Save The Odeon campaign, wrote to the Salisbury Journal wondering why they had bothered. They had recently visited the cinema and were surprised to find there were no concessions for senior citizens for evening screenings. Attending Screen 3 ('which is rather like sitting in a biscuit tin') they were saddened by the 'drab dilapidated appearance', which 'surely could be smartened up with some paint and decent furnishings'. It didn't help that the Lyons' had not enjoyed the film (Hope And Glory) itself, and on the way home they reminisced about the cinema experience of 40 years earlier when 'for a modest sum we usually saw good films plus a news reel and no commercials, and all this in comfortable surroundings.'

Desmond Fitzgerald responded in the Journal and admitted he agreed with the Lyons to some extent. He explained that the two smaller screens tended to fill up quickly in the evening and it was felt senior citizens could attend earlier screenings more easily than other customers (and thus cheaper tickets were only offered at those times) – this approach had ceased after similar complaints and concessions were now available on all screenings.

The legacy of having two small screens could not be avoided but improvements were being undertaken and planned: £8,000 had been spent on a new chimney; £3,000 was to be spent on refurbishing Odeons 2 and 3 - £2,000 worth of paint having just been delivered; £2,600 had been spent on new telephones to link with a newly computerised box office, to be installed in a new kiosk in the Hall of John Hale at a cost of £17,000 – subject to English Heritage agreement.

The cinema had just had its best year ever with the high point being the total of 30,119 seats sold for Crocodile Dundee. As well as introducing afternoon screenings, Saturday morning pictures had been revived with the support of the Journal's 'Brown Street Gang'. Franchises were being considered for the restaurant and bar, a coffee lounge was planned and Dolby sound and new heating was in the pipeline. In January 1988, the Odeon held a special reception for locally - based extras appearing in the latest Merchant Ivory film, Maurice, which had largely been filmed on the Wilbury Estate near Newton Tony.

 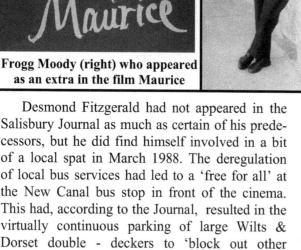

Frogg Moody (right) who appeared as an extra in the film Maurice

Desmond Fitzgerald had not appeared in the Salisbury Journal as much as certain of his predecessors, but he did find himself involved in a bit of a local spat in March 1988. The deregulation of local bus services had led to a 'free for all' at the New Canal bus stop in front of the cinema. This had, according to the Journal, resulted in the virtually continuous parking of large Wilts & Dorset double - deckers to 'block out other operators.' Mr Fitzgerald's concern was that this obscured the frontage of the cinema for most of the day, making it harder for tourists to find.

That same month Mr Fitzgerald's departure was announced, as he relocated to the Southampton Odeon. The assistant manager at Southampton, John Ferris, returned to take over in Salisbury on a temporary basis. This regular changing of management cannot have helped the stability of the Odeon given the challenges faced in recent years, but the next permanent manager would stay longer and see the cinema through another period of significant change.

Graham Dilks had spent his working life as a manager of Rank cinemas in London and the Midlands before retiring at the age of 47 to enjoy his narrowboat, Silhouette. However, after five years or so he had a chance encounter with a former colleague, which resulted in him returning to the company as an assistant manager at the new £7 - million state of the art cinema in Sheffield. Now, a year later, he was brought in as manager in Salisbury. With a reputation as something of a trouble - shooter, Mr Dilks told the Salisbury Journal 'There are ways in which I can improve the service here, but it is early days and I am still absorbing the atmosphere.'

Also in March, there was controversy over the localised banning of the film Scandal – the dramatisation of the 1960s Profumo Affair. The film had been rated as 18, and therefore unsuitable for families. It had been shown in Salisbury for three weeks, including on Sundays, but it was a condition of the cinema's licence that films to be shown on Good Friday had to be specifically approved by SDC. In this case Councillors resolved that the film should not be screened as it was considered 'unsuitable family entertainment on a Good Friday.'

Unfortunately, due to the Council's Committee scheduling cycle, the decision arrived after cinema publicity had already listed the 8.30pm screening of Scandal, resulting in disgruntled punters at the booking office. Louise Whitten, of Burford Avenue, told the Salisbury Journal 'It's really bad. I'm very annoyed that somebody should be able to enforce their opinions on us', before joining the growing queue for A Fish Called Wanda. Others opted for Disney's Lady and The Tramp but many simply walked out.

Salisbury's only remaining cinema is unique in the country if not the World - long may it last!

The Journal dedicated an editorial to the incident - Gareth Weekes' view was that the reasoning behind the decision was 'absurd' as an 18 certificate film being shown at 8pm was not intended for 'family' viewing. He hoped councillors would repent their decision and suggested that the 'Good Friday' condition should be removed from the cinema's licence, leaving censorship to the BBFC.

Angela Evans of Devizes Road felt compelled to write to the Salisbury Journal in November 1989, to thank the Odeon for its 'imaginative programming over the last year or two.' Ms Evans commented that this had allowed the viewing of good 'minor' films that might otherwise have necessitated a trip to London, although she did recommend using part of the foyer area as a bar. Graham Dilks thanked Ms Evans for her comments, and Mrs C Maude of Wilton endorsed her comments on programming but was unhappy about the amount of litter in the cinema – the policy being to clear up after every second showing.

The end of the line for the Plaza Cinema Amesbury

A cautiously triumphant decade for the cinema in Salisbury thus closed, but the story in Amesbury was not so happy. The Plaza had finally closed and was demolished in 1993, to be replaced by the St Melor surgery building.

In that same year a 70 - seat fourth screen was created in part of the former restaurant area of the Odeon, and in 1995 a fifth screen in the former front stalls area with a seating capacity of 278. The modern day Screen 1 was originally the circle of the Gaumont Palace cinema when it opened in 1931. Screen 2 contains the remains of the lower half of the original proscenium arch and the edge of the stage - all now painted deep blue but with the plasterwork intact. Screen 5 retains extensive original decorations and a side door leading into a storage area which was once the cinema's restaurant. As previously noted, the original full stage with associated changing rooms, corridors, fly tower and most of the equipment is still in place.

In terms of technology the equipment used in the modern cinema is similar to that used in the home. Satellite dishes, receivers, digital discs, sound systems and metre on metre of connecting leads all play their part. There is still of course a skill in setting the modern systems up and making sure the entertainment runs smoothly and on time, and the ability to fix problems that extends beyond the 'try re - booting it' approach. However, those with expertise in the perhaps more specialised aspects of film projection skills are becoming a rare breed.

John Paul Getty Junior (left) and Alan Richardson

2003 saw the death of the still - anonymous benefactor who had funded the legal representation for the Save The Odeon campaign at the planning PI in 1986, and had pledged further support if the Hexagon group had taken on the running of the cinema. With the benefactor's passing Alan Richardson felt able to reveal that it was none other than John Paul Getty Junior – the great philanthropist!

Having survived a major threat to its very existence during the 1980s, Salisbury's last cinema is now in its 90th year and has met the challenge of TV (including multiple specialist film channels – some free-to-air), home videos, various digital products and platforms, and a growing range of competitive activities – including the showing of films at the Arts Centre and by mobile companies in some of the outlying villages.

At the time of writing the cinema is closed due to Covid-19 restrictions. However, Salisbury should be proud of its central city five screen complex – partially housed in the only Grade I listed building in the country still used in connection with a cinema. Unlike so many other towns, where there is no cinema at all and punters have to drive out to some remote industrial site to see a film in a vast impersonal 12 screen complex that provides little more than small viewing rooms, Salisbury's only remaining cinema is unique in the country if not the World – long might it last!

SAVE THE SALISBURY ODEON

4 Hamilton Road
SALISBURY
WIlts

(0722)   334714

8 August 1986

Dear

We are pleased to be able to bring you news of the result of the Public Inquiry concerning the Odeon Cinema, Salisbury, which took place in January of this year:

THE ODEON IS SAVED FROM DEMOLITION!

In brief, the Inspector found as follows: -

- The Odeon is an important listed building.
- Bath & Bristol Estates Ltd, the developers, failed to demonstrate that every possible effort was made to continue its use.
- Rank Theatres Ltd failed to offer the Odeon on the open market, as required by the Town & Country Planning Act, and failed to put forward acceptable reasons for doing so.
- The demolition of the Odeon would not be justified by the benefits of the development.
- Servicing arrangements for the proposed development were inadequate.
- The need for shopping development in Salisbury was not considered to be a material factor in this case.

There is currently some uncertainty as to who will be running the cinema as Rank Theatres Ltd are still considering the Inspector's very lengthy report and are unable to comment as yet – but the building is safe from demolition. It is our hope, of course, that those who run the cinema in the future, whoever they may be, will invest in the building and its equipment, and exploit its sadly under-used potential to the full. If you would like, at any point in the future, to know the current position, please do not hesitate to contact us.

We would like to take this opportunity of thanking you most sincerely for your support during the campaign; it is entirely due to the generosity and interest of people such as yourself which has enabled our hope of saving the Odeon, Salisbury, from closure, demolition and redevelopment, to become a reality.

We would like also to tell you of another group of cinema-goers currently fighting a campaign against closure – the Save the Regal Trust, Henley on Thames. The Chairperson of the Trust, Tony Lane, of 28 Western Road, Henley on Thames, will be pleased to hear from anybody willing to help, or lend their name, to the campaign there.

Once again, very many thanks for your support for the Salisbury Odeon campaign.

Yours sincerely

SAVE THE ODEON CAMPAIGN GROUP

CHAPTER SIX:
THE MAN WHO SAVED THE ODEON
(Alan Richardson)

From a very young age, Alan Richardson's life was closely entwined with the cinemas in Salisbury, particularly The Gaumont Palace – the name that he persevered with using way beyond the physical and titular changes that led to 'The Odeon' as we know it today.

In 1981, referring back to the day in 1929 when the man with an Alsatian dog walked into his mother's needlework shop in Catherine Street, Alan wrote of the building he was destined to save: 'Our shop was indeed to become an entrance to a Palace, and was to see more patrons passing on their way through to the cinema than we ever did see customers purchasing needles and wool in our shop. Our upstairs rooms were to become the manager's flat, and our garden which seemed vast, its paths never ending to small legs on tricycles, would disappear and the stage of the new cinema with the giant silver screen would replace the green lawn with the pampas grass growing in the middle where we children used to play.'

'Those of us who remember the glorious days of old can still see and enjoy the Gaumont Palace much as it was in its hey - day. Only now, when looking over the edge of the circle into the dark void below, now empty of seats, is it my imagination that among the flickering shadows of the silver screen I see the children that played in that garden...or are they the shadows of countless thousands of satisfied patrons, young and old, who enjoyed the show on the silver screen through the thirties and forties, and afterwards made their way out into the real world of Catherine Street where I was born?'

Alan was born at 28 Catherine Street on 3 December 1923. Following the sale of the property to the cinema builders the family moved to Kent. Alan was educated at Sutton Valence

School near Maidstone. In 1942 Alan joined the Royal Naval Volunteer Reserve, with initial training in Portsmouth and Dartmouth. On 6 June 1944 - D-Day - he found himself a First Lieutenant at Sword Beach in Normandy, in a landing craft packed with explosives and ammunition. This was obviously highly hazard-ous in itself but there was the added danger of sitting on the beach whilst the landing craft was unloaded – sometimes having to then wait until tide conditions allowed for a re - launching. This role was considered by many to be a suicide mission.

Speaking to the Salisbury Journal on the 40th anniversary of the Normandy landings, Alan said 'One of my most visual impressions of D - Day was looking out from our landing craft on the sand of Sword Beach and seeing the bodies of soldiers that had been killed, drowned, shot...and across it all the strains of Glenn Miller's Moonlight Serenade from the landing craft that were there. The music I had always associated with dancing, yet here it was, still coming across.'

On his successful return from the 'suicide' mission, Alan was on a night out dancing with a friend in Southampton, when the band started to play Moonlight Serenade: 'My mind slipped back to that scene on the Normandy beach only a few hours before, and she wondered why the tears were streaming down my face.' Having earned the 1939 - 45 Star, Atlantic Star, Defence Medal and 1939 - 45 War Medal, in 2016 Alan was awarded France's highest honour - the Legion d'honneur, presented by Josette Lebrat, the French Honorary Consul, for his involvement during the landings on D - Day.

After the war Alan followed his youthful dreams of working in film, completing his education with a course in Kinematography in London. Having taken advice from the eminent film director David Lean, in 1949 Alan started a 27 year career at the BBC. As Assistant Film Librarian at Alexandra Palace he was instrumental in building the Corporation's film archives into something which was later considered to be the biggest and finest in the World. From there he moved on to the film department working on the Television Newsreel – a new concept of reporting the news 'live', which of course we all take for granted today.

Seven years as Telerecording Manager followed, before organising film operations at Ealing Film Studios and overseeing such classics as Dad's Army, The Two Ronnies, Morecambe and Wise, The Liver Birds, Monty Python's Flying Circus and many more. He also produced several BBC films, including Nation To Nation, about Eurovision on its 21st anniversary. Two of Alan's daughters followed in his footsteps at the BBC - Louise making documentaries and Sara joining the Design Department and having a career as a Production Buyer.

Despite his busy working life Alan also devoted time to his family. His passion for film overflowed into the family garage where he built a fine mini - cinema, complete with proper seats, where he screened many films for the benefit of his daughters and the youth of Ruislip. He also made many teenagers in the 1960s and 1970s deliriously happy with trips to Top Of The Pops

and opportunities to meet The Beatles, The Who and The Rolling Stones. He also shared his love of books with his daughters, took them to the theatre and the cinema (of course), sang the funniest of songs and recited crazy rhymes or beautiful verse which tugged at the emotions.

Alan retired from the BBC in December 1976 and returned to live in the Salisbury area, initially at West Gomeldon and then at New Street in the city. Alan had a great sense of humour and most notably, after moving back to Salisbury, saw the funny side when an enormous hot air balloon crash landed in his garden, just over the Close wall – 'God's Back Garden' as he fondly called it - the balloon having narrowly missed the Cathedral itself and leaving the then bishop in a state of nervous hysteria. Alan on the other hand was rather more sanguine in his reaction, noted the balloon had made a rather fine landing on the lawn and then continued on his way to Elizabeth Gardens with his dog Marmaduke. Alan told the Western Daily Press 'It was all very amusing and rather startling. I wasn't expecting any visitors.'

In his retirement Alan wrote and lectured widely on the subjects of the BBC, film and cinema and theatre history, both in Salisbury and more generally. He also became heavily involved in Salisbury's glorious architecture, green spaces, culture and arts, becoming a city guide, a Cathedral steward, guide and Tower Tour guide. He relaunched and edited the Cathedral News, sat on the Board of Directors at the Playhouse (where he was a highly effective fundraiser), was President of the Theatregoers Association, created the Theatre archives and gave great business to local booksellers. Alan also lectured widely on his D - Day experiences and led tours to the Normandy landing beaches.

As we have seen, even during his long exile as a child and younger man Alan kept up a keen interest in Salisbury affairs. This included an excellent archive on local cinemas and several volumes of press cuttings from the Salisbury Times and Salisbury Journal, covering a range of local topics and continuing in to his retirement years. Alan's daughter Sara kindly donated his cinema archive to the researching of this book and we are pleased to report that – following a fortuitous discovery in a Salisbury charity shop - we were able to reunite this with a number of clippings folders that had seemingly gone adrift.

Alan Richardson died on 28 October 2018, aged 94. He had lived in New Street until 2015 when he moved to Braemar Lodge in Stratford Road. His daughter Sara said 'the respect and kindness they [the Braemar Lodge staff] showed to him and their unwavering support to our family was awe inspiring.' Alan's funeral service was fittingly held at Salisbury Cathedral, and Sara said 'To me, my brother and my sisters (Karen, Stephen and Louise), he was the most loving and committed father. To our mother, Pauline, he was her knight in shining armour - a gentle, kind and loving husband - and to his friends and colleagues he was a loyal, respectful and charming gentleman.'

Having by then already led an interesting and varied life, the events for which Alan is probably best remembered by the Salisbury public took place in the mid - 1980s. These events are of course set out in previous chapters so we leave his final eulogy in this context to the then Salisbury Journal Editor Gavin Weekes (writing in the edition dated 10 July 1986):

If Salisbury had its own honours system there would be an outstanding candidate for a knighthood this year – Alan Richardson, the man who saved the Odeon. Sir Alan – or should it be Lord Richardson of New Canal? – mounted a brilliant campaign against the demolition scheme.

By his inexhaustible enthusiasm and determination he:

- Mobilised public opinion;

- Formed an action committee;

- Inspired the support of some of the top names in the British film industry;

- Found a mystery backer prepared to finance not only the planning appeal but an independent company to buy the Odeon;

- Forced major concessions from the developer and finally…

- Helped persuade the inquiry Inspector to find against the redevelopment scheme.

There is no doubt in my mind that without the persistence of Mr Richardson and his committee Salisbury's last remaining cinema would now be in ruins. Without their ceaseless campaigning the developers would not even have offered to build a substitute. The Inspector's decision is a triumph of People Power, proof that the developers and their powerful backers can be beaten, and that ordinary people with enough guts and intelligence can outwit them.

The Journal – which shamelessly supported the Save The Odeon campaign – offers its congratulations to the committee and to Mr Richardson in particular. For two years of nagging and cajoling and plotting, thousands of local people will want us to say: 'Well done, and thank you.'

APPENDICES

Ernest Frank who was a junior usher at the Gaumont Palace 1931

APPENDIX ONE: BRIEF TIMELINES OF THE MAIN SALISBURY CINEMAS

COUNTY HALL
South west corner of junction of Endless Street with Chipper Lane
1889 Opened as public hall and theatre
1908 First films shown
1910 Renamed Palace Theatre
1931 Closed
1968 Building demolished
Site most recently occupied by The Karma Centre

NEW PICTUREDROME AND THEATRE
West side of Castle Street
1910 Opened
1913 Renamed New Theatre
1932 Closed
1957 Building demolished
Site now occupied by office building named Cheviot House

PICTURE HOUSE
North side of Fisherton Street
1916 Opened in converted Methodist Chapel
1937 Closed
1979 Building demolished
Site most recently occupied by Baileys of Salisbury (Retail Beds)

GAUMONT PALACE
South side of New Canal
1931 Opened in converted house and china shop
1955 Renamed Gaumont
1966 Renamed Odeon
Now Salisbury's only remaining cinema
Closed at time of writing due to Covid 19 restrictions

REGAL
North west corner of junction of Endless Street with Chipper Lane
1937 Opened
1963 Renamed ABC
1969 Closed
Site most recently occupied by Buzz Bingo/Sultan's Cut Barbers

NEW PICTURE HOUSE
North side of Fisherton Street
1937 Opened
1948 Renamed Picture House
1950 Renamed Odeon
1961 Closed
Site now occupied by City Hall
In use as Covid 19 vaccination centre at time of writing

APPENDIX TWO: ACRONYMS

ABC:	Associated British Cinemas
ABPC:	Associated British Picture Corporation
AGM:	Annual General Meeting
AKC:	Army Kinema Corporation
ARP:	Air Raid Precautions
ATS:	Auxiliary Territorial Service
BBC:	British Broadcasting Corporation
BBE:	Bath and Bristol Estates
BBFC:	British Board of Film Censors/Classification (latter since 1984)
BFI:	British Film Institute
BIP:	British International Pictures
CFF:	Children's Film Foundation
CMA:	Circuits Management Association
CND:	Campaign for Nuclear Disarmament
DSO:	Distinguished Service Order
DVD:	Digital Versatile Disc
EMI:	Electric and Musical Industries
ENSA:	Entertainments National Service Association
FRIAS:	Fellow, Royal Incorporation of Architects in Scotland
GWR:	Great Western Railway
ITV:	Independent Television
KCB:	Knight Commander, Order of the Bath
LP:	Long Player (Record)
M&S:	Marks & Spencer
MBE:	Member of the Most Excellent Order of the British Empire
MC:	Military Cross
MGM:	Metro-Goldwyn-Mayer
MP:	Member of Parliament
PC:	Police Constable
PCT:	Provincial Cinema Theatres
PI:	Public Inquiry
QC:	Queen's Counsel
RAF:	Royal Air Force
RCA:	Radio Corporation of America
RSC:	Radio Speakers of Canada
RDC:	Rural District Council
RKO:	Radio-Keith-Orpheum (Pictures)
SDC:	Salisbury District Council
SFS:	Salisbury Film Society
SoS:	Secretary of State (for the Environment)
UFO:	Unidentified Flying Object
UK:	United Kingdom
VIP:	Very Important Person
WCC:	Wiltshire County Council

CREDITS

We would especially like to thank Anne and Ruby as always.

INDIVIDUALS

The following have provided material, information, support and inspiration, in some cases without even knowing it:

Chris Abbott; Mandy Biddle; Ruth Butler; Roger Collins; Fiona Crowther; Naomi Doman (Salisbury Odeon – Her guided tours are recommended); Terry Grace; Sara Hoggan; Sara Hubbard; Geoff Lang; Val Lewis; Peter F Mason; James McCarraher; Arthur Millie (Salisbury Playhouse Archivist); Roy Nash; Gemma Newbold; Barbara Parker; David Richards; Alan Richardson; Bryan Rowe; Nigel Rowe; Kevin Rowland (The original Projected Passion); Roxy (Salisbury Odeon); Jodie Scott; Jim Slater; Ken Smith; Isabel Stone; Mick Stone; Dave Todd; Hilary Ann Topp; Neil Tonge; Simon 'Wiggy' Wigglesworth; Ian Wheeler; Chris Usher.

PUBLICATIONS

Kelly's Directory of Salisbury and Neighbourhood (Kelly's Directories) (Various Years)

Salisbury Gaumont Opening Programme (1931)

Salisbury New Picture House Opening Programme (1937)

Salisbury Regal Opening Programme (1937)

Amesbury Plaza 21st Anniversary Programme (1956)

The Buildings of England: Wiltshire (Nikolaus Pevsner – revised by Bridget Cherry) (Penguin 1975)

Ancient and Historical Monuments in the City of Salisbury (Royal Commission on Historical Monuments of England) (Her Majesty's Stationery Office 1977)

Salisbury Odeon 50th Anniversary Programme (1981)

The Cinema Theatres Of Salisbury (Alan A Richardson) (IMS 50th Anniversary Special, Odeon, Salisbury, September 7th, 1981)

The Whites: Salisbury City FC, The First 60 Years, 1947 to 2007 (David Thear, Richard Walker, Peter Waterhouse and Peter Wood) (Citywhite Publishing 2007)

Hold Tight! (Voices Of The Sarum Sound 1945-1969) (Frogg Moody and Richard Nash) (Timezone 2010)

Durrington & Larkhill Design Statement (Durrington Town Council 2012)

Salisbury City Hall: Through The Looking Glass (James McCarraher) (James McCarraher 2013)

Salisbury In The Great War (Neil G M Hall) (Pen & Sword 2016)

Page 131

PERIODICALS

Cinema Technology
Fisherton Informer
Kinematograph Weekly
Salisbury ADnews
Salisbury Journal
Salisbury Times (and South Wilts Gazette)
Sarum Chronicle
The Spectator
Southern Evening Echo
Sunderland Daily Echo and Shipping Gazette
Western Daily Press
Western Gazette
Wiltshire County Mirror

WEBSITES

Fisherton History Society Facebook Group

www.amesburyhistorycentre.org.uk

www.fovanthistory.org

www.wiltshire.gov.uk

www.cinematreasures.org

www.cinemauk.org.uk

www.imbd.com

www.bbfc.co.uk

www.historicengland.org.uk

www.british-history.ac.uk

www.wikisource.org/wiki/Dictionary_of_National_Biography

www.maps.nls.uk

www.britannica.com

www.parliament.publications.uk

www.ancestry.co.uk

www.beatlesbible.com

www.margaretthatcher.org

PHOTOGRAPHS

All attempts have been made to contact copyright holders of photographs, where known, and they have been credited accordingly. Apologies are offered to any copyright holders who we have not been able to contact. Where this is the case, please contact us and we will rectify matters in the event of any future editions of this book.

ABOUT THE AUTHORS

Frogg Moody is an award winning Salisbury historian. He has conducted the research for six books on local history and in 2007 co-created Timezone Productions. (timezoneproductions.com) He also has his own weekly Salisbury Journal column entitled 'Bygone Salisbury'. In 2017 he founded the Fisherton History Society and the Fisherton Informer magazine - this in turn resulted in the Salisbury History Festival, which is now in its fourth year. As a musician he brought into existence two critically acclaimed musicals on Jack the Ripper and the Titanic Disaster.

Richard Nash was raised in Downton, near Salisbury, in a house named after a song from South Pacific – his parents had seen the film on the same day that they obtained planning permission for the plot. He has written articles for a number of publications and has worked on local history projects in Downton.

Frogg and Richard have previously worked together on the following projects:

Hold Tight! – Voices Of The Sarum Sound 1945-1969 (Timezone Publishing) (2007)

Endless Beat – Voices Of The New Sarum Sound 1970-1999 (Timezone Publishing) (2010)

Walls Of Sound (Exhibition at Salisbury and South Wiltshire Museum) (2010-2011)

Haunted Salisbury (History Press) (2012)

Lectures on the above subjects plus Salisbury Pubs

Fovant 11
Francis, A J 20
Francis, Jack 24
Francis, Mrs 84
Francis, Ralph 52
Frank, Ernest 128p
Franki Compressed Pile Co Ltd 28
Friary Lane 79
Friary, The 70
Friese-Green, William 2
Frome 18, 31, 44, 48
Fry, J 80
Furse, W J & Co Ltd 25
Fury, Billy 66

Garrison Theatre (Salisbury) 43-44, 43p
Garrison Theatres: Bulford 11, 23, 49, Codford 11,
11p, Fovant 11, Heytesbury 11, Hurdcott 11,
Larkhill 11, 11p, 23, 49, Salisbury Plain 10-11,
Sutton Veny 11, Tidworth 9-10, 10p, Westdown
Camp 49
Garton & Thorne Ltd 25
Gas Lane 41
Gaumont (company) 4, 5, 14, 20, 28, 30-31, 32, 33,
34, 44, 48, 50, 52, 65, 91
Gaumont (Salisbury cinema) 5, 5-7, 6p, 7p, 16, 16p,
18, 19-22, 19p, 20p, 21p, 28, 31, 32, 33, 34-35, 34p,
35p, 36p, 37p, 38, 39, 40, 42, 47, 47p, 48, 51p, 52,
53, 53p, 54-55, 56, 60p, 62, 63, 65, 66, 81, 90, 92,
117, 121, 122p, 124, 128p, 129
General Infirmary 13, 48, 71, 89
George Street 69
Getty, John Paul Junior 122, 122p
Gigant Street 22
Giorgi, Louisa 94
Girlings Ferro-Concrete Co 25
Glasgow 65
Glen, William 5, 24-25
Goddard, Jill 88
Goddard's 106
Golan & Globus 5
Golding, Pam 64
Golding, R C H 28
Golding, William 86p
Gooding, Barry 81
Goodlatte, D J 55
Goodman, H 80
Gorman, John 108
Gosney, PC 51
Gough, E G 56
Graham, George 80
Gratwick, G 28

Great Wishford 80
Green, Frank 76
Green, Stephen 109-110
Grey Wolves, The 118
Griffin's 28
Griffin's Court 30
Grimstead 119
Guildhall 8, 53, 98, 120
Guinness, Alec 76, 108

Hall & Dixon Ltd 25
Hall of John Halle 16, 19-20, 20p, 63, 94, 95, 99,
101, 104, 105, 110, 110p, 117, 119, 120
Hall, John & Co 59
Hall, Amy 85
Hall, Stephen 88
Halle, John 5, 5-6, 21, 84-85
Halle, William 6
Hamilton, Gabrielle 79
Hamilton, Michael 79
Hamnett, Mr and Mrs Dennis 77
Harding, Michael 13
Harker, Gordon 24
Harnham 48, 53, 89
Harnham Road 85
Harnwood Hospital 48, 71
Harrold, Mr 8
Hart, Romaine 104
Hart, S 28
Hartley, Alison 82
Harvey, Alex 106
Haugh, Michael 64
Hawes, Lionel 95
Hawkes, Barbara 111
Hawkins, Jack 53, 70
Hay, Will 10
Haywards Ltd 26
Heath, Ted (bandleader) 53p, 66
Heath, Ted (former Prime Minister) 99
Hems, Harry 7
Henry VII 6
Henson, Leslie 43
Hexagon Enterprises Ltd 104, 106, 107, 108, 122
Heytesbury 11
Higgins, Brenda 74
High Post 32
High Street 6, 9, 79
Hill, Candy 96
Hollies, The 66
Holly, Buddy 60p, 66, 119, 119p
Hope, Bob 10, 65
Hopkins, Ernie 117, 117p

Old Mill Hotel 53
Oldham 75
Oliver, Yvonne 62
Olivier, Laurence 43, 70
Ostrer, Mark 20
Otto's 90
Overton, Jack 16, 65, 117p
Owen, David 110
Owen, Sandra 90
Oxford 4

Palace Garage 24, 66
Palace Theatre 7, 8-9, 8p, 10, 16, 17, 18, 18p, 20,
22, 24, 65, 66, 66p, 129
Palmer Road 77
Park Street 22, 110
Parker, Alan 108
Parker, David 96
Parkinson, Terry 110
Parratt, Les & Mrs 91
Parrott, Kay 91
Parsons, William 51
Pathe Equipment Co Ltd 25
Paul, Robert William 2, 3, 79
Pauls Dene Road 82
Payne, Sampson 6-7
PCT 4, 14, 31
Pearce, Mike 111
Peck, Gregory 88
Peerless, W F 28, 45
Pembroke, Earls of (and Family) 19, 20, 21, 42, 77,
79, 83, 90, 91, 92
Penarth 26
Pennells, Reg 84
Penny, Myrtle 39, 45
Penny, R 80
Perry, Simon 112
Pevsner, Nikolaus 7
Pewsey 73
Pickernell Family 9-10
Picknett, Susan 79
Picture House 5, 12, 12p, 12-14, 15-16, 18, 23, 27,
28, 28p, 30, 31, 43-44, 50, 52, 63, 76, 78, 112p,129
Pilbeam, Nova 30, 31, 32
Pinewood Close 81
Pinniger, Misses 18
Pitcairn Campbell, General 11
Pitton 98
Platters, The 66
Plaza 23, 57-59, 57p, 58p, 59p, 72, 74, 93, 94, 95p,
96, 97, 99, 102-103, 103p, 107, 114, 118-119, 118p,
121, 121p

Polley, V H Ltd 30
Portland Avenue 96
Portman, Eric 43
Portsmouth 38, 41, 109, 124
Portswood 92
Poultry Cross 105
Powell, Christine 90
Pride, F H 25, 29
Primitive Methodist Chapel 12, 12p, 76, 129
Pugin, Augustus 6
Pullen, Francis 13
Pullin, R J 85
Purdy, F Daphne 97, 104, 111, 114, 116
Puttnam, David 90, 91, 108
Pyke, Rosemary 96

Quayle, John 91
Queen Alexandra Road 64

Radnor House 11
Radnor, Countess of 30, 30p, 32
Rampart Road 117
Randall's 32
Rank Organisation 5, 38, 48, 56, 58, 63, 65, 69, 70,
73, 75, 78, 79, 82, 83, 84, 89, 91, 93, 94, 95, 98,
98-99, 100, 101, 104, 105, 107, 108, 109, 110-111,
112, 113, 115, 116, 119, 120
Ray, Ian 90
Rectory Road 18
Red Lion Hotel 39, 96
Redlynch 95, 96, 97
Regal 5, 24-27, 24p, 25p, 27p, 32, 33, 40, 43, 45,
49, 51, 51p, 52p, 53, 55, 55p, 56, 56p, 59, 65, 65p,
68p, 69, 90, 92, 129
Reindorp, George 79
Richard, Cliff 66
Richards Way 93
Richardson L F 25
Richardson, Alan 15, 16, 34, 49, 63, 64, 69, 70,
85, 89, 90, 91, 92, 94, 95, 95-97, 98, 98p, 100, 101,
101p, 103, 105, 106, 108-109, 112, 113p, 114,
114-115, 116, 117, 119, 122, 122p, 124-126, 124p
Richardson, Karen 126
Richardson, Louise 125, 126
Richardson, Pauline 126
Richardson, Sara 125, 126
Richardson, Stephen 126
Rideout, J H 15
Ridley, Nicholas 115
Rigg, Diana 66
Riman, C 85
Rising Sun 66

Rix, Brian 10
Robbie The Robot 56, 56p
Roberts, Ramon 83
Roberts, Ray 91
Robertson, John 49
Robeson, Paul 97
Robey, George 66
Robson, Flora 43
Robson, Ken 39, 45
Robson, Major 31
Roeg, Nicolas 108
Rogerson, Barry 77
Roget, Peter 2
Rollestone Street 9
Rolling Stones, The 66, 125
Romsey, Lord & Lady 91
Rose, R 80
Rowe, Bryan 54-55, 54p, 56-57, 61, 66
Royal British Legion Hall 95
Ruderham, Gaynor 105, 107, 116
Ruislip 63, 125

Salberg, Reggie 76
Salisbury & Wells Theological College 80
Salisbury Amateur Operatic Society 9, 62
Salisbury Civic Society 111
Salisbury Corinthians FC 71
Salisbury District Council 82, 85, 88, 91, 94, 95, 96,
98, 99, 100, 101, 103, 104-105, 106, 109, 113, 116,
120-121
Salisbury District Hospital 38
Salisbury Exhibition 53
Salisbury FC 71-72
Salisbury Film Society 72, 72p, 73-74, 77, 78, 83,
84
Salisbury Journal 14, 16, 52, 55, 91, 92, 94, 95-96,
96, 97-98, 100, 101, 102, 104, 106, 107, 108, 109,
114, 116, 119-120, 120, 120-121, 121, 125, 126
Salisbury Motor Club 32
Salisbury Plain 10-11, 12, 49, 53, 82
Salisbury Playhouse(s) 52, 63, 73, 76, 76p, 79, 83,
85, 90, 105, 125
Salisbury Press 14
Salisbury Times 13, 19, 22, 40, 43, 53, 56, 59, 61,
63, 65, 66, 67, 68-69, 69-70, 70, 72, 73, 74, 75, 78,
79, 80, 81, 81-82, 82, 83, 88, 89, 90, 93, 125
Salt Lane 27, 39
Sanders, F 47
Sarum Mobile Film Shows 50
Saunders, J D 20, 21, 30-31
Save The Odeon 95-96, 95p, 96-97, 97p, 98, 98p,
99, 99p, 100p, 101, 103, 104, 105, 106, 108-109,

108p, 111, 111-113, 111p, 112p, 113, 114, 113p,
114p, 114-115, 115p, 116-117, 119, 122, 123p, 126
Scorey, Chief Inspector 51
Scots Lane 81
Scott, Mr and Mrs 53
Scott, Ronnie 10
Seabourne, Barry 73-74
Serviour, Roy 44
Shadows, The 66
Shaw, Sandie 66
Sheffield 107, 120
Sheldrake, Leonard 18, 117p
Sheldrake, Winifred 18
Shepherd and Hedger 59
Shepherds Bush 4
Sheppard, Betty 72
Shingler, George and Mrs 74
Shipton Bellinger 6
Shirley 75
Sidney Street 64
Silver Street 76
Sim, Alastair 10
Sim, Sheila 78
Sinden, Donald 108
Sinden, Mrs M 85
Singleton, Samuel and Jamie 85
Sleeman, S G 95
Smith, Anthony 101-102, 101p
Smith, Jim 27, 27p, 45, 48, 49, 90
Smith, Mary 49
Smith, Maudie 50p
Snook, Councillor 63
South Wilts Grammar School 77
Southampton 7, 41, 64, 70, 75, 78, 90, 92, 97, 109,
114, 120, 125
Southern Electricity and Gas 94
Southern Evening Echo 105
Southey, Violet 22
Southon's 90
Southsea 46
Springfield, Dusty 66
Spruce, David 93
Squires, Rosemary 49
St Francis' Church 47, 80
Standard Metal Window Co Ltd 26
Standard Pavements Co 25
Stanger, Peter 90
Stannard, Don 48
Star Associated Holdings 69, 70
Stephens, Roger 95
Stephenson, Douglas 89, 90, 91
Stephenson, Margaret 90

INDEX OF FILM TITLES

Lightning Source UK Ltd.
Milton Keynes UK
UKHW030234241121
394422UK00003B/249

9 781914 407130